The looking machine

MANCHESTER
1824

Manchester University Press

ANTHROPOLOGY, CREATIVE PRACTICE AND ETHNOGRAPHY (ACE)

SERIES EDITORS: PAUL HENLEY AND ANDREW IRVING

Anthropology, Creative Practice and Ethnography provides a forum for authors and practitioners from across the digital humanities and social sciences to explore the rapidly developing opportunities offered by visual, acoustic and textual media for generating ethnographic understandings of social, cultural and political life. It addresses both established and experimental fields of visual anthropology, including film, photography, sensory and acoustic ethnography, ethnomusicology, graphic anthropology, digital media and other creative modes of representation. The series features works that engage in the theoretical and practical interrogation of the possibilities and constraints of audiovisual media in ethnographic research, while simultaneously offering a critical analysis of the cultural, political and historical contexts.

Forthcoming titles

Paul Henley, *Beyond Observation: Authorship and Ethnographic Film*
Christian Suhr, *Descending with Angels: Islamic Exorcism and Psychiatry – A Film Monograph*

In association with the Granada Centre for Visual Anthropology

The looking machine

Essays on cinema, anthropology
and documentary filmmaking

David MacDougall

Manchester University Press

Published by Manchester University Press
Altrincham Street, Manchester M1 7JA, UK
www.manchesteruniversitypress.co.uk

British Library Cataloguing-in-Publication Data is available

ISBN 978 1 5261 3411 0 paperback

First published 2019

The publisher has no responsibility for the persistence or accuracy of URLs for any external or third-party internet websites referred to in this book, and does not guarantee that any content on such websites is, or will remain, accurate or appropriate.

Typeset by R. J. Footring Ltd, Derby, UK

For Colin Young

Contents

Figures

Series editors' preface

THE aim of the series Anthropology, Creative Practice and Ethnography (ACE) is to explore the ethnographic understandings of social, cultural and political life offered by visual, acoustic and textual media. It will be offered in a range of formats, including comparative and general works, monographs, edited collections and audiovisual media.

New technologies enable the documentation of the embodied, experiential and sensorial dimensions of social and cultural life to unprecedented degrees but these representations urgently call for the ethnographic grounding and understanding that anthropology brings to creative, audiovisual and technical practice. We shall be particularly interested in working with authors and Manchester University Press to explore the various ways in which written texts may be placed in a creative dialogue with online resources. Our aim is to go beyond the standard study guide model in which the printed and audiovisual components are merely juxtaposed or whereby the book offers little more than an explanation of the audiovisual resource or vice versa. Instead, we envisage a range of different formats through which the book and the audiovisual components may inform and extend beyond each other or alternatively exist in a productive tension.

We are delighted to be able to launch the series with *The Looking Machine*, a timely and important collection of essays by David MacDougall, in which he writes with characteristic elegance about the related fields of cinema, anthropology and documentary film. MacDougall brings new insights into cognition, sensory perception and the act of looking, drawing on a wide range of literary, theoretical and cinematic inspirations, as well as his unrivalled career and influence as an ethnographic filmmaker. Other works by senior figures in visual anthropology and film are currently in production. We are also keen to encourage submissions from new authors from a broad diversity of backgrounds, including those from outside the English-speaking world.

We very much look forward to hearing from authors interested in contributing to this collective adventure in contemporary ethnographic representation.

Paul Henley and Andrew Irving
Granada Centre for Visual Anthropology, University of Manchester

Acknowledgements

THE writing of these essays has been made possible by the support of a number of institutions and individuals. The Research School of Humanities and the Arts at the Australian National University has provided a congenial place to work and institutional support for both my filmmaking and my writing. I am grateful to the Australian Research Council for an Australian Professorial Fellowship and a Discovery Project grant that allowed me to continue my visual research on institutions for children in India and to conduct the collaborative project 'Childhood and Modernity: Indian Children's Perspectives'. Much of this book was written in India while engaged in these activities. I am particularly indebted to the Delhi School of Economics at the University of Delhi, which hosted me on several occasions, to Rishi Valley Education Centre in Andhra Pradesh, where I wrote a number of the essays, and to Seva Mandir in Udaipur, which helped me in countless ways during my stay in Delwara.

I am also grateful to a number of colleagues and friends who have provided inspiration, friendly encouragement and sometimes actual physical space for my writing. They include Andreas Ackermann, Peter Crawford, Anna Grimshaw, Frank Heidemann, Paul Henley, Radhika and Hans Herzberger, David Howes, Peter Loizos, Judith MacDougall, Howard Morphy, Christopher Morton, Luc Pauwels, Paolo Piquereddu, Rossella Ragazzi, Ivo Strecker, Colin Young and Salim Yusufji.

Several essays in the book have appeared elsewhere, some in slightly different versions. For permission to include them here, I should like to thank the following publishers: Berg Publishers for 'The experience of colour' (chapter 7), published in *The Senses and Society*, vol. 2, no. 1, March 2007: 5–26 (© 2007 Taylor & Francis. All rights reserved); Ashgate Publishing for 'Anthropology and the cinematic imagination' (chapter 10), published in *Photography, Anthropology and History*, 2009: 55–63; and Sage Publications for 'Anthropological filmmaking: an empirical art' (chapter 11), published in *The Sage Handbook of Visual Research Methods*, 2011: 99–113. A portion of 'Camera, mind and eye' (chapter 3) appears in *Anthropology as Homage: Festschrift for Ivo Strecker*, published by Rüdiger Köppe Verlag, Köln, 2018.

Introduction

Most of the reflections on films and filmmaking in this book were written in the intervals between days and weeks of filming. For that reason they tend to focus on the immediacy of film images, both on the screen and, perhaps as much, when seen through the viewfinder of a camera. My underlying aim has been to bring the two experiences closer together, shifting that of the film viewer a little nearer to that of the filmmaker. This is a book of personal observations based on my own practice and film viewing rather than a book of general film history or theory. I can therefore make no claim to being encyclopaedic, whether writing about documentary or about fiction films. In many ways these are speculative essays, reflecting both convictions and uncertainties, and the intermediate position of someone whose career spans documentary filmmaking and anthropology.

The book is in three parts, moving from a personal to a wider view; from the immediacy of filmmaking to the ways that films address us as viewers; and from the growth of documentary cinema as a genre to its role in anthropology and public discourse. Part I is concerned with the filmmaker's eye and mind behind the camera; the constraints, both public and self-imposed, that filmmakers face in filming what they witness; and some of the strategies that may help them to give a better insight into the life experiences of others. Part II looks at the ways that images and sounds evoke emotions and physical sensations, and how filmmakers have come to place increasing emphasis on human perception and bodily experience. Part III is primarily concerned with documentary cinema's powers of representation in academic and public life. Particular attention is paid to the development of observational cinema and visual anthropology. Here I discuss some of the misconceptions, theoretical questions and practical problems that arise in this work. In the closing chapter I cast a broader glance at the history of documentary and call for a reinvestment in the ideas that originally inspired it.

Writing about these subjects has meant taking account of the complex relationships between filmmaker and film subject, relationships that ultimately guide the filmmaker's decisions. It has also meant focusing on those moments in which the filmmaker responds second by second to the events taking place in front of the camera. These events are often as unpredictable to the people filmed as to the filmmaker. In them, filmmaker and subject become bound up in a common experience. The resulting films trace both a course of events and the consciousness of their passing. Much as in fiction filmmaking, they seize upon a gesture here, an object there, or the fleeting expression on a face. They require as much attention to the commonplace as to the rare moments of revelation. They also require the ability to resist looking away from the subject, out of impatience or embarrassment. This does not come automatically to filmmakers; it is something that must be learned over time: not to retreat from the disturbing face of reality, as we constantly do in daily life. It demands both the novelist's unsentimental eye and the journalist's resolve to record what he or she has seen.

As this applies to the individual filmmaker, so it applies to documentary films generally. One aim of this book is to question the odd tendency of the genre to withdraw from examining life as we experience it – to remain so often in the safer zone of the authoritative report, the inspiring message, the conventionally beautiful image.

If the new directions taken by documentary films in the 1960s had a principal aim it was to reduce the gap between the viewing perspectives of the filmmaker and the film viewer – between the world shown on the screen and what was actually happening around the filmmaker at the time. This was basically a question of how much the viewer would be allowed to see. Widening the conceptual frame of the film meant including, at least implicitly, the filmmaker as part of the event, and respecting the ability of viewers to observe filmed events and apply their own deductive reasoning to them. This meant relinquishing some of the control that went with cinematic professionalism: the power of films to amaze and mould the responses of their audiences.

These moves were not so much driven by a spirit of egalitarianism as by a wish to let others see what the filmmaker had seen. They were perhaps also a response to the dominance of fiction films and their taken-for-granted artificiality, as opposed to the desire of documentary filmmakers to convey a sense of the historical moment. They challenged the assumption of so many earlier documentary films that images were to be taken as emblems of things in the world rather than glimpses of the world itself. Too often, the 'facts' of these films had come to stand for something other than themselves – for heroic ideals, social problems, personal passions. Against this background, filmmakers began to suspect that the real strength of documentary lay in acknowledging the camera's limitations rather than its sleight of hand. The question then, as now, was not what the images meant but what viewers would be allowed to make of them.

Each film has its maker and its viewers. The filmmaker is the first and keenest viewer of a film, during the actual filming and, later, in the editing. Every film exists twice. The first film is an uncertain enquiry in which new discoveries appear at every turn. For the filmmaker, this is a time of all-consuming engagement with life, compared with which the film's completion sometimes seems irrelevant. The second film is the one prepared for others to see. Now the film, instead of being fluid and expansive, becomes a work of consolidation. It begins to take on the intricacy of a network, where strands are linked across great spaces, where shapes and resonances converge and coalesce. Here one strives to make connections not noticeable in the raw materials, and yet, if one is careful, to preserve some true sense of their rawness and indeterminacy. The elements within a film often have little independent meaning; they acquire it through their connectedness. Of the two films I have described, the first belongs essentially to its maker, the second to its viewers. As time goes on, its audiences will change and be replaced, and different viewers will find different things in which to take an interest.

Several essays in this book pay attention to how viewers respond to films with their senses – how they grasp the textures of objects, the indefinable presence of human beings, the openness or confinement of spaces. Films let us experience a coherent world that we also recognise as experienced by the people in them. But this evocative power, although it appears in many forms, should not be taken as an end in itself. The human sensorium is only part of a much larger complex in which we engage in multiple ways with objects, words, each other and the social forces around us. Evoking physical sensations, although a vital element of cinema, can easily become insular and coercive, forcing viewers into fixed responses, much as the manipulative music and authoritarian spoken commentaries of documentaries did in the past. That tendency is still with us today in varied forms – in the elaborate packaging, spectacular imagery and multi-track sound designs of many films, employed in some cases simply to hold the wavering attention of television audiences. We should welcome films that deepen our sensory experience, but not at the cost of our independence as viewers.

Part I: Filmmaking as practice

Dislocation as method

A T my university I had a fencing instructor who taught us a tactic called *second intention*. It consisted of making an attack on one's opponent not in order to score a point but in order to put oneself in a better position to do so. It created a new angle and a new opportunity. There are similar tactics in chess and, I would guess, many other games. Over the years I have wondered whether the principle of second intention might apply to filmmaking in some way. There are at least some parallels. When you are filming someone who is camera-shy, it's quite natural to begin by focusing on something comparatively neutral, to put the person at ease. Or if you are filming a group of people, you may shift your camera to a new framing, not primarily for the sake of the new frame but as an intermediate step, to move more easily from it to a third frame. These things are done for social and aesthetic reasons, and they are not so different from what we do in many other situations in life.

But there is another sense in which the principle of second intention applies to filmmaking and I believe that it lies at the heart of the cinematic process – in what makes filmmaking fundamentally different from other forms of art or human enquiry. Cameras impose special ways of engaging with the world and these often force filmmakers to step outside themselves and adopt intermediate positions, not knowing the outcome. These changes in behaviour produce changes in perception, and sometimes new kinds of knowledge.

In science it is first intentions that generally matter most. If you don't have some idea of what you are looking for, there will simply be a muddle of undirected interests. Rather than asking many questions simultaneously, it is far better to ask one question and then pursue whatever new questions arise from it. A kind of theoretical armature is established, around which the research takes place. This is normal practice, not only in the physical sciences but in many of the social sciences as well. The outcome can often be predicted from the questions being asked. Much of the work serves to test or substantiate conclusions already guessed at. Just occasionally this approach opens up some wholly new line of enquiry, but when that happens it is considered exceptional and not part of the original intention.

In music and literature, painting and sculpture, the approach is not so different, although sometimes left more open to chance. Artists may be less sure of their first intentions than scientists are, but they try to clarify them as their work progresses. Often an artist starts with only the barest idea – a germ or rough schema of what will be produced. In music this may be a phrase or a structure to be developed. In literature it may be a character who comes to mind or a situation to be explored. In sculpture it may literally be an armature, to which bits and pieces are added, or a sketch of something to be constructed. Then the process becomes one of elaboration and refinement.

There are resemblances between this process and anthropological research. The anthropologist goes into the field to learn how another group of people think, feel and do things, usually with some general questions in mind. These questions are almost always altered or replaced as time goes on. Things that at first seemed of crucial importance tend to be superseded by others. Fieldwork is not a tidy, coherent process, as most written accounts make clear. However, when anthropologists sit down to write a monograph or journal article, the process changes. Then they attempt to express their knowledge in a more systematic form, by presenting an argument or set of findings and supporting this with the observations and pieces of evidence they have gathered. At this stage the ideas are clarified and re-examined and are then rewritten in a form very different from the anthropologist's field notes.

But if anthropologists try to film in this more systematic way, they often encounter problems and frustrations. The underlying structures they have identified remain elusive, and the visual evidence that crowds in upon them often seems too fragmentary to be conclusive. What they discover is that filming is more like the experience of fieldwork itself, more exploratory and less orderly. It produces material that generally fails to make the kinds of explicit points that they would like to make. Furthermore, the material it produces – the actual film footage – is unalterable; that is, the images cannot be rewritten, although they can be presented and edited in a variety of ways. One solution frequently found, often as a last resort, is to revert to a spoken commentary, for which the film material ends up serving primarily as an illustration.

These problems highlight the different qualities of film and written texts. Although film can demonstrate some kinds of findings, such as how something looks, or how something is done, or in a general way why someone did something, it is not essentially a theoretical or propositional medium. Indeed, it is relentlessly specific. Its attempts to generalise take the form of examples for which some sort of unity is implied, but these are far from definitive. Indeed, it tends to produce material no less complex and ambiguous than the subject it is exploring. Instead of stating relationships, it can only suggest them; and it is annoyingly inefficient at coming to conclusions. Thus, to an anthropologist, constructing models of society with images and sounds must seem very different from constructing them

8

in writing. Unless film images are circumscribed by words, they tend to be awkward instruments for making anthropological statements.

This does not mean that these films lack intellectual purpose or are concerned only with immediate experience, or that they lack powers of explanation. When such films show *how* things occur, they often reveal *why* they occur and bring to light previously ignored factors. In fact, in an era in which society is thought to be governed largely by economics, politics and ideology, part of the value of film lies in drawing attention to causes that may have been overlooked, such as good manners, stubbornness and aesthetic choices.

One hope that used to be held out for film, although expressed less often now, is that it could provide accurate and comprehensive accounts of human events. This hope has been disappointed. Cameras, it could be said, are particular rather than catholic in their tastes. They see narrowly. What is put into a film is very different from what one sees in daily life. It is a set of brief glimpses squeezed into rectangular frames. To make any sense (in the sense that words make sense), the frames must then be arranged according to principles that are understood by the viewer. For those who don't know the principles, or who are unsympathetic to them, the result may seem an incomprehensible jumble.

The counter-argument, of course, is that because cameras are made by human beings they are made to see like us as a species, rather than, say, like insects. The conventions (or grammars) that guide them are also human. Therefore film 'language' – if it can be called that – is a language anyone can learn because it is modelled on human perception and psychology. It is often pointed out that audiences all over the world, even if they've never seen another film, can immediately understand one about Charlie Chaplin.

And yet if film is a language, what a strange language it is. It lacks many of the abstract and descriptive qualities of writing or speech, and yet possesses qualities that they lack. A film cannot say 'All oaks produce acorns' or 'This is not a pipe' or (except in a roundabout literary way) 'Someday I shall go to Venice'. But it can say 'Look at this girl's hair' or 'Look at that man's eyebrows'. It can show the smoothness of glass and the redness of red. It can present the key steps in a process, or a complex group of simultaneous events. It can show, as words never could, the struggle to learn, as when a child attempts something repeatedly and finally gets it right. It can show us the fear on someone's face or in someone's posture, or a glance of understanding between two people. It can show us a stream of water disappearing into dry earth, a plant growing or a cell dividing.

Many of these achievements, nonetheless, are no more than mimetic or technical extensions of human vision. For many filmmakers, the most distinctive and important quality of film lies elsewhere, not in advancing the technology of vision but in transforming the positions from which human

9

beings see. Most scientific and artistic activities are conducted from the relatively secure position of someone working with a known set of materials. In filming (unless we follow a script) we relinquish this first position of the self for a second position less in control of the situations it encounters. This is perhaps not so different from an anthropologist choosing to be immersed in the life of another society in order to learn more about it. The difference is that anthropological texts are created afterwards, in a process of reflection upon experience, a process that often has a reductive or normalising effect. In filming, by contrast, the final inscription occurs moment by moment in the filmmaker's engagement with the subject and cannot be recast or recreated in retrospect. The materials may be shortened, juxtaposed and re-biased in various ways through editing, but they carry the indelible stamp of the original encounter and the decisions the filmmaker made at the time.

As a filmmaker, I can either resist this state of affairs or embrace it. If I embrace it, I will typically put myself in situations in which my expectations are upset, revised or superseded as I film. I choose to enter a zone of indeterminacy, not because I lack objectives but because I want my objectives to be recast by the particular experience. I make a wager this will happen. To some, this may seem an odd way of approaching knowledge, for knowledge – or at least scholarly knowledge – is supposed to be built up more systematically. Here the outcome is unpredictable and open to sudden shifts of direction. To work in this way often means entrusting yourself to strangers, and there is always the risk of becoming a stranger yourself. That may be why this approach is little favoured by thesis supervisors or television commissioning editors, who prefer their successes guaranteed in advance. But for the filmmaker it is more than a calculated risk: it's a voluntary act of dislocation.

This kind of self-dislocation has something in common with the way in which our minds sometimes come up with a solution, or retrieve a word we have forgotten, only when we stop concentrating on it. Neuroscientists suspect that in these cases those parts of the brain that make unexpected connections temporarily overpower more literal thought processes.[1] This sidestepping of the logical processes of thought is capable of producing important insights in science (the 'Aha!' or 'Eureka!' moments) and powerful metaphors in the arts. Typically this occurs when the mind is relaxed and open to a wide range of connotative associations or homologies of form, as when we are just waking up, halfway between dreams and reality. Or it may happen when we are tackling a stubborn problem and, having exhausted all the conventional approaches, find ourselves at a dead end. What then takes place is a radical shift of perspective. We either see our way around the problem, or we realise that we were tackling the wrong problem all along. Just as the fully awake mind can sometimes inhibit our creative faculties, so too our familiar ways of seeing can make us blind to what we might otherwise have seen from the very beginning.

Filming produces ways of looking at the world that differ from the ways we conventionally see it. The differences are partly optical, partly social and partly structural. The optical differences are well known – the effects of different lenses on perspective, depth of field, magnification and so on. The camera itself produces these technical shifts in perception. Each filmmaker also inevitably sees the subject of a film more comprehensively than the viewer does when watching the film. These two visions are therefore in tension, since the viewer is always displaced from the filmmaker's position. Dislocation one might say, both physical and perceptual, is already, even at this stage, at the heart of cinema. There is also the peculiar enhancement that filming imparts to ordinary objects, which the Surrealists called *photogénie*. This phenomenon results partly from the ways cameras produce images, but it is also caused by the way in which framing separates objects from their surroundings and intensifies our awareness of their foreignness, their indifference to our existence. This effect, of the material world revealed in its autonomy, is experienced not only by viewers of films but also quite frequently by filmmakers in the act of filming. Through the viewfinder, filmed objects and people can take on an unexpected beauty or significance.

The social differences, on the other hand, are bound up with the oddity of trying to interact with others while operating a camera; with the presumption of 'taking' their images; with the very idea of creating an image of the present to be seen in the future. Filming fixes, photographically or electronically, the process of looking, which was once an ephemeral activity considered as ordinary as talking or breathing. Now that freedom to look as we please is called into question. Looking has overspilled its boundaries as a local, personal act. Filming also induces in the filmmaker a hypersensitivity to others that seems to negate or bypass language and other cultural differences. It is not unusual for filmmakers to feel more affinity with complete strangers than with their own close relatives and neighbours.

The structural differences are perhaps the most radical. The process of filming restructures perception through the disciplines it imposes. Just as poets for centuries have expressed themselves through sonnets, triolets and octaves, so filmmakers filter their experiences through arrangements of frames, shots and sequences. Filming requires a constant stream of decisions about what to frame, how to frame it and how to relate it to previous and future frames. It produces an analytical mode of thought specific to film, in which the filmmaker is sensitised at every moment to the particular significance of an object, a movement, a word or a facial expression. These decisions are sometimes rational, sometimes intuitive. They involve the filmmaker's body as it moves, selects, finds the right distances and repositions itself. Constructing a filmic reality in this way may be a little like writing, except that this is writing of the instant, a creative response to something outside the filmmaker's control. It is more like the instantaneous responses required

11

of an athlete or jazz musician. As in those cases, it works best when there is a synchrony between the observer and the action, an instinctive sense of what will happen next and a visceral (as well as intellectual) pleasure in responding to it.

In these situations the camera may act as an intermediary with others. Even when the filmmaker is not engaging directly with the people being filmed, the camera becomes a way of interacting with them as it responds to their actions. It acquires a personality through its use, much as each person present expresses a personality through his or her behaviour. This may be as important a presence as another observer whose primary function is simply to see, to understand, and to be known to have seen and understood. Without a camera the filmmaker would behave very differently. When interpreting the world with a camera, the filmmaker is also living through it.

Filmmaking is the only recording method I know that is three dimensional – not in the sense of producing a three-dimensional image on the screen, although there are 3D movies, but in creating a three-dimensional view of human events. It is possible for a filmmaker just to record what is directly in front of the camera, remaining more or less aloof from it. But the experience of most filmmakers is that every event can potentially be seen from a variety of positions, each producing a different understanding of it. Even a slight movement of the head contributes to three-dimensional vision, a displacement that can be duplicated by the movement of the camera. Filmmakers therefore attempt, through their filming and editing, to convey a three-dimensional understanding. This need not be achieved through a fragmentation of images, but rather through the filmmaker's living response to what is happening. A first-intention position could be described as two dimensional – approaching a subject from a conceptually fixed point – and a second-intention position as three dimensional, combining several different perspectives. This can be compared to the experience of musicians playing instruments in an orchestra. Each player experiences the music from a different position. Put all those positions together and you begin to approach a three-dimensional conception of the music.

Documentary filmmakers today, working alone with digital video cameras, are in a far better position than their forebears to become what Edgar Morin (1962: 4) called *ciné-plongeurs* – 'filmmaker-divers' who plunge into life without predetermined scripts. Jean Rouch (2003: 155) spoke of his approach to filming as a 'model of disorder'. By this he seems to have meant a way of destabilising the ordinary to gain a better purchase on it. Provocation – of reality, of consciousness, of 'normal' cinema – became Rouch's working method. 'We enter the unknown', he said, 'and the camera is forced to follow. [...] In most of the sequences I start to film, I never know what's going to be at the end' (2003: 149). 'In the field', he noted, 'the observer modifies himself' (2003: 100).

We tend to think that we learn about the world experimentally, through experiences that we just fall into. These give us new perspectives and new ways of thinking. We say these things just 'happen' to us, but I believe that, on another level, we also invite them. We often give practical reasons for making our decisions, but underlying them may be an unacknowledged wish to be taken by surprise. This drive towards dislocation suggests an unconscious strategy of second intention.

To see differently requires a certain openness, or renunciation. To find new bearings, one may need to get a little lost. When Rouch speaks of disorder, he is issuing a challenge to established cinema. The camera plays its part in creating this disorder, for it changes both the observer and the observed. In operating a camera, the filmmaker becomes an ambiguous object, taking on some of the qualities of a machine, but a machine also invested with something human. Filmmaking, says Rouch, 'is what lets me go anywhere' and 'do things I could never do if I didn't have a camera' (2003: 154).

An example of this is Rouch's filming of spirit possession at a harvest ritual in the village of Simiri in Niger. 'It seemed to me in particular that the individual observer who confronted the phenomenon of possession, of magic and sorcery, merited critical examination himself' (2003: 183). Reflecting on filming the ritual, he says:

> I myself was in a sort of trance that I call a ciné-trance, the creative state, which allowed me to follow very closely the person who was about to be initiated. The camera played the role of a ritual object. The camera becomes a magic object that can unleash or accelerate the phenomena of possession because it leads the filmmaker onto paths he would never have dared to take if he did not have it in front of him, guiding him. (Rouch, 2003: 183)

Whether in this case the presence of the camera reinforced the phenomenon of possession (we have only Rouch's word for it), what we undoubtedly see here is the role of the camera in altering his own perceptions and behaviour.

The relation of a filmmaker to a film subject may or may not have this symbiotic quality. What is more significant is that the camera propels the filmmaker from non-involvement into a stream of creative activity that runs parallel to the actions of the people being filmed. It is inspired by them but nevertheless maintains a certain independence. Rouch sometimes claimed to provoke a trance-like state of possession in the people he was filming, but in most cases the possession is all on the part of the filmmaker, who can feel possessed, sometimes entranced, by the persons and events seen through the viewfinder. This is both a spiritual and a bodily response, from which the filmmaker never remains wholly detached. In its risks, pleasures and experimentation it requires effort, but it is also much like play.

Play in filmmaking includes the physical sensation of moving fluidly and skilfully, if one is filming well. It is also part of the mimetic creation of a new event (in the theatre, called a 'play'), the pleasure of identifying with others (when observing them closely) and the excitement of the unexpected. These pleasures are apparent in many other kinds of play, such as games and make-believe. (Word-games and jokes depend upon making unexpected connections.) Similar pleasures are part of the appeal of team sports, which guarantee the surprise of a final score and the joy of free and coordinated body movements. A 'play' in sports is also a planned action, and in card games we say 'It's your play'. Above all, filming, like all play, involves a measure of trial and error; it is a way of taking risks, trying one's luck, testing one's skill. In a sense this is true for all the arts that try to distil something from reality, for each art creates its own equivalents for the forms, textures and emotions experienced in daily life.

The camera is both an instrument and an instigator of dislocation. It changes the filmmaker's visual and social perspective. In the process it becomes a guide in more than one sense, able to lead the filmmaker across the frontiers of culture, class, age and gender. In some societies certain persons are thought to be mediums for spirits of the dead. If mediumship involves a dislocation of the spirit, then perhaps filmmakers are mediums for the living. For it is not uncommon to feel inhabited by someone you have filmed. Their gestures, their tones of voice, even their phrases of speech can come back to haunt you in your own mind and actions.

In 1949 the philosopher Gilbert Ryle dismissed the Cartesian notion of the conscious mind separate from the body as 'the dogma of the Ghost in the Machine' (1949: 13). Writing some fifty years later, Gilberto Perez (1998: 28) described the images in films as ghosts of the material world. I believe the true ghosts of cinema are neither metaphysical nor material, but the phantom traces of the filmmaker's experience. Films may be machine-made, but they are also human. In my films the ghost is me.

Notes

A slightly different version of this chapter was delivered as a keynote speech at the Visual Evidence conference, held in Canberra, Australia, in December 2012. I should like to thank Frank Heidemann, Peter Loizos, Judith MacDougall, Rossella Ragazzi and others for their comments and suggestions on earlier drafts.

1   See for example Bowden and Jung-Beeman (2003) and Kounios et al. (2008).

2

Looking with a camera

Film is the only method I have to show another just how I see him.
Jean Rouch

WHEN you walk down any street in the world you watch others, and they watch you. Other creatures also watch: the dog at the corner looking for something to eat, the startled bird that flies away, the cat that (so the saying goes) can look at a king. A woman may hide her face behind a veil, a man may turn his back, a child may hide behind its mother, but in the economy of looking there remains an innocence and ease, like the freedom we have to think our own thoughts. We look, and the world looks back. Looking is considered an essentially private matter, as spontaneous and carefree as breathing. But in most societies the freedom to look has it limits and is governed by convention, and the conventions are by no means uniform. What I may look at in some circumstances, such as in my own family or the intimacy of a friendship, may be considered quite improper if I am an outsider.

Seeing is one thing, looking another. The two can sometimes be distinguished by their intention or intensity, but each shades off imperceptibly into the other. And intention, like the privacy of our thoughts, is hard to read. We may just happen to see something, or we may put ourselves in a position to see it; we may look casually or with obvious interest. Duration is critical here. A glance, one of our most instinctive and involuntary acts, can, if prolonged, quickly turn into a stare.

Acts of looking satisfy our desires and answer to a variety of needs, whereas seeing serves chiefly as a means of navigation and recognition. We look if we are attracted by a sound or a movement, out of curiosity to see how someone reacts to another's words or actions, to learn how something is done or what has happened, or simply because we take pleasure in the appearance of an object or an expression on a face. We also look involuntarily, since our eyes are always roving, catching at something here or there. Looking continuously reframes our interest as we move through different social and physical settings. During a conversation our attention may shift from one face to another, as if in a series of close-ups. When we enter a room filled with people, a quick glance may suffice to identify a friend. If we look more carefully, it is usually to work out the prominent features of an unfamiliar place. In a more familiar place we tend to notice little, needing only a few landmarks to confirm where we are. In effect, we see but don't look.

Throughout history various instruments have been devised for looking, from the *camera obscura* of antiquity to spectacles, microscopes and telescopes. Even shading the eyes to see better is a kind of instrument. Pictorial art is another. Preserving a semblance of what we have seen is as old as the cave paintings of Lascaux and Altamira, but it has always borrowed something from the imagination. Drawings and paintings capture an aspect of looking, but they are essentially retracings of the physical act, concrete memories of having looked.

The invention of photography changed all that – as it changed the way we see. Berenice Abbott, photographer of city streets and champion of the once neglected photographer Eugène Atget, observed of Atget's photography that the 'act of seeing sharpens the eye to an unprecedented acuteness. [...] As [Atget] scans his subject he sees as the lens sees, which differs from human vision. Simultaneously he sees the end result, which is to say he sees photographically' (see Goldberg, 1981: 255).

Photography, and now electronic image-making, fixes the act of looking and has upset the balance between the observer and the observed. It does so in two fundamental ways – by opening up the act of looking to others and by extending the possible time for it almost indefinitely. The glance of the shutter becomes the permanent gaze of the photograph or film. While photography may have important consequences for recording history, it has also allowed people to have second thoughts about what they have seen. Once looking is preserved, the act of looking as one wishes no longer remains transient and private, no matter how much one may want, like a diarist, to engage in it for purely private and personal reasons. When preserved, looking creates a document that can be interpreted and reinterpreted by any number of people, including those who might see it in an adverse light, not to mention the people photographed, who might think their appearance and activities best forgotten. It's one thing to imagine how others see you, another to see them looking at your image. Films and photographs also bring the past vividly into the present, in scenes that would otherwise have faded from memory. What we remember may have repercussions in the present, but replacing it with images can be far more disruptive. We are often happier that the past is irrecoverable than that we can retrieve it in films and photographs.

Fixing the look also transforms it physically, as cold transforms a gas or liquid. The look now becomes invested with all the qualities of an object that can be lost, found, bought, sold, kept private or made public. In gaining a new status it also gains substance, just as transforming spoken words into writing emphasises their meaning. The words are no longer presented as they were spoken, each replaced by the next as soon as it is uttered, but take concrete form on the page. You can see this clearly in the subtitling of films. Sentences appear not in their linear flow but as whole units on the screen. Printing them not only translates the speech but adds to it the *gravitas* of a text.

For all these reasons, the ability to look freely with a camera is subject to cultural and legal constraints. It shares this with the ability to write freely in the press. But those who control photography and filmmaking – unlike the Beaverbrooks, Maxwells and Murdochs of publishing – are now more likely to be faceless institutions like television companies, censorship boards, film finance corporations and academic committees. Underlying them are other, more deep-seated forces of constraint. These are the rules and conventions that have become so ingrained in us that they appear to be natural laws. That they are not, and can even be harmful to us, should be a matter of concern.

CONVENTIONS

Looking with a camera imposes its own routines and disciplines. Filmmakers surrender many of their ways of looking to more regulated systems. Photography and cinematography impose their own technical constraints – for example, in their earlier years the inability to reproduce colour. But cultural conventions impose even more. In fiction films these take the form of condensing time, fragmenting actions and framing scenes in formally prescribed ways. These conventions may be acceptable and even essential in fiction films, but when they spill over into documentary they can begin to erode its ability to reflect the extraordinary range of human perception.

In both fiction and nonfiction films, a physical process is typically broken up into a series of shots, each representing a step in the process and reducing the time it takes to unfold. The same approach is often applied to a social process, such as an argument. As tempers rise, the film progresses through a series of quickening shots of the actors from different positions, adding to the tension. Other conventions govern how abstract ideas are presented, such as the passage of time. Hollywood films of the 1930s and 1940s developed a special kind of montage for this purpose, with pages fluttering off a calendar, clock hands rapidly revolving and newspapers rolling off the presses. This required such specialised treatment that an expert was often called in to create the sequence. The most famous of these was Slavko Vorkapich. Even today, this type of sequence is known as a 'Vorkapich montage'.

Audiences readily understand such conventions as cinematic shortcuts, but other practices tend to collapse more subtly the differences between human and filmic perception. Commercial film production, especially for television, demands professional efficiency. The director is under an obligation to 'cover'

17

events and get the necessary establishing shots and cutaways for editing. An implicit standard of *relevancy* creates further pressure to streamline the representation of events and produce a coherent narrative. This may mean leaving out distracting material that gets in the way of establishing clear-cut characters or furthering the film's forward momentum. In documentaries, several events are often compressed into one and people are portrayed as holding simpler views than they do in reality. The ambiguities are simply smoothed away.

Efficiencies of this kind clearly have the potential to misrepresent the situations filmed. Although reducing complexity is often explained as necessary to avoid confusing the audience, there is a further tendency that might be called the 'cosmetic effect'. Here, certain conventions are observed not out of any particular aim at clarity but because of a broader consensus that films, especially documentaries, should be discreet. Socially conscious films are allowed a certain frankness when this serves a morally or politically approved purpose, but otherwise filmmakers are encouraged to gloss over the smaller realities and indignities of life. Filmmakers may be willing to show the horrors of war, the pollution of the land and extremes of violence but be reluctant to show much more common events. Few films, fictional or nonfictional, portray with any accuracy the most ordinary human activities or the unglamorous ways people typically see their own bodies. Even sex scenes, in which the cinema abounds, remain highly stylised and circumspect. Rarely do films show anything as routine as making a bed, brushing teeth, bathing, dressing, washing clothes, preparing a meal, reading or writing – much less sneezing, scratching, coughing or using a toilet. We are left with a habit of turning away from these things, as if we were to blame for their existence. Of the many details of modern living, films seem to have singled out only a few for repeated attention: driving cars, going in and out of doorways, drinking alcohol and (until recently) smoking. Still photographers have been far more courageous and wide-ranging in this regard. Among American photographers alone, Wayne Miller, Sally Mann, Robert Frank and Danny Lyon are notable for recording the many small particularities of everyday life, whether painful, awkward or pleasurable.

It's not that we necessarily want filmmakers to fill their films with such material, but rather that they should feel more at liberty to do so. At a certain point the cinema goes into retreat, drawing a veil over whatever it judges to be awkward or inappropriate on the screen. Most filmmakers will stray only so far from the public consensus, even if it means producing sanitised or highly edited accounts of what they have witnessed. Sometimes films about extreme events such as wars or disasters bypass these conventions, but those dealing with everyday events seem bound by narrower rules. Many details of the fine grain of human experience thus remain invisible to film, either because they are considered too ordinary to merit attention or because they are viewed with shame. For such an avowedly realist medium as film this is surprising, since it is one of the best technologies we have for recording just how we see the world. The loss is not simply a benign absence. It produces a lop-sided account of human experience, even implying that the act of looking is somehow reprehensible.

There is also film's temporal dimension. From the beginning, the cinema has been modelled on the theatre, and films have also had to fit the spectators' capacity to stay seated. Whereas most forms of writing – novels, memoirs, biographies – adopt a relaxed approached to time, it is rare for films to do so. They tend to rush ahead as though pursued, and they lack the gaps and quiet moments that occupy so much of our lives. A few filmmakers – notably Michelangelo Antonioni and Andrei Tarkovsky, but others too, such as Abbas Kiarostami, Nuri Bilge Ceylan and Sergei Loznitsa – have tried to restore some of the flexibility of time as people experience it. Some, like Andy Warhol, have carried their experiments to an unwatchable extreme. Yet today, with so many viewing formats available, the older constraints seem less necessary. Nonfiction films such as Agnès Varda's *The Gleaners and I* (2000) and Wang Bing's *West of the Tracks* (2003), many recent drama series for television, and fiction films such as Bernardo Bertolucci's *1900* (1976) and Terence Davies's autobiographical films resist the pressures of conventional cinema and use more essay-like and novelistic structures.

The conventions of filmmaking, however, were not invented just to make things easier for directors and film editors. They are also recipes for regulating the thinking of the viewer. In film after film, cinema audiences are trained to cooperate in certain ways of looking at the world. This has become a kind of shorthand and, indeed, the foundation of an artistic tradition. But like all such traditions, it has come at the cost of narrowing the horizons of artists and their audiences. If a filmmaker wishes to look at the world in a different way, this has to be done by a calculated departure from the norm, just as writers, at their peril, can stray only so far from the conventions of written language. A noted authority on James Joyce's *Finnegans Wake* has admitted that he has never quite managed to read it through.[1] In filmmaking, as in the other arts, there is always a kind of balancing act between convention and innovation – between observing the rules and breaking them. If you take a risk in one direction, you may have to offset this by following more accepted practices in another. The familiar thus serves as an anchor and a point of departure for change. Pioneering film directors like Alfred Hitchcock and Jean-Luc Godard underpinned many of their cinematic experiments with melodramatic plots and glamorous actors, giving audiences something attractive and reassuring to hang on to. For documentary filmmakers, the choices are necessarily more limited. Yet they often 'cast' their films as surely as Hollywood directors, looking for the most expressive protagonists. Documentary films are also expected to provide more overt forms of explanation than fiction films. Robert Gardner, breaking several documentary conventions, refused to include either subtitles or an explanatory commentary in *Forest of Bliss* (1985), his film about the cycle of death in the city of Benares. By refusing to explain certain practices, he was criticised by anthropologists for reinforcing popular misconceptions of India.[2] For analogous reasons, many middle-class Indians accused him of a touristic approach, exploiting the exotic and sensational aspects of Indian culture. Both failed to grasp the film's complexity and serious intent.

The characteristic response to a film that offends is moral outrage, not only because it appears to violate good taste but because, in many cases, the filmmaker seems to be getting away with what others would hesitate to film. Luis Buñuel was attacked throughout his career for ignoring the codes of propriety – those of the church, of bourgeois society, of the law. From the time of his association with the Surrealists he presented the hidden, the painful and the perverse as perfectly ordinary. In *Los Olvidados* (1950) a pack of children rob and beat up a blind beggar, something that no doubt happens somewhere in the world every day. In *Viridiana* (1961) he jokes about *The Last Supper* by having a woman lift her skirt to 'photograph' a group of beggars in the poses of Leonardo da Vinci's famous tableau. In *Le Fantôme de la liberté* (1974) people sit around a table shitting instead of eating. Many years before these feature films were made, Buñuel made his mock documentary *Land without Bread* (1933), which parodied the posturing of educators and reformers. His films take for granted the dishonesty of all moralists and their institutions. Buñuel's response to the restraints felt by filmmakers was to reply with excess. Most documentary filmmakers are less inclined to do so, while those attracted to oddities and excesses often simply mirror the public's conservatism in reverse.

There are other, more understandable reasons why filmmakers may choose to avoid or exclude some aspects of what they film. They may withhold material that could be damaging or embarrassing to those they have filmed. The voluntary withholding of such material has been called a 'moral pause' and may take priority over other concerns.[3] If we accept that documentary films almost always intrude upon their subjects' lives in some way, in most cases filmmakers have an obligation to try to minimise the negative effects of their intrusion. Without some such understanding, they could hardly gain the trust of their subjects necessary to make their films. The dilemma for all filmmakers, however, is how to balance this obligation against the imperative to give an honest account of what they have seen. Achieving such a balance is not as simple as it sounds. Even assuming that the filmmaker is sympathetic towards a film's subjects, which is not always the case, most filming situations are still full of ambiguities and conflicting loyalties. The relationship between the filmmaker and film subject is a fluid one. Trust is not a given; it must be built over time as the filming progresses. Added to this, the subjects' views are likely to fluctuate, not least when the film is shown to others. The easiest solution is to establish rules and protocols for the filming in advance. But fixed rules, such as the obligatory use of release forms, are blunt instruments. They fail to recognise the evolving nature of the relationship between filmmaker and film subject. Imposing an artificial and formalised structure tends to encourage the making of safe and predictable films. Unsurprisingly, institutions and their legal teams favour such an approach, but more often to protect their own interests than those of the film subjects. More perceptive documentary films usually result from a shared belief by filmmakers and subjects in the importance of the film, even if they believe in it for different reasons. People who have been filmed will very often agree to the inclusion of disturbing or embarrassing scenes provided they feel the film was made in good faith and gives an honest account of the events shown.

There are some circumstances in which other priorities may override the wishes of the film subjects. Although the physical safety of people in a film should always be protected, this does not necessarily hold true for their personal feelings. Frederick Wiseman has argued that the public's right to know what goes on in publicly funded institutions may take precedence over the right of those institutions to prevent their activities being shown, even if this means some of the individuals in them suffer indignities or criticism as a result. This principle is evident in such films as his *Titicut Follies* (1967) and *Hospital* (1970), in which the camera refuses to look away from distressing conditions and individual suffering. In other cases the aim may be precisely to expose a person or group to criticism, as in Nick Broomfield's *The Leader, His Driver and the Driver's Wife* (1991), about the South African white supremacist Eugène Terre'Blanche. In these cases, right is not necessarily on the side of the film subject. Not all films can or should be respectful and polite.

POLITENESS

In 1984 Pauline Spiegel published an article entitled 'The Case of the Well-Mannered Guest'. She argued that 'outsiders tend to become insiders when studying their subjects closely'. At the time, a new subgenre of autobiographical and biographical documentaries was beginning to give an unprecedented look at the lives of ordinary people. But according to Spiegel, when

> watching them, one senses that something is missing, that more could be said, that they show us less than they could. What characterizes many of these films is a sense of politeness, of reticence towards their subject. It's the politeness of the frequent, privileged guest. [...] What this implies is an agreement, stated or unstated, with the subject to produce a film that shows the subjects the way they see themselves. [...] The implicit contract between the filmmaker and the subject leads to self-censorship. (Spiegel, 1984: 15–16)

Self-censorship among filmmakers is often reinforced by the conditions under which films are made – of collaboration, commissioning and sponsorship. The more filmmakers owe to their subjects or sponsors, the more they are likely to be bound by their perspective and complicit with their desires. The misrepresentation that then occurs typically results from a combination of two factors: collusion between filmmakers and their subjects and filmmakers suspending their moral judgement. Initially, protecting the subjects may mean no more than omitting material they might find embarrassing, disagreeable or critical. But further along, the filmmaker's judgement can be compromised by accepting (or concealing) acts that he or she would usually find unacceptable. This can sometimes be justified on the grounds of respecting cultural differences, but it may eventually lead to concealing or condoning cruel or even criminal acts. If the film is about a group of political dissidents, how far should the filmmaker go in recording their acts of violence? If a group believes in genital mutilation or inhumane punishments, should the filmmaker agree to film such scenes? The filmmaker's moral position becomes even more dubious if, as sometimes happens, such acts are performed as demonstrations for the film.

The politeness of a guest easily extends to overlooking community discord, a central character's wrongdoing, a government official's lies or an institution's dangerous conditions. As the recipient of a gift – the subject's cooperation – it is all too easy for the filmmaker to respond with compliance. The misrepresentation that results may not be of a serious nature, but it is misrepresentation nonetheless. Perhaps no film can show everything, or should even attempt to do so. Indeed, specialists often criticise films for leaving things out, and demand excessive detail. But there is a crucial difference between avoiding this kind of overload and suppressing facts that a filmmaker knows full well but elects to leave out. All too often filmmakers are put under pressure to avoid embarrassments, iron out complexities and shield reputations. The truth of nonfiction films is undermined less by the shortcomings of visual representation than by their makers' bad faith.

Filmmakers who violate the boundaries of propriety or good art are apt to be seen as brash or incompetent. They may be, but it is important to look more closely at their films. Have they given us any new understanding of how life is lived? The majority of filmmakers are content to stand back. They would prefer to view their subjects from afar, coming close only in predictable ways. But as Jean Rouch (2003: 38) has pointed out, this is a surveillance mentality, a desire to see without responsibility, as if from a distant observation post. Filming honestly may mean showing what others are reluctant to show. Although documentary films inevitably reflect the character of their times, they are also capable of reaching beyond them. Films have allowed us, for the first time, to see in concrete detail how and what others see. Like the other arts, they help create a shared consciousness among us, but about the outer world, beyond our powers of creation. There are many gaps in what filmmakers have been allowed or have allowed themselves to film, but the dream to fill those gaps has always existed. It is a fragile dream, and one to be protected.

Notes

1 This was supposedly Sebastian D. G. Knowles, as reported in the NB section of the *TLS* (*Times Literary Supplement*), 18 December 2009.
2 See reviews of the film by Alexander Moore (1988), Jonathan Parry (1988) and Jay Ruby (1989), all appearing in the *Society for Visual Anthropology Newsletter*.
3 This concept is put forward in the book *Image Ethics*, edited by Larry Gross, John Stuart Katz and Jay Ruby (1988: 32). In arguing for media restraint, the editors in their Introduction took this phrase from a court case in which a Federal judge asked if CBS Television couldn't have waited a week – taken a 'moral pause' – before releasing videotapes that could have prejudiced the drug-trafficking trial of John Z. DeLorean. DeLorean was eventually acquitted.

3

Camera, mind and eye

Camera and mind

Documentary filmmakers sometimes have literary ambitions. Robert Flaherty always insisted that film commentary should be written as poetry. Pare Lorentz, in his two documentaries of the 1930s, *The Plow That Broke the Plains* (1936) and *The River* (1938), edited his images to a text that was more poetic incantation than prose. A few years earlier W. H. Auden's verse formed part of the commentary of the GPO Film Unit documentary *Night Mail* (1936).

But these have been the exceptions. Most documentary films that rely on a spoken text are wedded to more prosaic language. Usually the commentary is based on the language of journalism or the academy. Occasionally everyday speech makes an appearance, but this is rare. There is sometimes an oratorical element. Newsreels of the 1930s and 1940s specialised in a grandiose style that borrowed heavily from the pulpit and politics.

Similar conventions apply to images. Today, most scientific, historical and public affairs television programmes, like the documentary films that preceded them, are built around images that illustrate a spoken text. These images vary from the inspired to the hackneyed – for overpopulation, a crowded street scene; for pollution, factory chimneys; and so on. If their own footage doesn't suffice, many directors will make do with images from a stock shot library. Their choices of images that match the subjects mentioned in the script are then more often literal than literary.

Finding the appropriate material isn't always easy. Television producers and filmmakers have good reason to regard both the concreteness and the indeterminacy of images with caution. A shot may be judged too specific to represent the general principle to be illustrated. Yet when specificity is required, the shot may turn out to be too general. Shots, like unruly children, may have to be brought into line with words, using voice-over commentary, titles on the screen or interviews. There are historical precedents for this. Long before the introduction of sound, documentaries were routinely ac-companied by lectures that interpreted the images for the audience. This pedagogical style has had a lasting and often stifling effect on documentary filmmaking.

Even when texts are less prominent in films, the way the images are organised often follows textual modes of presentation. Nonfiction films, like academic papers, will typically be built around an introduction, an exposition, the development of an argument and a concluding summary. Booklets on filmmaking used to recommend a similar approach: start with a wide-angle 'establishing' shot, then use several close-ups to identify the main characters, use medium shots for the action, and finally another wide shot to pull everything together.

This way of organising visual material mimics the structures found in speech and writing – exposition, argument, counter-argument, induction, deduction and so on. Even so, such structures rarely correspond to the ways we actually think, and even less so to the varied ways we experience the world. The consciousness of most of us is more disorganised. Our ideas tend to emerge from a rich jumble of glimpses and fragments that only occasionally coalesce into a pattern of words. In describing the mind's activity, William James in 1890 compared it to the 'flights and perchings' of a bird.[1] Until we have grasped something non-verbally, we often have no way of formulating a coherent statement about it. By the time we are able to pose a question in words, we often already have a good idea of the answer. The sorts of mental questions we ask rarely take the form of written questions. They express themselves in speculations, doubts and uncertainties. Similarly, film images, and the conventions by which they are put together, depart from the ways we actually see, which is both more wide-ranging and less systematic. We tend to gather up visual impressions omnivorously, mixing relevant and irrelevant details within a broader view. We position ourselves strategically in relation to those objects that have meaning for us. For reasons that perhaps reach back to our biological past, we are especially drawn to faces; we note people's features as familiar or unfamiliar and respond to their expressions.

If spoken texts in films represent a particular, stylised mode of thought, the organisation of the images attached to them tends to be no less stylised. Our minds admit many less disciplined forms of language, and combine visual images, sounds, sensory impressions, memories of the past, imaginings of the future, and beneath all this a stratum of desire and potential action. Words play a part, but often in unexpected ways – as experimental sentences, things we might have said, snatches of music, nursery rhymes and bits of remembered conversations. A few filmmakers have tried to capture this upsurge of the subconscious into our thoughts. Clément Perron, in *Day after Day* (1962), includes on the soundtrack the sorts of uninvited phrases that invade the minds of workers during monotonous hours of factory work.

Some films, and many individual scenes in films, dispense with words altogether. There are long stretches without dialogue in the films of Robert Bresson (*A Man Escaped*, 1956; *Au hasard Balthazar*, 1966) and Michelangelo

Antonioni (*La Notte*, 1961; *L'Eclisse*, 1962), and in later films, such as Michelangelo Frammartino's *Le Quattro Volte* (2010). These films implicitly question the importance of language in our lives and the extent to which films reflect our day-to-day experience. Is life really as full of words as films imply? Have films, whether fictional or documentary, let themselves be too easily dominated by them? What if films paid more attention to the diversity of sounds around us? What if they more closely followed our actual patterns of thought and perception, not just the ideas or the images we formulate for others?

We can explore this possibility further if we ask how films pose questions. They can of course do so verbally, in titles or spoken commentary. Titles asking questions can be found in a number of Soviet films of the silent era. In Sergei Eisenstein's *The General Line* (1929) one inter-title reads: 'Why a tractor?' More often, however, films ask questions by means of narratives. These films seem to be asking 'What will happen next?' or 'Who is this person?' or 'Why did he or she do that?' Another way of asking a question is less direct. In form, it closely resembles the way we examine and assess the objects around us. Simply showing something poses few questions, but watching it closely, looking at it intently, is a way of saying: 'I am drawn to this thing, I demand something from it: to know more about it, to learn its true nature, to discover what, if anything, it means to me.' This kind of questioning seems pre-linguistic, yet it is a mode of enquiry that is funda-mental to our patterns of observation and essential to the way we acquire most kinds of knowledge.

Most documentary films tend to give answers to questions rather than ask them. More speculative films tend to be made by filmmakers with an intuitive approach to the cinema. For filmmakers like Chris Marker, Johan van der Keuken and Agnès Varda, the camera is never simply used as a recording device or a way of imparting information but an extension of the mind and body – a means of connecting with the world on personal terms (figure 3.1). Their films often have literary qualities in their use of voice-over commentary, but these qualities are extended by concrete observations of the physical world. What literature evokes verbally, their films are able to express more directly, through objects, faces and gestures.

At certain moments in such films there is a merging of the mind, the body and the camera. We see not only the enquiring mind at work but more complex expressions of thought and feeling. In commercial documentary films, on the other hand, the aim is generally to project an air of certainty and authority, and the footage shot for them generally reflects this purpose. Footage shot by more adventurous filmmakers will often lack such economy and predictability. On the contrary, it may contain passages of blankness, searching or simply waiting. It can also take the form of a conscious exercise in looking. Richard Leacock (1997) has said that when he was working with

3.1 Framing a detail in Agnès Varda's *The Gleaners and I*

Robert Flaherty on *Louisiana Story* (1948), the two of them often spent hours filming spiders' webs, clouds, birds and water lilies.

Human memory is imperfect and coloured by the concerns of the day. A camera's memory is technically perfect and highly selective, but it is also inflexible. Someone once pointed out to me that the camera's images can in some instances supplant one's own memories. The film's testimony is more vivid and concrete – but at the cost of undermining the pictures of one's imagination. I had filmed this young man as a child, and a portion of his childhood, he said, had been fixed and defined by being filmed. In a similar way, our knowledge of world events is largely formed by the photographs and films we see of them. As time passes, the dominance of film and photography increases, as those with direct memories of the events die out.

Institutions tend to present the camera as a neutral instrument, all the better to prove that their view of the world is correct. They expect us to believe what we see and accept the camera's way of showing it. This assumption dominates most documentary films and nonfiction television. It is reinforced by a standard repertoire of camera set-ups: the establishing shot, low angle, close-up, reverse angle and so on. But as we know from the work of directors like Renoir, Welles, Ozu and many others, filmmakers are capable of framing the world in quite diverse ways. The images in them become immediately recognisable as theirs, and one would not mistake them for those of another director, any more than one would mistake Stravinsky's music for Rachmaninoff's, or the writing of Faulkner for that of Hemingway. In nonfiction films, the camera style of Flaherty, for example, is clearly different from that of Basil Wright, even though they have things in common.

As in these cases, the authorial voice in documentary films is particularly evident when the camera is in the hands of the director. Even in the hands of an amateur, a camera can reveal specific patterns of thought. Imagine a camera that is constantly roving but never quite coming to rest on any subject, as can often be seen in home movies. The camera is nervous and overexcited, reflecting a mind unsure of itself, hunting for something worthy of such a powerful technology but never quite finding it. Typically, in these cases, the camera glides over the surface of things in the belief that this will somehow gather up reality and allow us to see more of it, when in fact the constant movement allows us to see very little. Imagine now a highly attentive camera that studies a subject for a sustained period. It may do so for a variety of reasons. It may be because of a special interest already established, or because it is drawn to a particular person or place. It may be waiting for something to happen, or watching out of fascination or horror, or looking purely for the sake of looking, for aesthetic enjoyment. Preoccupation with a face may indicate more than a wish to know the feelings of the person being filmed: it may signify complicity or desire on the part of the filmmaker. This particular kind of looking often seems like a form of communion, as if reaching out to the person being filmed.

The camera, far from being a neutral instrument, is thus capable of registering a complex range of responses to the world, from indifference to professional competence to feelings that are deeply personal. The clues to these states of mind must, of course, be interpreted by a viewer, and this requires some common ground of cultural and psychological experience. But the process may also involve something more primitive – our innate animal responses to certain sights and sounds: to facial expressions, postures, cries and sudden movements.

Several other factors also play a part. The physical distance between a filmmaker and the subject can reflect either cultural conditioning or a degree of personal engagement, or both. At times, the personal engagement may be strong enough to overcome social conventions, as when the camera draws unusually close to a face or, on the contrary, disregards the ostensible subject of the scene in order to inspect something quite different, such as the clothes a person is wearing or another event going on nearby. One of the strongest indicators of the state of mind of the filmmaker is how the camera moves, or when it does not. Shifting the camera from one framing to another usually indicates a change of interest, but it may also indicate a desire to reveal a link between two objects or people, or demonstrate a cause and its effect. It may also suggest a metaphorical or thematic connection.

28

Even moves that are apparently unconscious can be clues to deeper feelings of empathy. Synchrony between the movements of the camera and those of the film subject – a synchrony that Jean Rouch (2003: 99, 184) compared to the dance – often reveals a strong cultural or personal affinity.

From fragmentary traces like these we construct the filmmaker's way of looking at the world, and that world itself. Sometimes filmmakers purposely defy our expectations. Jean-Luc Godard, in *Vivre sa vie* (1962), keeps the camera firmly fixed on the back of Anna Karina's head throughout her conversation with an unseen man on her right, both of them seated at a bar; her face appears only indistinctly in a mirror (figure 3.2). The next shot is of the man, also seen from the back. This perverse withholding of information, while witty, also creates a sense of mystery. In *Weekend* (1967) Godard makes the camera travel impassively past everything happening in the frame, purposely ignoring it. Hitchcock often plays with our expectations for a strictly narrative purpose. In *Strangers on a Train* (1951) he holds a shot on a crowd of spectators at a tennis match. We see that only one man in the crowd is not turning his head, following the ball (figure 3.3). He is Bruno, the protagonist's enemy, and his fixed look creates a sudden thrill of danger. In these films, two dramas are being enacted on the screen: one the event being filmed, the other the filmmaker's way of filming it.

3.2 A scene shot from behind the actors in *Vivre sa vie*

3.3 The gaze of the enemy in *Strangers on a Train*

CAMERA AND EYE

Camera technology sets certain limits on a filmmaker's expressiveness yet at the same time may be turned to the filmmaker's advantage. In 1982 the anthropologist Ivo Strecker published a paper that, given the temper of the times, seemed meant as a provocation (Strecker, 1982). He gently reproved those scholars who would rather deliver themselves into the hands of media professionals than attempt to make films themselves. As for himself, he had discovered the virtues of the only camera he could then afford, a Bolex 16 mm camera with a mechanical spring drive, capable of making shots of no more than twenty-four seconds. His essay begins with technology but ends with broader implications for how we see.

By the 1980s the technology of silently running, battery-driven hand-held cameras such as the Éclair and Arriflex was well established. These were now the preferred cameras of documentary filmmakers, replacing the cumbersome 35 mm equipment that had originated with Lumière and Edison. Sound recorders had undergone a similar transformation, becoming ever more portable. In earlier times, documentary filmmaking had gradually adopted the methods of fiction filmmaking, with pre-planned camera set-ups and the subjects acting act out scenes based roughly on their own lives. The technology that emerged in the 1960s allowed the filming of much more spontaneous events in almost any situation. It largely did away with big film crews, cameras on fixed tripods and sound recorders attached to noisy generators and lengths of heavy cable.

Thus liberated, filmmakers began to explore the possibilities opened up by the new portable equipment. One of these was to follow the course of unpredictable events. Another was to film the things that made an event distinctive rather than those that made it typical. This was contrary to the usual documentary practice, which, as Dai Vaughan (1999: 12) observed, aimed to 'portray a "type" of incident, not to record a particular one'. The new approach often led to the use of longer camera takes. Filmmakers often became more interested in showing the development of events in their own time than reconstructing them in the editing. Since revelatory moments could not be scripted in advance, they had to be caught as they occurred. Documentary filmmaking thus began to be more about observing human events in their wholeness than about building them up later, in shots taken from different camera positions. The film editor's job, instead of putting fragments of film together, became more one of selecting and linking entire scenes.

Against this background – with cameras capable of making shots of ten to twelve minutes (or even hours, if the filmmaker so arranged it) – Strecker began to discover the virtues of his spring-drive Bolex. In describing this he was not trying to promote the use of short takes as a method; he simply offered it as an alternative. The limitations of the Bolex camera, he wrote, could teach the filmmaker an important lesson: 'not to confuse the filmic representation with reality itself, and to realize from the start that his film will be a reduction, an iconic resemblance, a model' (Strecker, 1982: 11). The shortness of the shots forced the filmmaker to think of the film as a construction rather than a copy of reality. Each shot had to be made in such a way as to contribute an essential piece to the accuracy of the model. Although the pieces would be combined later in the editing, the selection and sequencing of them had to be done at the time of filming.

It will be obvious that, in some respects, this approach resembles the sort of documentaries that the newer film technologies had largely replaced. Strecker pointed out, however, that it suited only some subjects, such as ritualised events, whose structures were already known. In effect, the film then illustrated the event, sampling it at various points to represent its different stages. At the same time, he went on to say, the weakness of such an approach was that 'you will be concerned only with what is standard and what is the norm. You will be concerned with patterns rather than [particular] events.' It was therefore not a way of gaining new knowledge but rather a way of demonstrating the knowledge you already had. And he added: 'But how do you find out how things are in the first place? Is not the finding out in itself an illuminating process? Doesn't the camera have a place in the very process of *exploration*?'

31

(Strecker, 1982: 12; original emphasis). Elsewhere in his writings Strecker describes this process as a quest for 'not the ideal but the real, not the reflective but the spontaneous' (Strecker, 1979: v). Using the camera in this way, as a research tool rather than a means of publishing previously acquired knowledge, had much in common with the approach of Jean Rouch, Marc-Henri Piault, Eliane de Latour and other, mostly French, visual anthropologists for whom filmmaking was first and foremost a method of research.

Strecker's experience with the Bolex brings to mind a discovery that several of us made in the 1980s when teaching anthropology students how to use video cameras. One disadvantage of using low-cost video was that it encouraged inexperienced filmmakers to shoot a great deal of material in the hope that it could eventually be edited into a coherent work. Almost inevitably, they discovered later that they had made the wrong shots for what they now wished to convey. Instead, we asked our students to edit their material as they were shooting it, in the camera. As well as limiting excessive shooting, this forced them to think of their filming as an analytical process – to think how the shot they were making at one moment related to the last shot they had made and the shot they might make next. They were structuring the material as they created it instead of hoping that by simply 'covering' a subject they could later provide an intelligent understanding of it.

Further changes in technology have helped make filmmakers even more aware of the selective nature of images. With modern video cameras, instead of looking through a viewfinder it is more usual to look at an LCD screen. This produces a miniature framed picture that the filmmaker holds in the hand. This experience is very different from looking through a viewfinder, with the impression that you watching the world through a little window. Here you are looking at the finished image itself. You are forced to think of it as an image only, to be put alongside other images.

The virtues of short camera takes are evident in the films of Jorge Prelorán, who, like Strecker, started his filming career using a Bolex camera. In making films such as *Imaginero* (1970) and *Zerda's Children* (1978), he began by recording extensive audio interviews with his subjects. It was only after this that he began filming. The two kinds of material were then combined in the finished films. The images, rather than merely illustrating what the subjects said, commented further on their lives, revealing their social and economic situation as well as Prelorán's feelings about them, and even at times the subjects' own subjective view of the world. The films become a collage of multiple perspectives. They give the impression of a filmmaker observing details with the same sense of intimacy that they hold for his subjects. Often these images have no strictly functional role in the film. They are the sorts of details that in many other films would be stripped away to make for a more streamlined argument. But here their presence is at the heart of the film and its subjects' lived experience.

In a later article Strecker notes that such small details may be 'seemingly accidental elements' that the viewer discovers half-hidden in films but finds particularly striking – details that may have been included for reasons that even the filmmaker doesn't fully understand. These elements are 'uninvited' but for that very reason they contribute to 'complexity, creativity and authenticity' (Strecker, 2003). They allow for random observations that give added resonance to the filmmaker's underlying interests. Such apparently gratuitous moments provide a key to Prelorán's art and, in part, to Strecker's. In Strecker's *The Leap across the Cattle* (1979, filmed 1975–6) and *The Father of the Goats* (1984), there are a number of such 'accidental' cinematic details. Strecker describes the filming of one of them:

> As the first warm rays of the morning sun were entering the goat enclosure of a Hamar homestead I was focusing my Blech-Bolex on a small white goat. The goat was doing some exercises to warm up after the long and cool night. It stood up and banged its front hooves against the fence of the enclosure. Then it rubbed its side against a pole and in a sudden fit of joy leapt into the air, spreading all four legs widely apart. As it came down to the ground again, it raced off and, after a moment, was back again.
>
> Now I began to film. Again the goat played at the fence. A few seconds passed until suddenly one of its forelegs got stuck in between two pieces of wood. First the goat tried to free itself, then it began to bleat. I continued to film and then saw the hand of a girl free the foreleg of the goat. The moment the goat was released, my twenty-four seconds were over and the camera stopped. (Strecker, 1982: 11)

Although it is important to distinguish between intention and accident, there is nevertheless a link between Strecker's inclusion of 'seemingly accidental' events and Prelorán's constant search for the telling detail. In filming the unexpected, Strecker opens his filmmaking up to what he can neither predict nor fully understand. His courting of such accidents becomes part of a larger strategy of intention.

In other films, short takes can have quite different meanings and effects. They can resemble a character's glances or a stage actor's 'asides'. For the filmmaker, they may hint at the inexpressible. I once made a shot of three peaches caught in flickering sunlight. On another occasion I made a shot of a schoolboy's feet and scuffed shoes under his desk (figure 3.4). Another shot is of a metal teapot filling up a cup.[2] It would be difficult to explain exactly why these shots were made or what their function is in their respective films. None is essential to the scene in which it occurs. Nor are these shots simply meant to give texture to the events shown, although they may contribute to it. Their metaphorical value, if any, is negligible. Rather, they function both as a kind of punctuation and more simply as tributes to objects in the material world. Then, too, they create for the viewer a brief suspension in the film's progress, as though to say: forget the film for a moment and only

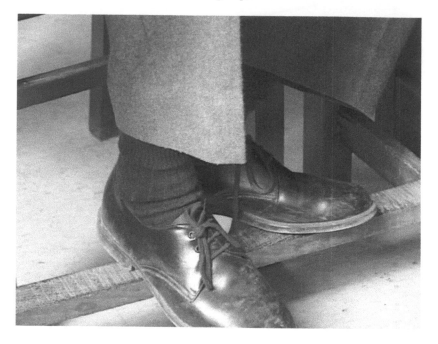

3.4 A student's shoes in *Doon School Chronicles*

look. These are the humble things that matter: the peaches, the scuffed shoes, the teapot.

The act of looking with a camera may be quick or lingering. Neither practice is necessarily better than the other: the choice depends upon the circumstances. A deliberate gaze – the long take of cinema – allows the viewer to observe events in the course of their enactment. It may lead to a better understanding of cause and effect, or show how something is done, or reveal the thoughts and feelings of the people in the film. A short take, like a quick glance, seizes an observation from the countless possibilities available – sometimes apparently at random, sometimes accidentally, but more often for some half-sensed purpose. It can yield unexpected insights and significant details. These images, because of their brevity, can also be filmed with great efficiency and then tucked away for future use. They may serve to illuminate a complex situation, such as the facial expression of someone caught off-guard or (as might happen in a Hitchcock thriller) the fact that a character is missing a finger. At other times their value may be less direct. A glance may link a physical object to someone's character or epitomise a certain social milieu. It may summon up sensory qualities such as the texture of an object, the way a person stands or a resemblance between two apparently dissimilar objects.

It might seem at first that there is a direct correlation between the short take and the close-up and, equally, between the long take and the wide shot, but this is by no means always the case. A quick glance from a distance can accurately size up a social situation such as an argument between two people, while a long take in close-up may register important details, such as how a particular procedure is carried out. In Robert Bresson's film *A Man Escaped* (1956) it is through such extended close-ups that we learn how an improvised knife is used to cut through a cell door, and in Nicolas Philibert's film *In the Land of the Deaf* (1992) how a deaf child is taught to speak.

Some years ago Norman Bryson argued that in paintings one could detect two different sensibilities, that of the gaze and that of the glance. The gaze, he maintained, is disconnected from personal experience and history. It is penetrating and sustained yet conceals its authorship, its humanity. The glance, by contrast, has the inadvertent quality of an everyday happening and is like a simple, fleeting artefact of personal looking. It can be innocent and casual, or carry a suggestion of stealth, lust or hostility. In painting, 'it does not seek to bracket out the process of viewing, nor in its own techniques does it exclude the traces of the body of labour' (Bryson, 1983: 94).

If in films a short take suggests a glance, it seems even more firmly linked to the act of looking than in painting, where its qualities must be inferred from the composition or technique. Perhaps because it also stands out more obviously in a film as clearly targeted, it seems more forthright, declaring its interest with little possibility of evasion. The filmmaker's glance becomes, involuntarily, the viewer's. It is tied to the moment and yet, as we have seen, it may convey a variety of intentions and meanings, from casual recognition, to shock, to pleasurable discovery. While never wholly arbitrary in the constructed nature of a film, its brevity nevertheless gives it an artless, accidental quality. A glance does not penetrate, it glances *off* its subject, almost as if out of politeness. The glancing look, having looked, moves on. If it judges, it does so lightly, like most of our glances in everyday life.

But in cinema the long take too (*pace* Bryson) easily carries the weight of a filmmaker's intentions. Far from being impersonal, it often reveals its authorship in the intensity of its scrutiny, its framing or the way it moves from subject to subject. It is rare for a long take in cinema to suggest the kind of blank gaze that might be produced by a surveillance camera in a bank. Mistaking its gaze for indifference may stem from the same confusion that equates observation with a lack of engagement. It was a common misconception among critics in the 1960s that *cinéma vérité* and Direct Cinema films represented a distanced, impersonal stance, when they were in fact even more personal and highly authored forms of documentary filmmaking than previous forms.

The majority of events that we witness in daily life are routine and predictable and they tend to be filmed in predictable ways. But others are erratic, exotic or volatile. Filming such unexpected events involves flexibility, requiring the filmmaker to be carried along, seizing whatever opportunities present themselves. Filming unpredictable situations tends to encourage a greater openness to the richness of the moment. Almost as soon as the filmmaker fixes the camera on a detail, it is likely to be swept away and replaced by another. Such details often have a transitory beauty and a wealth of associations. They may involve gestures or facial expressions or particular objects that seem to evoke a person's physical presence or personality.

Filmmakers fix such transient observations in short, glance-like shots, often made during moments seemingly stolen from filming more weighty events. They may be shots of objects that have a routine familiarity for those being filmed, such as the tools they use, the utensils they eat with or the clothing they wear. On other occasions the shots may capture characteristic postures or gestures that the filmmaker has seen frequently repeated. Sometimes they reflect the idiosyncratic interests of the filmmaker; at other times they represent intrinsic features of the world in which the film's protagonists live and act.

I have suggested that there are at least two ways in which films indicate the thoughts and feelings of the person behind the camera. The first is through the behaviour of the camera itself, such as its movements from one frame or subject to another, indicating a shift of interest; or when the camera follows a person or object within a shot; or through less obvious signs, such as an unusual persistence of attention. The second is through patterns of filming that reveal the filmmaker's more general underlying interests, sometimes expressed inadvertently, sometimes more purposefully. The most revealing patterns tend not to be those dictated by cinematic conventions, such as the use of reverse angles and reaction shots, but those that stand out more clearly as exceptions. Shots that represent a filmmaker's glance fit this description, since they often interrupt the film's progress and seem to be in the film largely for their own sake. If at first they appear accidental, or to be private indulgences, they may in retrospect have a resonance that haunts the memory. In making *The Song of Ceylon* (1934), Basil Wright incorporated a number of glance-like shots of kingfishers flying over water. Their symbolic meanings have often been discussed, but this in no way exhausts their continued mystery and power. As Wright himself expressed it in interview:

> I had these extraordinary, inexplicable inner impulses, which made me shoot sequences and things that I couldn't have logically explained. But as soon as I got into the cutting room, they all fell into their places, like the birds flying up, that sort of thing. I had no reason to shoot them; in fact, they were shot at a time when I'd finished shooting for the day and was very tired, but something forced me to shoot a number of shots and the thing built up to a tremendous amount of inner tension, breaking out into expression, coming from one's subconscious very much, I think, and this was all. (Levin, 1971: 53)

In his own practice, Strecker attributed this sort of phenomenon to 'hidden analogies'. In the example of the girl's hand freeing the foot of the goat, the invisibility of most of the girl is crucial to the scene. The hand has its own agency. We do not know who the girl is, but at some level her act is emblematic of the care the Hamar exhibit in raising their animals, and perhaps their dependence on them. Moreover, by reducing the girl to a hand and the goat to a foot, we may feel a subtle correspondence between the goat's vulnerability and hers.

Strecker has identified the accidental features of certain shots as 'co-presences', by which he means us to understand that in these shots there are elements that are both connected and disconnected from what appears to be the shot's purpose (Strecker, 2003). They are disconnected in having their own parallel existence but are connected by occupying the same frame, with or without the filmmaker's knowledge. The viewer may make further connections, finding some common thread or, more interestingly, by speculating on the significance of their co-presence. Thus, the sight of butterflies hovering over freshly made pottery drying in the sun (one of Strecker's examples)[3] may bring to mind a butterfly's attraction to moisture or the flower-like shape of the pots, but equally it may point to the juxtaposition of such fragile lightness with the heaviness of clay. Films, despite their resemblance to everyday vision, also create artificial ways of seeing. A camera may record long stretches of human interaction in a fixed shot, whereas we are much more likely to observe such interactions by shifting our attention from one person to another and allowing our eyes to wander and occasionally fix on sometimes irrelevant details. It can of course be argued that it is possible, within long camera takes, to let our eyes wander too, and it may in fact be one of the functions of film editing to limit this and impose its own control over the viewing process. Yet when filmmakers resist this kind of editing in favour of longer takes, they also accept the consequences of ignoring the possibilities inherent in the short take, one of which is surely its affinity with the glance. If the gaze, and particularly the male gaze, has gained something of a bad reputation in film theory, the glance has so far remained relatively untouched. It may owe this immunity to being a more polite and less possessive form of looking. At the same time, we must acknowledge that the short take, like the glance, can be an instrument of great precision. Quite apart from its value for cinema, it should encourage us to re-evaluate the often neglected benefits of this way of looking. In reclaiming the short take for cinema we may rediscover the wisdom of the glance.

Notes

1 'As we take, in fact, a general view of the wonderful stream of consciousness, what strikes us first is the different pace of its parts. Like a bird's life, it seems to be made up of an alternation of flights and perchings' (James, 1890: 36).

2 In, respectively, *Tempus de Baristas* (1993), *Doon School Chronicles* (2000) and *With Morning Hearts* (2001).

3 Strecker takes this example from the film *Diya* (2001) by Judith MacDougall.

4

Environments of childhood

INNER AND OUTER WORLDS

Children present a puzzle to the filmmaker. They belong to an elusive social group, with its own rules and rituals. They jealously guard the secrets of their private lives. Their relations with adults are ambivalent and variable. They can be distrustful and keep their distance and yet at other times show astonishing candour and affection. They have their own distinctive ways of speaking and thinking – a fact now confirmed by neuroscientists, although long assumed by Jean Piaget and many developmental psychologists. So why film children? To find out where we adults came from? To discover other ways of being? To learn, perhaps, where the human experiment went wrong?

For adults, approaching children is a little like stepping into a time machine, trying to recall what it was like to be a child. In doing so, they are likely to make mistakes. Adults may not know what to say to children, and if they do manage a conversation with a child it is frequently on some arcane subject the child knows better than they do. It is often better to watch and listen. By doing so, an adult may at least earn a child's tolerance, if not respect.

Filming children's lives can be a form of ethnography, even if the children belong to the filmmaker's own society. Children have their own subcultures, different from those of their parents. They learn a great deal from each other – probably more than from adults. In another country they can teach the filmmaker things that local adults never would. They are well placed to do so, for they are always trying to understand what adults are up to. Children are the keenest students of their own culture because they have to be.

Most films about children seem content to reproduce the current stereotypes of childhood. The children who are filmed rarely have a voice of their own. Although filmmakers often interview adults, they rarely think of interviewing children, perhaps because they don't believe children have much of importance to say. For their part, many children who could say a lot are reluctant to do so because they doubt adults would take them seriously. If filmmakers listened more to children, they would discover that they can be just as profound and just as banal as adults.[1] Understanding children is more difficult when they are very young, before they fully develop language skills. Few children have sufficient mastery of another medium to impress adults, although there have been exceptions, like Mozart and Picasso – or Jacques Henri Lartigue, whose virtuosity in photography belied his years. Until recently it was thought there was no reliable way to gauge the knowledge of babies or find out how they viewed the world. Unable to speak, they were a 'black box' phenomenon. But then cognitive psychologists such as Elizabeth Spelke devised ingenious experiments to explore the minds of very young infants, relying on measuring their attention to controlled changes in their environment. This suggests we might investigate similar possibilities with older children, looking more closely at how they respond to their physical surroundings and bypassing the difficulties of language. In any case, speech has its limitations. It tends to be overemphasised in films, often dominating them at the expense of other kinds of expression. In fact, only a small part of our daily life is taken up with speech. Most of the time we engage with the world non-verbally and through the physical objects around us.

Objects are the anchors of our consciousness and mediate our relationships with others. Writers of fiction employ them as markers, having limited ways of conveying their characters' subjective experience. They can, of course, make assertions about their thoughts and feelings, but the reader must take these on faith. An alternative is to find objects to represent their emotions, or to try to recreate the sensory environment and events the person has lived through, in the hope that this will evoke similar feelings in the reader. T. S. Eliot called this process creating objective correlatives of their experience – objective, in a literal sense, referring to the objects in their lives. For filmmakers this approach is even more useful, since they lack a writer's ability to make statements about a person's interior life. Filmmakers possess one advantage, however. Writers must evoke the material world by means of a verbal code. Filmmakers are able to evoke it more directly, through visual images and sounds. For filmmakers, creating objective correlatives is not a matter of verbal constructions but of exploring the experiential world in material terms.

Fiction filmmakers discovered this before documentary filmmakers. In Jean Vigo's *Zero for Conduct* (1933) there is a well known scene of lyrical disorder. In a school dormitory, a pillow fight escalates until the pillows break open and feathers fill the room. The idea was not new – two early Lumière films portray similar scenes. But in Vigo's film the feathers embody the sudden release of oppression under which the children have been living. The point is not that the feathers symbolise their freedom but that they are a direct physical manifestation of it. Later, the scene turns to slow motion as the boys parade dreamily through the clouds of feathers in a triumphal procession. Here it can be said that Vigo moves from something grounded in reality to a level of fantasy. The scene becomes the expression of an imagined freedom. But earlier, when the pillows first break open, there is a brief moment of material and spiritual unity.

4.1 The boys ride their horse in *Shoeshine*

A similar vision of freedom is created by Vittorio De Sica in *Shoeshine* (1946) when the two boy protagonists buy a horse (figure 4.1). It might seem at first that De Sica fails where Vigo succeeds – that the horse remains separate from them, a figure of their dreams and a mythic emblem of their tragedy. And, indeed, their adventure into horse ownership is a kind of escape from their daily reality, which is the difficult life of post-war Rome. But it is also deeply rooted in the life and traditions of the Roman working class, where owning horses has long carried with it a special pride and prestige. Thus, for the boys, having a horse represents an achievement of status in the masculine world of Roman society. It is not only a figure of their dreams but a physical expression of social success.[2]

In Roberto Rossellini's film *Germany, Year Zero* (1947) the unity of a child and his surroundings is more obvious, although the boy himself remains an enigma. We never fully understand why he commits suicide, but our bafflement is also, in a sense, his own, living in a seemingly irrational landscape of urban destruction. The empty shells of bombed-out buildings are not just symbols of his emptiness or the legacy of a Nazi upbringing but are part of his daily reality. In this case, as in Vigo's, the filmmaker has found a concrete extension of human consciousness. There is a unity of the child's surroundings and his interior life.

4.2 The juvenile detention centre in *Shoeshine*

De Sica is at his most successful in evoking childhood experience when he shows the physical surroundings of the boys in *Shoeshine*. His depictions of life on the streets, negotiations for black market merchandise and, above all, the walls of a juvenile prison (figure 4.2) convey the boys' emotional life far more effectively than his dramatisations of childhood loyalty and betrayal. What we see around them defines their world and the subjects of their thoughts and feelings. This tendency of the Italian Neorealists to show the impact of an exterior environment on the inner life of individuals was carried a step further by Michelangelo Antonioni in *Il Grido* (1957) (figure 4.3) and such later films as *L'Avventura* (1960) and *Il Deserto Rosso* (1964).

The importance of environment in childhood comes through clearly in two early domestic comedies of Yasujiro Ozu. In *I Was Born, But...* (1932) a conventional household in a new suburb is the setting of a revolt by two boys against the social climbing of their father, who has shamed them by his fawning behaviour towards his boss (figure 4.4). The very ordinariness of the house signals the narrowness of their father's aspirations, which the children challenge by a hunger strike and by escaping to the rougher world of a children's gang outside. By contrast, in *Passing Fancy* (1933), Tomio (played by one of the actors in the earlier film) lives in the chaotic household of his feckless, working-class father, whose wife has left him some years before.

4.3 Father and daughter in the Po Valley setting of *Il Grido*

4.4 The two boys and their father in *I Was Born, But...*

Clothes and food are scattered everywhere and, like Jackie Coogan's character in Chaplin's *The Kid* (1921), it is the child who does his best to keep order in the house and take care of the adult. In both Ozu films the children live in tension with their surroundings, but their personalities have already been shaped by them. Tomio is inwardly as chaotic as the two brothers are ultimately respectful of authority.

The spaces children inhabit, and their understanding of them, are clearly delineated in these films. In *I Was Born, But...* there are zones of safety and zones of danger, which the two brothers must quickly learn to distinguish in their new environment. The zones of danger – beginning beyond the gate of their house and including the school and the no-man's-land of gang territory – are areas they venture into with extreme caution. As they gain confidence, some of these boundaries begin to dissolve or are reconfigured in their minds. As viewers, we learn about this wholly through the behaviour of the children themselves. The landscape becomes patterned and defined by their inner life.

Filmmakers often look back on their childhood with a sense of loss. It seems to matter little whether theirs was a happy or unhappy childhood; the attachment remains. What they miss, and what they sometimes try to recapture in their films, is the memory of a certain freshness of perception. Places stand out in sharp visual flashes, along with precise evocations of smells, tastes and sounds: the scent of spring rain, the taste of a special food, the screech of streetcars – each person will recall a different set of impressions. What seems most common to these remembered sensations is the accompanying sense of independence, the memory of exploring the world on one's own, apart from adults. It is this emotion, never quite grasped again, that seems signally to define childhood. Even in the horrific conditions shown in Vitali Kanevsky's *Freeze – Die – Come to Life* (1989), a film set in a filthy gulag mining town in post-war Soviet Russia, the child is fully attuned to the nuances of his surroundings, accepting and curious about them. The same is true in *Empire of the Sun* (1987), based on J. G. Ballard's semi-autobiographical novel of a child's life in a Japanese prison camp. In film after film about childhood, a child's sensitivity to small and precise details stands out and, with them, places. In *The Spirit of the Beehive* (1973) it is the magical aura of an isolated house and a forbidding landscape. In *My Father's Glory* (1990) it is almost the opposite, Marcel Pagnol's love of the openness of his Mediterranean hills. In *Murmur of the Heart* (1971) it is clearly the adolescent hero's discovery of his own body. In *I Was Born, But...* it is the open field where the children spend precious moments while escaping from school (figure 4.5).

Harmony of place and self may be the norm for most children, but occasionally the dissonance between a child's situation and surroundings manifests itself in a transformation of the child's consciousness. The child comes to

4.5 The brothers enjoy their escape from school in *I Was Born, But...*

be defined by reversals and discontinuities. This is elaborated in such films
as Andrei Tarkovsky's *Ivan's Childhood* (1962) and René Clément's *Forbidden
Games* (1952). In each film the child is thrown into an unfamiliar situation.
In each case the cause is warfare. Tarkovsky dramatises the contrast by
opening his film with a sunny image of idealised childhood, almost certainly
a remembered image in Ivan's mind. This is soon followed by a scene of
him dragging himself through a swamp at night, a spy delivering a message.

In *Forbidden Games* the transformation has already begun at the opening
of the film, with a small girl and her family escaping from the enemy along
a country road. Her parents are killed by gunfire from a strafing aircraft and
she wanders off the road into farmland. The rest of the film concerns her
confrontation with a rural way of life she has never seen before. It seems to
be the director's intention to convey the girl's discovery of this world through
our own discovery of it, for it is an image of rural France that few viewers
would know first-hand. Everything that is strange to her becomes part of
her newly emerging state of mind. Her developing obsession with death and
burial (figure 4.6) is a manifestation of her wartime ordeal superimposed on
the abundant animal life around her at the farm.

Children out of place, as in *Ivan's Childhood* and *Forbidden Games*, are acutely
sensitive to their surroundings as they try to rebalance themselves – sometimes,

45

4.6 Michel and Paulette bury a dead animal in *Forbidden Games*

one might say, as they try to begin their childhood over again. It is therefore appropriate that Rossella Ragazzi, in her documentary film *La Mémoire dure* (2000), concentrates her attention on the classroom in Paris in which a group of migrant and refugee children are making the transition from life in Asia and Africa to life in France. The film begins by moving up the stairs to this special classroom, which is a kind of cocoon from which the children are expected to emerge reborn. Most of the film is shot here, in a place which we come to know intimately over the course of the film. For the children it is a place of mixed emotions, of both suffering and sanctuary, as they struggle with a new language, a new culture and their often traumatic memories. In its informality it is very different from the classical schoolrooms of European cinema, which are always imagined as a kind of prison, each child shackled to a desk – a vision that has remained essentially unchanged from *The Blue Angel* (1930) and *Zero for Conduct* (1933) to *The 400 Blows* (1959) and *Entre les murs* (2008).

In documentary films, images of the physical world – objects, processes, gestures, landscapes – are clearly shown, but any links with the interior world of the film's subjects are often purely accidental. The possibility of connecting the two is ignored or is thought self-evident, although this is not always the case. Basil Wright's *The Song of Ceylon* (1934) is founded on a convergence of the exterior and interior worlds. The throwing of a fish net, the climbing of a sacred mountain, the movements of children's bodies in a dance – all serve to construct a world view and coherent way of life. Robert Flaherty, too, found the images of objects the most effective expression of an individual's consciousness; for him, perception of objects was a near equivalent to being. This is suggested in *Nanook of the North* (1922), and even more strongly in *Moana* (1926) and *Man of Aran* (1934), but it reaches its full expression in *Louisiana Story* (1948). The tale of the Cajun boy is told almost exclusively through the objects he sees.

In *Zerda's Children* (1978), a documentary film by the Argentine filmmaker Jorge Prelorán, an impoverished family survive by clearing the brush from great tracts of land owned by a wealthy landowner. The children vary in their abilities, but Zerda, their father, values each child for what he or she can contribute to the family. The film is relentlessly concrete. Whether Prelorán is showing children cutting the brush, repairing a truck engine or attending school, he ties each child to physical objects, and from this we gradually begin to grasp each child's outlook. The film is at its most concrete in showing an operation to remove a gigantic cyst from one of the boys' lungs. It is through Prelorán's insistence on the physical that he ultimately builds up his remarkable tribute to an unknown family and their particular experience. There is no need for heroics or expressions of sentiment. The particular experience is enough.

In Johan van der Keuken's film *The Eye above the Well* (1988) a group of young boys are being trained to be Brahmin priests in South India. The sequence is reminiscent of the scene in *The Song of Ceylon* of children learning to dance, but the implications are very different. After a regimen that includes ritual bathing and the chanting of the Vedas (figure 4.7), accompanied by an almost violent manipulation of their bodies, the boys move towards an opening in the building that allows them to look across the river. There on the far bank are the *dhobis*, the laundry men, rhythmically slapping the wet clothing on the stones in the same cadence as the verses the boys have been chanting. Here, the mechanics of the everyday world seem to merge effortlessly with a form of training that is hard to distinguish from brainwashing. Are the minds of the *dhobis* as vacant as the minds of the children after such treatment?

Film is a medium well suited to expressing materiality, yet during the last century it has become primarily concerned with the dramas of people's lives. Through cinema, the visible has become a magical pathway to the invisible: to speech, time, the mind, the emotions and the full range of the senses. Films have evolved to such an extent that many need refer only minimally to the material world. It is left to the imagination of the viewer to fill in the rest. In the hands of a great filmmaker like Robert Bresson, this ability to evoke the larger world through a few limited images becomes a poetic means of expression. In most other films, however, and particularly in

47

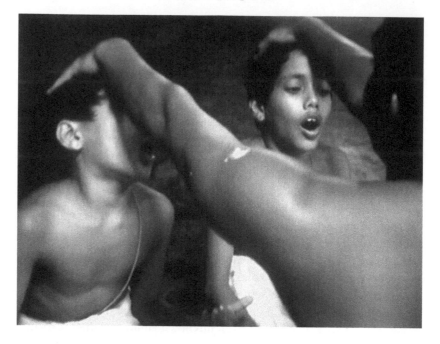

4.7 The training of Hindu priests in *The Eye above the Well*

television, it has become a retreat from engagement with the sensory world. This can be a serious limitation in films about children, for whom physical experiences loom large. If there is now a renewal of interest in the sensory potential of cinema, as some recent films suggest, the cinema of childhood can only benefit.

FILMING IN INSTITUTIONS FOR CHILDREN

I began filming in institutions for children at the invitation of a colleague who was doing a study of three schools in northern India.[3] It was an intentional step into the dark, for I had always felt that children's social worlds were among the most difficult for adults to enter, and childhood itself notoriously clouded in myth. Children are a marginalised group, dismissed as inferior by adults in most circumstances and at most times in history. In much of the world they work hard and get little credit for it. Yet they make important contributions to society, culturally and economically. They introduce new energy and ideas into the more staid world of their elders and are important generators of change. But when famine or disease strikes, they are the first to suffer. They are often trafficked and abused. Even when they are indulged and protected, they are still generally assumed to be incomplete human beings. Making films about children led me to question this assumption, and to explore the intellectual, emotional and physical experiences of children in their own right.

I filmed children at both ends of the socio-economic spectrum. I began at two famous Indian boarding schools. At the Doon School, a boys' boarding school in Dehra Dun, and later at the Rishi Valley School in South India, I filmed children growing up in elite middle-class institutions.[4] I was doubly an outsider, an adult and a non-Indian – perhaps not the best-qualified person to take up this task. But my foreignness also offered me protective cover. I reasoned that the children might feel less threatened by me – lacking, as I did, both knowledge and authority – than by the Indian adults around them. In many respects this proved to be true. At Doon School I found myself being treated by the students as a sympathetic but innocuous observer. The camera gave me privileged access to their lives, for they accepted that I was an outsider with a job to do. But it also let me see them in specialised ways: as an anatomist, isolating faces, arms, legs, hands and feet; as a chronicler of narratives; as a witness to exchanges and private moments; as an audience for performances; and a sometime receiver of confidences. I became a compiler of voices, postures and gestures, and a recorder of countless nuances and details, such as how a pen is held, a shoe tied, a smile given.

The camera also helped me understand the relationships between the students and their physical surroundings. This included the role of specific objects in their lives, such as their clothes, beds, desks, sports gear and eating utensils, and how they occupied the dormitories and other spaces in the school, even as the school itself organised them through its own activities and rituals. At this time I began to combine still and moving images as a way of fixing some of these observations, something I still do by extracting and printing stills from video footage.

The longer I stayed, the more I lost my sense of the difference between children and adults, despite the school's insistence on it. It was hard to think of the boys as less capable than adults, so confident were their judgements and so distinctive their personalities. Just as in other societies in which I have lived, where the strangeness of the culture soon faded, they became for me simply an assortment of complex individuals. I developed a sort of age-blindness in which many of the boys struck me as more sensible and reliable than their often quite eccentric teachers.

My approach to the school as an institution was to record small events in the boys' lives, their personal relations, their conversations with one another or with me, and their material surroundings. Their surroundings, which initially I would have put last in importance, turned out to be a more interesting and productive resource than I expected. The buildings, grounds, furnishings and school uniforms physically contained the boys but also acted as extensions of

4.8 Boys at their desks at Doon School

them. This was true in a double sense, first because the setting reflected the particular stratum of Indian middle-class society that had produced boys such as these, and second because the boys' own presence was a significant part of the school's physical being (figure 4.8). And the longer they stayed there, the more they took on the colouration of their surroundings. The school was what they saw, heard, touched and smelled, and it could be said that they ingested it through all their senses. Their consciousness was permeated by their sense of place and the smaller objects that filled their lives and shaped their habits – quite ordinary items such as food, eating utensils, clothing, toothbrushes, cupboards and beds. These material objects became saturated, not with meanings but with familiarity.

At Doon School I found that even small actions became significant signs of the boys' relationships with the world and their sense of control, or lack of it, over their lives. One boy had an unusual way of tying his shoes. Another made his bed in a particularly fastidious way. A third could never tie his turban properly. At other institutions, too, I saw that children rearranged their dormitories, decorated the walls and organised the insides of their lockers in distinctive ways. At each place they defined and reshaped the spaces around them both materially and in their own imaginations.

At Doon School the larger dormitories contained long rows of beds, all with green or blue bedcovers. Here was an image of orderliness. The floors were grey and the walls were painted with white distemper. The colours were few. I found this monochrome environment strangely monastic at first, but as time went on I came to see it as restful and part of a more extensive restriction of colour throughout the school. Where there were colours, they were limited and repeated, producing regular figures against a more neutral ground. This was most obvious in the school uniforms, which varied from grey to black-and-white to shades of blue. The type and colour of the uniform worn depended on the time of day, with evening uniforms the most lacking in colour. It seemed as if this control over what the students saw was part of a larger strategy to reduce the stimulation of colour on their senses. If so, it could be regarded as a kind of visual conditioning.

In other ways, too, clothing played an important part in the Doon School environment. Not only did the school uniforms make everyone look superficially alike, but different uniforms were required for different activities. As a result, a disproportionate amount of the students' time was taken up with dressing and undressing. Clothing was part of the reward and punishment system, further focusing the children's attention on what they wore. High achievement in games or studies was rewarded with special blazers. Breaking minor rules was punished by making the boys run back to their dormitories in the morning break and change their uniforms two or three times in succession. Clothing, cloth and colour thus became dominant elements in the students' personal experience, closely related to their awareness of their own bodies and their physical appearance. These elements provided a common backdrop for their differences but also created an atmosphere of performance, even theatricality, in school life.

I found I could convey some of this density of experience by filming situations in which the repetitive features of life were most evident. Their effects on individual boys, however, could only be deduced by observing their handling of objects, their attention to their clothing, and their relations with one another. Much the same could be said for the rituals of eating and the boys' daily exposure to the same tables, utensils and foods. Food was a major preoccupation, as it often is in childhood. Away from the dining hall, the boys hoarded and shared clandestine supplies of 'tuck'. In certain seasons they ate green mangoes and lychees from trees on the school grounds.

Institutions that cater to large numbers of inmates tend to standardise the ways of providing for their needs. This produces a multiplication and magnification of facilities. Food preparation becomes an industrial process, and eating hardly less so. The same could be said for sleeping, bathing and sanitation (figure 4.9). The result is rows of identical beds, tables, desks, bathing stalls, basins, toilets and urinals, all of which have the power to overshadow the individual. The standardisation and control of bodily processes and activities was much in evidence at Doon School, as it is in most other institutions. It created an unusual childhood for the boys, perhaps comparable only to that

4.9 A communal washroom at Doon School

experienced by adults in the army or religious orders. Depicting it on film meant building up inventories of the sights and sounds they encountered routinely.

I was helped in this by a boy who became interested in my filming. He used to direct my camera at objects around us and tell me what he thought it was seeing, sometimes checking the reflection in the lens to make sure. Once he had me turn 360 degrees as he gave a running commentary on our surroundings – or, more precisely, on what attracted his notice. In this way I accumulated a number of visual and verbal inventories of material culture, based on what he saw in the school environment. He was an experienced observer of boarding schools, having lived in one since the age of six.[5]

Do children and adults see things differently? Clearly, they notice different things, having different interests. But do they organise them differently? This is a difficult question because there are great variations in the perceptions of individual adults and children, and there is little empirical evidence on the subject. In Nicolas Philibert's film *Etre et avoir* (2002), about a French country school, there is an intriguing moment in one of the scenes. A small boy, Jojo, is told by the teacher to wash his hands. He goes in and out of the room to wash them and shows them to the teacher. At one point he says, 'There's a wasp.' He doesn't seem frightened that the wasp will sting him. Is he simply trying to draw the teacher's attention to the existence of the wasp? Is it part of his developing awareness of strange things that can be encountered in life? Or is he making some further connection that we cannot understand? The film doesn't tell us.

While filming at Doon School, I focused for a time on a boy who lived with twenty-nine others in a dormitory for first-year students – a so-called 'holding house'.[6] The boys were twelve and thirteen years old. Although the house was very bare, containing little more than rows of beds, the boy contrived to make his portion of it a personal space. His bed was at one end of a dormitory, so that he had a corner to himself. There, without changing anything on the walls or any of the fixtures, he created an imaginary room. He domesticated this space not so much by defending it, for it was continually overrun by other boys, but by his attitude and behaviour. The focal point was his bed. He would walk around it and observe it with proprietary interest. In cold weather he would muffle himself up in his *rezai*, or quilt, and treat the bed with obsessive care, endlessly rearranging and smoothing the bedcover. He seemed to be trying to reassure himself that this space was his, and that he belonged in it. It was an important buttress for his sometimes precarious sense of himself. I understood him better through his imaginary room than through any of his words or other actions.

Several years later I filmed children at the opposite end of the social spectrum, at a combined shelter and juvenile detention centre in New Delhi, the Prayas Children's Home for Boys.[7] The building itself was a monumental four-storey structure in Jahangirpuri, on the outskirts of the city. Seen from a distance, it rose above the adjacent fields and houses like an unfinished sculpture or a toy left behind by giants. Closer to, it revealed rusted windows and balconies, with an occasional face peering out from behind a grille (figure 4.10). It had clearly cost a great deal of money to build, but little seemed to have been left over for maintenance, for inside it the plumbing was broken and the electrical fittings dodgy. The rooms were arranged around galleries overlooking cement courtyards (figure 4.11). The walls were painted an institutional green, and when the light reflected off them even the most healthy faces took on an unhealthy pallor.

The boys in the home came from a variety of backgrounds. Some were runaways from abusive families, others were orphans and a few had simply been lost in the chaos of the cities. Many had lived by their wits on the streets before being picked up by the police for minor crimes. Not surprisingly, they regarded adults as powerful but unreliable beings. Although my aim was to study the home as an institution, I felt that in many ways an institution is best defined by the lives of those who live in it. How could I convey the experience of growing up in such a place? Of what were the children more conscious: their memories of the past or their current surroundings?

In general appearance, many of the children would not have seemed out of place in an Indian middle-class school. Thanks to the food provided by

4.10 Looking out of a window in *Gandhi's Children*

4.11 Early morning, an interior gallery in *Gandhi's Children*

the institution, they had the same nimble bodies and clear complexions, the same brightness of expression. But if you looked closely, as you do when filming, you could identify signs of previous abuse in burn marks and facial scars. Some boys were frightened or withdrawn. Some were undersized for their age or had sight or speech impairments and other physical problems. There were boys who limped and boys with tics.

It was clear that life was difficult, but probably much less difficult than it had been on the streets. The boys got regular meals, they had clothes and beds to sleep in, and they were protected from the dangers of the outside world. About half were confined to the building by a magistrate's court order. Many therefore considered themselves prisoners. The hardships they faced stemmed partly from institutional indifference and partly from a breakdown of facilities. The mattresses on the beds were by now dirty and stained. There were rats in the rooms by day and night. Usually only one dim tube light worked in each of the dormitories. There were no buckets in the bathrooms (they were kept locked away in a storeroom) and there were few showers, only cold-water taps on the walls. Few boys had towels, so in the cold months of November and December they would wash under a tap, pull on their clothes over their still-wet bodies and hunt for patches of sunlight in which to warm themselves. The ground-level toilets tended to back up, so the floors were often wet or covered with faeces. As a result, when the boys entered in the morning they would take aim to pee from as far as away as possible. In fact, they peed nearly everywhere. If you walked along the galleries, the volatile reek from the bathrooms struck you like a solid wall.

And yet life was tolerable. The boys made a great effort to keep clean, despite the primitive facilities and the dust that kept blowing in from the unpaved road outside. They washed their own clothes and could often be seen carefully folding their shirts in a professional manner. They swept and mopped the dormitory floors, pushing their beds out on to the galleries to do so. They found endless ways of amusing themselves despite having few possessions. They made small toys out of paper and bits of plastic. Nearly any object could serve as a ball, cricket bat or set of cricket stumps. The things they made, and their talent for improvisation, were concrete expressions of how their minds worked. All this, I found, could be filmed.

While living in the home I got to know a group of pickpockets aged between eleven and fourteen. My daily filming encouraged them to demonstrate to me their pickpocketing techniques and talk about their encounters with the police. What struck me most forcefully, apart from their air of self-reliance, was the extent to which they lived side by side with adult society and yet collectively and morally apart from it. They were less complicit with adults than the more privileged children I had filmed at middle-class schools. They spoke of honesty and skill at stealing as equally desirable qualities. While being filmed they freely admitted to crimes they had refused to confess to when being beaten by the police. Yet I observed far less bullying among these boys than at Doon School, perhaps because they had seen more of personal misfortune or were more tolerant of one another's differences. The camera created occasions when they spoke about subjects that they would otherwise have considered too personal or improper to mention, such as their feelings about their lost families or sexual practices in the home. They sometimes volunteered more than I felt comfortable about recording.

The camera also gave me insights into aspects of their personalities that I had not often seen in children of their age. There were signs of resilience and strength of character that I was surprised to find in these children, including an ability to understand and accept social forces larger than themselves, to take pride in their skills as individuals, independent of adults, and to value friendship above caste, class, religion or personal possessions. Curiously enough, these were the same egalitarian values that Doon School was attempting to instil through its enforcement of rules and austere living conditions.

The camera also let me to examine more closely the environment in which the boys lived. I tried to compare my own experience of living there with what I could tell of theirs. The dormitories were crowded with double bunk beds. The bathrooms and toilets had no privacy. The windows had bars and, like the doors, were often locked. I tried to film the bare spaces in which they lived – the tiered galleries rising around four sides of concrete courtyards, the dusty ground where they played improvised games and the cavernous canteen where they sat in rows on the floor to eat. I noted the care with which they washed, dried and stored their clothes, their endless efforts to remain clean in the midst of refuse, dust and overflowing sewage, and how they guarded their few possessions. But there were some experiences the camera could not capture, perhaps thrown into greater relief by what it could, such as the cold of the December mornings, the pervasive smell of urine from the bathrooms and the grit under one's shoes and fingernails.

The building resembled a prison, but one without cells. The prison atmosphere came primarily from its echoing open spaces. The galleries surrounded the void of a courtyard. I could look across it and watch boys emerging from their dormitories and leaning over the railings. By contrast, the dormitories were less austere, with beds crowded together, colourful cotton quilts and a grilled window that looked out on a balcony. Sometimes the grilles were unlocked and the boys could go out on the balconies. Some older boys used them as areas to dry their clothes or watch activities on the nearby rooftops. A few boys kept pigeons there. Whereas the boys at Doon School seemed like parts of a well oiled machine, those at the home were more like temporary inhabitants of a derelict factory.

The building itself was a powerful presence. The boys were dwarfed by it. They were small figures dashing up and down staircases or running along the galleries or hanging their clothes over the railings. Yet no one commented on the design of the building or complained about it. It was as if everyone expected it to be like that, although occasionally new boys would peer around anxiously and hunch their shoulders as if feeling the building's weight. If the place oppressed the boys, this was not immediately apparent. They seemed resigned to it and, as in so many things, able to adapt to it.

It was finally the arrival of a new boy that heightened my sense of the building and led me to film it in a new way. There was a great disparity between this child's background and the surroundings in which he suddenly found himself. He was an eight-year-old village boy who had never before left his home in Bihar. One day he had been abducted by a man – why, we don't know – taken to the city, and then lost or abandoned. Someone found him and brought him to the home. One night I heard a distant sound of crying coming from one of the galleries. It was two or three o'clock in the morning. I switched the camera on, left it at my doorway and went out to investigate. At that hour the galleries and staircases were deserted, although brightly lit, as if by floodlights. I found the boy huddled by one of the railings, crying in despair. I stayed beside him for several hours on one of the stair landings, and despite all I could do to console him he continued to cry until he fell asleep, exhausted. During the following weeks I spent many more hours with him, trying to make him understand that steps were being taken officially to get him home, for he had given up hope of ever seeing his family again. It was through this incident that I later came to film the building in the middle of the night, empty but brightly lit, the pale green walls towering above the courtyard. I wanted others to see it as he had seen it that night, in all its terrifying desolation.

On other occasions, too, unexpected events prompted my filming. Often it was only later that I understood what I had done or what purpose it might serve. One day I saw a rat swimming in an open drain that ran past the home. It seemed to be losing strength against the current. As it weakened it drifted towards a collection of floating refuse, and despite its efforts to use this for support disappeared beneath it, where it presumably drowned. Its death was part of a larger system. There was a sewage pumping plant next to the home, where all the drains of the district converged. At a certain hour each day the plant would start pumping. A stream of black sludge would shoot out from one of its four giant pipes and run off into an adjacent field. Since the plant was just outside my window, and the pumping of sewage one of the most regular events in our lives, I got into the habit of filming it, and this eventually became a recurrent image in the film.

As a rule, I tried to film in all the places where the boys spent their time: in the dormitories, galleries, stairways, balconies, bathrooms, kitchen, canteen and so-called 'informal' classrooms. There were also some dusty grounds around the building where improvised games were played and physical exercises were conducted each morning. By filming the things the boys saw regularly, and the places that were most familiar to them, I hoped to build up a filmic equivalent of what they saw themselves, the mental backdrop of their thoughts and feelings. Yet this was only a beginning. Places children know are inscribed more deeply. They map them out in their minds as minutely as adults map out rivers and continents and cities. Each corner is familiar, and many have names. There are also secret places, holding special associations, even in such an impersonal institution as the Prayas home.

As part of my agreement with Prayas, the non-government organisation that ran the home, I trained five boys to use a video camera. Two were homeless, two were orphans and one was a former pickpocket confined to the home under a court order. They chose a topic to film, and I soon realised that how they filmed it could be a guide for my own filming. They were unexpectedly frank about filming what they saw around them. They seemed indifferent to adult taboos and never shied away from a subject if it was part of their common experience. They had chosen water as a theme because, as they pointed out, it flowed through every aspect of their lives. Apart from the sewage flowing past the home, it was part of cooking, cleaning, bathing, washing clothes and drinking. It was also, they said, in one's body and one's tears. They filmed a small boy crying and others urinating. If they had found someone bleeding they would have filmed that too. They filmed boys bathing and squatting over toilets. They made no special point of this; these were simply the sights they saw every day.

Following their example, I tried to be equally open to my surroundings. I hoped my filming would accurately convey the reality of their lives, without filtering it through an ethnocentric or even a specifically adult view of things. Otherwise, I thought, it would not only misrepresent what I had seen but also produce a false account of the boys' experiences. Although my primary aim was to study the life of the institution, a secondary aim was to produce a visual report for those in the higher echelons of the organisation who were distanced from the actual conditions in the home.

Along with the building they lived in and their few personal possessions, the children's reality was also made up of their own collective presence (figures 4.12 and 4.13). An environment not only consists of inanimate objects; it includes the bodies of others. This human presence is the shared reality in which most of us live. The boys were often crowded together in their dormitories or when standing in queues waiting for meals. They ate and bathed together. Often two or three would sleep in the same bed, which were sometimes pushed side by side to allow for this. Their physical closeness encouraged them to think of themselves as an extended family, and many of the boys told me they regarded the other boys as their brothers, for apart from them they had no one else. This perhaps accounted for the kindness they often showed one another.

The boys were well informed on sexual matters. Along with the more predictable sexual activities of boys living in such close quarters, they were aware of cases of sexual abuse in the home. Several told me that older boys would promise gifts to younger ones for sexual favours. Some also reported that adults routinely abused boys at other institutions in which they had stayed. But homosexuality was generally frowned upon. Younger boys were anxious not to appear to have too close liaisons with older ones. I filmed both older and younger boys talking about these subjects.

4.12 Waiting to bathe in *Gandhi's Children*

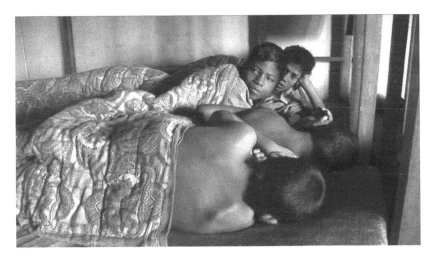

4.13 Sharing dormitory beds in *Gandhi's Children*

Each boy had a locker and a drawer for clothes. These were the only private places they controlled, and the lockers tended to be turned into miniature shrines of their hopes and dreams. Here boys kept their valued possessions, which usually amounted to no more than a piece of soap, pictures cut from magazines and a few small toys. Religion was practised casually, if at all. Some unclaimed lockers were used as sacred places, decorated with coloured paper and pictures of the gods. Half-embarrassed, a few Hindu boys showed me how they performed *pujas* at these lockers, for this was as close as most of them got to a temple. Religious pictures and posters of Hindi film stars and sports heroes were put up on the walls of the dormitories. Although there were many Muslim boys in the home, I never saw any of them praying.

Place, possessions and people – all these influenced the boys' sense of who they were and constructed the world they inhabited, even when they protested against it. To the village boy, such a life either confirmed his determination to become a city dweller or his desire to go home again. As well as filming the general conditions of the boys' lives, I learned the histories and followed the fortunes of several individual boys and their varied responses to being at the home. The earlier lives of some of them had been so horrific that they regarded the home as a place of sanctuary. For others, having been wrenched unexpectedly from their earlier lives, the home itself was horrific. For still others, life at the home was something to be tolerated for the meagre gains it provided, or as a temporary measure. But for most there was no choice: they had nowhere else to go, no other life to imagine for themselves.

PORTRAYING CHILDHOOD EXPERIENCE

In filming children, the filmmaker should not underestimate the importance of their material lives. This includes not only the objects that surround them, but their own material being – their bodies and their sense of living within them. It is against this background of the material self that children experience every other object, whether this be the clothes they wear, the utensils they use or the physical presence of other children and adults. The child has a skin with which to feel, as well as eyes to see and ears to hear. If films can convey the sensory qualities of the objects that surround a child, they may be able to suggest the sensations that constitute the child's experiential world. If they can combine this shared experience with the individuality of each child's personality – one child's ideas, another's expressions, another's characteristic ways of speaking and moving – we may come closer to extricating children from the oversimplifying myths of childhood.

Children can do much to dissolve these myths themselves if they have the opportunity. The limitations and restrictions placed on them, however, are increasing rather than diminishing, especially in European and American life. Children who once had the freedom of the streets now live in a much more restricted environment of home, school and supervised play. Fears for their safety, meant to protect them, also limit their independence. The places that children are allowed to occupy, and the decisions they are allowed to make about their physical, moral and economic lives, are increasingly controlled by adults. When I conducted a video workshop among middle-class children in South India, I was surprised by their hesitancy to film the embodied, material aspects of their lives. By contrast, the five boys I taught

60

to use video cameras at the Prayas home were quite fearless. They would have been astonished by the inhibitions of these middle-class children and their lack of independence.

Adults have long known the power of images and have used them as important tools in their relations with children. In books, toys, television and advertising, images are marshalled to show children their proper place in society. One of these uses is to protect the terrain that adults consider their own. Among the adult preserves that children are not supposed to encroach upon are religion, politics, sexuality and – except as consumers – money.

Images of children in general have come under more severe adult censure, with increasingly restrictive rules about what can and can't be shown about them. On television children are routinely shown out of focus, or with pixelated faces. This is presumably to protect their identity, although for reasons that are not altogether clear. A contributing factor is no doubt the proliferation of images in advertising and print media and new delivery systems such as the internet. Child nudity is immediately assumed to be pornographic. Contrary to our assumptions about living in a more liberated age, it seems that images of children are now perceived as far more threatening than they were in Victorian times. The effects of this are passed down. Adult fears ultimately create a sense of shame and anxiety in the children themselves.

The tightening of restrictions on children's lives appears to coincide with a re-emerging desire in middle-class society to maintain an idealised notion of the child at any cost. Unfortunately, this is often at the expense of the children themselves, reducing their sense of autonomy and their will to exercise it. At the same time, many adults appear more isolated from the realities of their children's lives. One reason for this may be a heightened protective instinct among parents, reacting to a world they see as increasingly unstable. Another may be that adults wish to keep children from challenging too aggressively the comforts of a hard-won middle-class existence, especially in countries where for many people a middle-class life is comparatively new. These insecurities are reflected in parents' tastes, politics and moral views. It could even be said that children are being re-infantilised in response to fears that they are growing up too fast, or that the traditional values of society are under threat. In journalism, academic research, broadcasting and the arts, the new imperatives tend to place children in a protective bubble, supposed to be for their benefit. But protection has also come to mean not only protecting the child but protecting specific cultural ideas of what a child should be.

These changes present a challenge to filmmakers far greater than the independent character of children themselves. If fears for children's safety grow, and restrictions on what can be said or shown about them tighten, the task of producing accurate accounts of their lives will increasingly mean going against the grain of public sentiment, and in some cases the law. The response of some filmmakers and photographers has been to publish ever more disturbing images of children in an attempt to call into question established views of them. An alternative is simply to report on children's lives more fully and frankly, resisting fear and political pressure. In the future we can expect an upsurge of both strategies, despite the risks.

Notes

This essay was first written, in somewhat different form, for the symposium 'Perceiving Children', held as part of the Nordic Anthropological Film Association meeting at the Moesgaard Museum, Aarhus, Denmark, on 28–29 August 2010.

1 Both the banality and the profundity of children are evident in *Seven Up!*, a British television programme of 1964 that interviewed a range of seven-year-olds. It was remarkable for showing how deeply ingrained the British class system was at the time, even among children of an early age, but perhaps even more so for having considered the views of children worth recording in the first place. Another film notable for listening seriously to children is Denis Gheerbrant's *La Vie est immense et pleine de dangers* (1995), its title taken from the remark of a boy hospitalised with cancer.

2 I am greatly indebted to Rossella Ragazzi for this insight into the place of the horse in Roman working-class society and its meaning in De Sica's *Shoeshine*.

3 This was Sanjay Srivastava, who was studying Mayo College, the Doon School and Lawrence School (Sanawar) for his PhD in anthropology at the University of Sydney. He later published a book based on his thesis, entitled *Constructing Post-Colonial India: National Character and the Doon School* (Routledge, 1998).

4 The resulting films include the Doon School quintet and a number of films made at the Rishi Valley School in southern Andhra Pradesh, among them *Some Alien Creatures* (2005), *SchoolScapes* (2007) and *Awareness* (2010). For further details of the Doon School filming project see MacDougall (2006). The five films made at Doon School are: *Doon School Chronicles* (2000), *With Morning Hearts* (2001), *Karam in Jaipur* (2001), *The New Boys* (2003) and *The Age of Reason* (2004).

5 See *The Age of Reason* (2004).

6 See *With Morning Hearts* (2001).

7 See *Gandhi's Children* (2008).

Part II: Film and the senses

The third tendency in cinema

LOOKING back, we can identify at least three tendencies in the topography of cinema. The first seems intrinsic to the earliest films and fundamental to the idea of spectacle and spectatorship. It is based on presenting something simply to be 'looked at' and predates the invention of cinema, since it includes everything from the circus to sports events, stage plays, paintings, sculptures and still photographs. Early cinema presented a framed moving photograph to the spectator. It was taken from a fixed position, was uncut and generally lasted less than a minute. Its framing was not unlike that provided by the proscenium arch of a theatre. The audience watched, was often fascinated and emotionally affected, but remained spatially disconnected from the action on the screen.

The second tendency emerged at some point around 1910, if not a little earlier. It was encouraged by other inventions of the nineteenth century such as the stereoscope, which began to insert the spectator imaginatively into a three-dimensional world, a world where the spectator could take up a number of different viewing positions. The discovery of film editing made it possible to extend this principle into the experience of film viewing. Within an edited sequence the viewer could (and in fact was forced) to adopt different viewing positions, corresponding to the different viewing positions of the camera. This was soon exploited by D. W. Griffith and other directors, so that eventually the spectator's point of view began to simulate the positions of the characters in the film. Thus a quite revolutionary possibility was born. From simply being allowed to look at a film as a performance, spectators were now able to engage with it in a new way, as if the story were actually happening around them.

It is possible to find a few scattered examples of this tendency even earlier in the history of cinema. The camera operators employed by the Lumière brothers experimented with innovations such as mounting a camera on a moving boat or streetcar, to create a shifting perspective within the shot. When Alexandre Promio first tried this in Venice, he was so worried that Louis Lumière would disapprove that he wrote him a letter of apology. But Lumière was delighted with it and promptly told all his camera operators to try the same thing (Frémaux, 1996).[1] The moving camera produced in the audience a feeling of personal involvement, with objects nearby moving past

5.1 An 'accidental' close-up in the 1896/7 film *Porte de France*

them more rapidly than those in the background. Oblique camera angles also produced a sense of three-dimensionality, as in the famous Lumière film of a train entering the station at La Ciotat. Another sensation was produced if the people being filmed came too close to the camera, creating an accidental close-up. We can see this in an early Lumière film shot in Tunis (figure 5.1).[2] Several pedestrians hurry past, casting curious glances at the camera. Another attempt to exploit this sort of effect occurs in Edwin S. Porter's shot of a cowboy firing his revolver point-blank at the audience in *The Great Train Robbery* (1903). This scene could be placed at the beginning or the end of the film and had no apparent connection to the story.

None of these devices produced quite the same effect as would later become a standby of fiction films and even some documentaries: the point-of-view shot, or shot–countershot combination. In this kind of editing the audience is first shown a person looking at something. Then it is shown what the person is looking at. Or the sequence is reversed: first the object or scene is shown, then the person looking at it. By this means the viewer's perspective and that of a character are bound into one – 'sewn' together, as one critic aptly put it (Oudart, 1969).

The third tendency goes beyond this commandeering of the spectator's point of view, with its nudge towards subjectivity. The cinema now becomes embodied in a new way. Initially it was mainly a matter of creating bodily responses in the audience. Filmmakers found that through editing and using certain images they could directly affect viewers physically, independent of any empathy they might feel for the people on the screen. Eisenstein, who had little interest in individualised screen characters or audience identification with them, had, on the other hand, a great interest in the kinaesthetic effects of cinema. He recognised, perhaps earlier than anyone, that movement within a shot, or movement from one shot to another, could generate sympathetic responses in the audience. Rhythms created by a succession of shots, or abrupt shifts in direction and angle between shots, could exploit some of the same mimetic systems that allow people to synchronise their actions with others in everyday life.

Addressing the audience in this way had little to do with the imagination, where most of the narrative power of cinema is created through identification with the characters. As Eisenstein had discovered, films can affect us almost as much through their composition as through our identification with characters on the screen (figure 5.2). Somewhere between the two lie the effects of posture and gesture. When these expressive actions are filmed, we respond to them both culturally and more personally. They stand for familiar patterns of social behaviour but also as expressions of individual emotion. A posture of lamentation may strike us as a formal convention but still engender feelings of pity in us. Even if we feel no identification

5.2 The power of diagonals in *Battleship Potemkin*

with the person on the screen, the posture can awaken in us memories of suffering, to which we respond directly. Filmmakers sensitive to these cues often make deliberate use of them in fiction films or incorporate them more instinctively in documentaries.

Filmmakers are thus able to reach out and affect viewers through a diverse range of cinematic effects. Some are subtly distributed throughout a film, while others are more obvious, as in the creation of stories. Narratives produce feelings of anticipation in an audience. They can induce an almost physical desire for forward movement and resolution. (A test of this might be a viewer's willingness to abandon a film at a crucial point in the story.) Another source of the filmmaker's power lies in editing. Tempos may be increased, or a sense of mounting pressure may be built up by sustaining a shot beyond its expected length, calling for the relief of cutting to a new shot. Effects such as these rely on the pattern of rhythms and conventions already established in each film. At the micro-level of editing, a particular cut may be triggered by a movement or sound that has little to do with the narrative. Filmmakers can of course disregard possibilities such as these, but at the risk of losing their hold on the audience.

The coming of synchronous sound in films had far-reaching effects on their construction and on film viewers' experiences. Combining sounds with images gave films new qualities of spaciousness and immediacy. The combined 'sound-image' had the power to stimulate the other senses as well, particularly the sense of touch. A scene such as a car door slamming and the car driving off produces in us a vivid sensation of the solidity and weight of metal closing on metal. We can sense vicariously the texture and grinding of the gravel beneath its tyres. Over time, the effect of sound was not simply to enhance the subjective qualities of silent cinema. It revolutionised filmmaking, altering styles of editing, acting and characterisation, and giving new impetus to the documentary film as an art form. The introduction of sound also represented a significant step towards a more fully embodied cinema. While narratives and the control of visual perspectives affected viewers largely through their emotions, increased emphasis on the qualities of the material world affected them viscerally.

The result has sometimes been called a sensory or haptic cinema, given the ability of films to stimulate a broad range of the senses, not least the sense of touch. That possibility had already been exploited in painting and had been discussed in essays on tactility by writers such as Adolf von Hildebrand and Bernard Berenson, culminating in Berenson's description of it in Renaissance aesthetics as 'giving tactile values to retinal impressions' (1896: 4).[3] But to speak only of cinema's sensory potential would be to underestimate the broader implications of this shift, or, one might say, its *destination*. Although evoking physical sensation imparts greater realism to films, the ultimate aim of this kind of cinema would seem to be to create a more profound relationship with the physical world itself. This suggests an indirect parallel between the sensory evocation of objects in cinema and closing the indexical distance between a film image and the objects it refers to. A photographic image can be seen as optically and chemically caused by the thing photographed, although it also stands apart from it. The emotion underlying embodied cinema indicates a desire for a greater connection to its source, one that takes a step beyond simple representation, carrying a greater charge of intimacy.

The desire for such a connection is evident in the way some films portray human beings. Most of the human figures in cinema are simply there, filmed as casually as other objects. In certain films, however – those of Bresson, Tarkovsky and Bergman come particularly to mind – our sense of a certain person's physical presence seems burned into the film, independent of any other purposes for which the film was made. Roland Barthes observed what he called 'the grain of the voice' in certain recordings of *Lieder* – evidence of the singer's body beneath the surface impression of the voice (1977: 185). In a similar way, some films convey a mysterious sense of another person's autonomous existence. This feeling of material and emotional presence would seem to require, at the very least, the viewer's sense of his or her own physical being, combined with a need to connect this sense of self with that of others, or sometimes the reverse. The result could be described as a feat of translation, by which the being of others is made assimilable to oneself. It allows the viewer to enter into the sensory world and even the consciousness of another, along with the erotic potential this sometimes implies.

Films make such responses possible partly through their power to evoke sensory detail, but also by remaining physically close to the actions of the people filmed, generating corresponding mimetic feelings in the viewer. The two responses may be linked. Here it is worth noting an observation of the Viennese art historian Alois Riegl. Riegl remarked on the difference between close-range and long-range vision, and then proposed a necessary link between close-range vision and what he called 'tactile space' – the ability of vision to evoke the sensations of touch. Riegl's important theoretical point was that although the eye can fulfil the functions of touch, it can do so only when it enters into the space of *close-range* vision (Deleuze and Guattari, 1987: 543). This leads to what, following Riegl, might be called a 'cinema of proximity', the first of its two components being the camera's physical closeness to the sources of sensation (acting as an extension of the viewer's perception, or creating a surrogate position for the viewer) and the other being the sense of an emotional connection with the people in the film. Ultimately, the two kinds of closeness become merged in a larger inter-subjective relationship involving filmmaker, subject and viewer.

Being aware of one's own body is one of the many additional senses that have been catalogued since Aristotle named the original five senses of vision, hearing, smell, taste and touch. Early in the twentieth century, C. S. Sherrington proclaimed a new sense, that of proprioception, the neural process that allows the body to know the position of its various parts and to control them without having to locate them by other means (Sherrington, 1906). It is what allows us to touch our nose or bring a glass of water to our lips in the dark. Sherrington's concept can be useful in discussing the relation between the filmmaker's body and the bodies of people filmed, and more specifically in sensing the bodily existence of others in cinema. Certain kinds of film seem to allow the viewer to share the sense of self that others have of their own bodies. Neurological research in fact suggests that specialised cells in the brain allow us to imitate and thus temporarily adopt the point of view of other persons.[4] This not only helps create empathy for them but can also in some circumstances generate physical sensations in us that mirror theirs. Under the right conditions, one may feel another's hand as if it were one's own. This opens up the interesting possibility that viewing other people on film can generate in the body of the viewer a sensation of their more extensive consciousness of themselves – in effect, a sharing of their proprioception.

Here we are on more speculative ground, because sensing the intimate presence of another person, a not uncommon experience in film viewing, may force us to confront an aspect of cinema that escapes from accepted ideas of filmic representation and signification. In most films the representation of human beings is nothing more than that – a visual record, comparatively neutral, comparatively conventional, comparatively predictable. It may be complicated by the expressiveness of a particular actor or by symbolic and cultural meanings. But it may also convey something more than this surface presentation – not simply the delineation of character, more or less efficiently rendered, but an existence independent of the film and its preoccupations. In fiction films this may be the actor rather than the role; in documentary films, the film subject beyond the personality revealed by the film. In these images a more fundamental quality of the individual persists, standing apart from its cinematic portrayal. It is the residue left when all else – verisimilitude, connotation, context and ornament – has been stripped away. We may recall it occasionally in those moments when we hear a few words in our minds, spoken in a characteristic tone, or a certain way of moving, or another person's gesture that at first we mistake for our own.

Embodied cinema is all about this sentient link. Our normal expectations of a film may be upset as something appears to break through its surface, like an apparition or double exposure. This can affect us like a touch, with a fleeting thrill of pleasure or pain. It may occur when viewing perfectly ordinary film material, produced by an expression on a face, a gesture, a sound, or the way light falls on an object. For a moment we are drawn into the sensation, so that the film itself becomes of secondary importance. Responses of this kind have little to do with the skill of the filmmaker or even the technical quality of the film. The roughness of the image may even enhance the effect, while at other times it can be produced by clarity and detail.

It would be a mistake, however, to assume that this phenomenon is always accidental. The filmmaker may have experienced similar feelings at the time of filming and then consciously or unconsciously communicated them to the viewer. Something may have occurred to reveal an unexpected side of the subject. Or the effect may result from the filmmaker's absorption in a highly charged atmosphere of personal involvement. For the viewer to respond in a similar way, we must assume there is some common feeling between filmmaker and viewer, or a sharing of sensibilities, for at these moments the camera seems to approach the very limits of consciousness of another human being.

During the past century, filmmakers have come to realise that being open to discoveries such as these creates a cinema that is capable of a more intimate engagement with life, rather than simply its 'to be looked at' qualities. One can see the tendency fully realised in Carl Dreyer's *The Passion of Joan of Arc* (1928) (figure 5.3), perhaps the greatest example of a 'cinema of proximity' of the silent era. It was realised that a persistent attention to detail provided a way to account for those episodes in life when we see our surroundings with a preternatural clarity, perhaps comparable only to the heightened

5.3 The cinema of proximity in *The Passion of Joan of Arc*

state of consciousness produced by certain drugs. As the century advanced, filmmakers no doubt came to value this possibility even more, as the sheer volume of trivial and clichéd films increased. The cinema could counter it by becoming more sensitive to small-scale events, producing works in which their uniqueness and special qualities could be felt. One response was a focus on everyday street life in the new genre of 'city symphonies' created by Alberto Cavalcanti, Walter Ruttmann, Jean Vigo and others; another response was the avant-garde films of Germaine Dulac, Luis Buñuel and Georges Franju. For the Surrealists, emphasis on detail was a way of reaching into the unconscious and providing evidence of the uncanny autonomy of the material world. For Realists, on the other hand, and particularly the post-war Neorealists, it was fundamental to rendering the experiences of ordinary people and the precise surroundings in which they spent their day-to-day lives (figure 5.4).

From the beginning, anthropologists have placed a similar emphasis on the material world. This is evident in the focus on objects and technological processes in many of the first ethnographic films, made around the turn of the twentieth century. It was later expanded to include a broader view of the physical environments in which people live. Accompanying it has been an increased focus on visual culture and cultural practices involving the body, including performances and religious practices. Some of the resulting films

5.4 A Sicilian interior in Luchino Visconti's *La Terra Trema* (1948)

have been essentially visual ethnographies of the senses, attempting to evoke the subjective experience of people in other societies. The tendency can be seen emerging in such early films as Robert Flaherty's *Nanook of the North* (1922) and *Moana* (1926) and in Basil Wright's *The Song of Ceylon* (1934). It is also a feature of later ethnographic films such as Hilary Harris and George Breidenbach's *The Nuer* (1971) and Robert Gardner's *Forest of Bliss* (1985). The risk attending such efforts, however, has always been that of conflating the filmmaker's sensory responses with those of the subjects.

The desire to communicate sensory experience and its significance in social life can also be seen in a broader range of documentary films. It is apparent in Sergei Dvortsevoy's *In the Dark* (2004), Stéphane Breton's *Ascent to the Sky* (2009) and Florian Geyer's *Sulfur* (2005). Films such as these emphasise the relationship of environment to work, and the hardships and anomie that often accompany it.[5] Two films – Ilisa Barbash and Lucien Castaing-Taylor's *Sweetgrass* (2009) and J. P. Sniadecki's *Demolition* (2008) – although dissimilar in some ways, can be seen as marking out an important new direction in documentary and ethnographic cinema, much as Jean Rouch's and Errol Morris's films expanded the possibilities of documentary several decades earlier (discussed in chapter 12). *Sweetgrass*, when it appeared, astonished audiences with the extraordinary immediacy with which it conveyed its presentation of sheep herding and herders' lives in the high country of Montana (figure 5.5). It accomplished this through extended camera takes that at times were intimate and unhurried and at other times expansive, and also by taking advantage of the potential of radio microphones to create a disjuncture between wide open spaces and the close-up sounds of voices. In

5.5 Herder and sheep in *Sweetgrass*

73

the film, this collapsing of the distance between image and sound, despite its artificiality, produces a powerful doubling of our perceptions, giving us at once a feeling of being at one with the herders' inner life and yet outside it, viewing the scene from a broader perspective, even the perspective of history. The film is seemingly of gigantic proportions, at one level taking in the lives of its two main protagonists with sympathy and irony and at another placing them in the distance, among the herds of sheep streaming up and down the mountains, vulnerable to the elements and the gradual dying off of the economy on which the herders depend. *Leviathan* (2012), a later film collaboration by Castaing-Taylor, made with Véréna Paravel, extends this cosmic view and use of sound to the point that human beings almost disappear from view, or are seen chiefly as living a harsh life exploiting other animals on the planet, a relationship very different from the close bond between sheep and men in *Sweetgrass*.

Sniadecki, while still a student at Harvard University's Sensory Ethnography Lab, a programme founded by Castaing-Taylor, made *Songhua* (2007), a short film that heralded his more ambitious film *Demolition* a year later. *Songhua* is composed of a series of long camera takes showing the varied activities of people along the shores of the Songhua River in north-eastern China.[6] It was notable for the subtlety of its choices and the care Sniadecki took in framing them. Simultaneously, it revealed his sympathy and respect for his subjects in allowing these observations to play out over time, instead of treating them, as in so many other documentary films, as mere impressions. In *Demolition*, Sniadecki applied these principles in a more considered and impressive way. The film makes use of long camera takes, starting with one of a seated man, apparently a supervisor at a construction site, and then turning 360 degrees to reveal the entire site before finally returning to him. In the scenes that follow, the film explores the dangerous lives of the migrant workers, contrasting the laborious breaking of concrete and hand-cutting of iron reinforcing rods with the dinosaur movements of the giant machines around them (figure 5.6). There are breaks for eating and washing, and casual conversations, some with Sniadecki. The film is true to the aims of the Sensory Ethnography Lab in revealing the tactile and auditory aspects of the workers' lives within a larger cultural and economic system. With *Demolition*, Sniadecki succeeds in creating a distinctive style of documentary, formally rigorous but at the same time delicately attuned to the particulars of everyday life, often viewing situations from a wry perspective. Although varying this style perhaps less successfully in his collaborations with other filmmakers, what remains consistent in his work is his fascination with using the camera to examine every nuance of lived experience. Sniadecki's later films maintain this interest, sometimes veering towards one-take *tours de force* in *The Yellow Bank* (2010) and *People's Park* (2012), but then pursuing it with great effect in *The Iron Ministry* (2014). Here, perhaps recognising

5.6 Workers and machinery in *Demolition*

the limitations of the long take, he moves towards freer and more allusive kinds of images of people and objects on long train journeys in China. Where his path and Castaing-Taylor's diverge is in Castaing-Taylor's broader view of human history and inclination to exploit the power of cinematic effects, as against Sniadecki's movement towards simplified technical means and a continued focus on the limitless details of human existence. In both cases one feels the filmmakers are immersed in the world of their subjects through a use of the camera that seems to defy and transcend the framing that surrounds their images.

One of the larger consequences of the alliance between film and the aims of ethnography has been a realignment of the camera with the body, not only through new ways of using the camera but through an emphasis on both the filmmaker's and the viewer's sense of being materially present in the film. This suggests the possibility of an emerging 'cinema of consciousness' that implicitly rejects the idea of documentary as a practical medium of information and public issues – what Bill Nichols famously termed 'films of sobriety' (1991: 29). Films of this kind seem primarily concerned with individual experience and admit forms of looking that documentary has traditionally excluded. Whether or not these efforts of present-day filmmakers result in a major breakthrough by so unreservedly addressing audiences' sensibilities, they may still serve to refresh the language of cinema, much as writers in the past have periodically stripped away the clichés and excesses of written texts to go to the heart of the matter.

In the end, the challenge of embodied cinema is not simply to create cinematic equivalents of sensory experiences at large in the world but, as films have always done, to perceive in them or invest them with value. A film invites us to enter into a particular experiential space with a subject. To the extent that it is experimental, its aim is to find out what filming can reveal about the subject. To the extent that it is analytical, it is to describe and explain it. To the extent that it is embodied, it is to insist on another way of knowing it.

Notes

1 The film in question was *Panorama du Grand Canal vu d'un bateau*. It was filmed from a gondola on 25 October 1896.
2 *Porte de France*, filmed in Tunis in 1896 or 1897 by Alexandre Promio.
3 Von Hildebrand writes in the Foreword to the third edition of *The Problem of Form in Painting and Sculpture* that the 'two different means of perceiving the same phenomenon not only have separate existence in our faculties for sight and touch, but are united in the eye. Nature having endowed our eyes so richly, these two functions of seeing and touching exist here in a far more intimate union than they do when performed by different sense organs' (1907: 14).
4 See Rizzolatti and Destro (2008: 2055) and Ramachandran (2010: 163–88). Ramachandran describes an amputee who felt physical sensations in his phantom hand while watching another person's hand being touched. He suggests that all of us might feel this if the responses of our mirror neurons were not blocked by 'null signals' that moderate their effect. 'Imagine: The only thing separating your consciousness from another's might be your skin!' (Ramachandran, 2010: 125).
5 In my films *Doon School Chronicles* (2000) and *Gandhi's Children* (2008) I attempted to locate sensory experience specifically in a community context. My aim was not only to evoke the sensations felt by members of the two institutions where I filmed but also the broader sensory environments of these institutions, which I believed were fundamental in shaping the inhabitants' consciousness and the decisions they made.
6 At about the same time, I was making *SchoolScapes* (2007), an attempt to create a film in which each scene was a single shot. New approaches to documentary such as this were clearly 'in the air' at the time.

6

Sensational cinema

THE director John Waters, known for his transgressive films, once said, 'If someone vomits while watching one of my films, it's like getting a standing ovation.' That is not a cinematic experience most of us would pay good money for. Nor is it how most people think of films, which are more often regarded as either enjoyable or instructive. Yet films are not always so amenable. They are capable of producing strong physical reactions in us, including tears, nausea and sexual arousal. Again and again, the cinema demonstrates the close links that exist between the mind, the body and the senses. The feelings we have when watching films are both physical and emotional, created within us by our reflexes, desires, culture and past experiences. If the cinema comes with a plan to possess us, we come more than halfway to meet it.

With films we watch images and hear sounds, but our responses are by no means limited to these two senses. We mentally fill in the sensory gaps. Combinations of images and sounds are capable of evoking a much wider range of sensations, including touch, smell and taste – although perhaps with decreasing intensity in that order. Why that disparity exists is one of the more intriguing questions in cinema. Touch and texture seem to be the most easily evoked, smell and taste less so, although this varies with individuals. Most of us do not have a sensation of sweetness when we see someone eating chocolate. Then again, certain images may arouse disgust – the sight of something rotting, for example – although we perhaps react as much to other associations it has for us as to its likely smell. In François Truffaut's *The 400 Blows* (1959), when Antoine Doinel is made to take a bag of smelly garbage downstairs to the rubbish bins, his revulsion is manifest in his face and posture (figure 6.1). As for viewers of the film, it's unclear whether they respond more to the sight of the garbage, his reaction to it, or to their memories of a similar experience.

The disparities in cinema's evocative power are especially puzzling when we consider that smell and taste are proximate senses – that is, they are both triggered by direct contact with some substance, whereas vision and hearing both depend upon receiving waves propagated or reflected from objects with which we are not in direct contact. This may suggest an inverse relation between distance and evocative power. But just as probably it has to do with

6.1 Antoine Doinel empties the garbage in *The 400 Blows*

the order in which, during childhood, we develop our sensory preferences. Babies may instinctively avoid heights but they will put almost anything in their mouths, and they are conditioned by what they are given. Much of our liking for certain tastes and smells, and our dislike of others, is a learned response, a process of cultural filtering similar to that by which we learn to speak the sounds of our own language but gradually lose the ability to speak those of others.

If you think of the many sensations evoked by films, such as the weightiness of an object, or the wetness of a foggy street, Aristotle's original five senses begin to look too restrictive. Since his time, other senses have been added to the list, among them equilibrioception (the sense of balance), nocioception (the sense of pain), the vomeronasal sense (sensitivity to pheromones) and other senses related to motion, temperature and time.[1] There is also no guarantee that we all share similar sensory impressions of things. Different individuals, and members of different societies, do not give equal weight to the senses or even experience them in the same way. The deaf and the blind compensate for deficiencies in one sense by the hypertrophy of others. In such fields as perfumery, wine-tasting and *haute cuisine*, a high degree of aesthetic awareness of one particular sense may give it precedence over another. In literate societies, it has been argued, vision has been awarded a heightened importance because of the intensive discrimination of shapes that reading and writing require (Goody, 2002: 19). Although the potential range

78

of the senses seems to be limited by human biology, given a certain amount of individual and cultural variation, the range of sensations we experience vicariously when viewing films is another matter, and more open. The cinema makes possible an almost limitless number of sensory impressions. Apart from the less obvious ones, we can add familiar sensations of space and distance, weight, pressure and texture. The last three of these should perhaps be considered derivative sensations, from touch and vision, but they are no less vividly experienced for all that. Where should we place the impression of wetness or dryness, the impression of viscosity? Each surely involves something more than touch.

It has been suggested by Michel Chion and other writers on cinema that when an image and sound are combined, the result is not simply one augmented by the other but a different and more powerful phenomenon in which the two become welded together (Chion, 1994). Film images seem to reach out and capture sounds, even when there is no direct relationship between them. Our minds produce the link and often a causal connection. The combination of a minimal image and a minimal sound (such as trees in darkness and a distant train whistle) is enough to evoke a vivid scene in the imagination. One explanation may be that since two quite separate systems of evocation are involved, the visual and the auditory, instead of a process of fusion taking place, the two channels together create a kind of overload. Or it may be that there is a synaesthetic leakage from one to the other, a cortical confusion, or even a rapid alternation of impressions – in any case, more than a simple doubling. A sound and an image may combine in other ways too, not to produce an enhanced sensation but to veer towards a different sensation altogether. The sight and sound of a rushing stream or the splash of water on a stone floor evokes both coolness (sensation of temperature) and wetness (sensation of touch), while seeing a hand stroking a cat's fur suggests sleekness or softness.

It's also important to take into account the sensory void in which such stimuli appear, at least when encountered in a cinema rather than on a computer or television screen. The typical cinematic environment is one of sensory deprivation. The spectators sit in a darkened room insulated from the sounds outside. They remain motionless in their seats. They are often separated from others in a state of blankness, anticipation and receptivity. It is no wonder that early theorists compared this condition to dreaming, and films to artificial dreams that invade our consciousness.

At the same time, images have their own reality, even as the shadows of absent people and objects. They would not exist if they had not been provoked by something in front of a camera, with which they share certain characteristics. Film images are perceptions of a kind, if only those of a machine. If the camera is our advance guard, our artificial eye, then it is up to the brain – and the assumptions and memories it harbours – to make sense of them.

However much we interpret the images of our imagination, they also act directly on the nervous system. Physiological responses to films are enhanced by the film viewer's powers of identification. Adam Smith observed in the eighteenth century that watching an activity such as walking on a slack rope (akin to tightrope walking) provokes in us an attempt to assist the balance of the walker, a sensorimotor response somewhat better understood now with advances in neuroscience (Smith, 1969 [1790]: 3–4). Sergei Eisenstein (1957: 80) noted that showing a film of farmers rhythmically scything grass caused the audience to sway back and forth in time with them. Today this would be termed a 'kinetic resonance'. In human evolution, such involuntary bodily synchronies may eventually have produced the more complex forms of empathy and understanding that allow us to live cooperatively as social animals. Even if not, they can help explain the mystery of why shadows on a screen can arouse in us such vivid sensations of the experiences of others, the ghosts of other lives being lived.

If it weren't for the absence of movement and sound, still photographs would seem almost as lifelike as films. Early possessors of Daguerreotypes remarked that those pictured in them appeared about to speak. Sound has a curious effect on the way we perceive images. We see an object falling and hear a sound, and the one seems to have been caused by the other. Connecting the two strikes us as a kind of proof, a sign of authenticity. This is not an intellectual conclusion but a perceptual one. We may even have been tricked if, as often happens in cinema, the sound was added later, as an effect. One of the odder aspects of adding sound effects to films is that they often create a more acute sense of reality than if the natural sounds had been used. Film editors add them precisely to give a sharper edge, a greater sense of presence, to the images. When certain sound effects are dropped into an aural void, as they often were in European films of the 1950s and 1960s (when the sound in most of these films was dubbed in later), the impression can be of great immediacy. The sound effects stand out more starkly, not competing with other sounds. And if a sound effect has been recorded at close range, it gives an impression not only of physical closeness but of a kind of privileged access to the moment. Our minds seem to welcome this essentialism, an abstract paring down of sensory stimuli.

In the short story 'The Photograph' by the Anglo-Indian writer Ruskin Bond, a grandmother studies a photograph of herself as a young girl.

> Those flowers at the girl's feet, they were marigolds, and the bougainvillaea creeper, it was a mass of purple. You can't see those colours in the photo, and even if you could, as nowadays, you wouldn't be able to smell the flowers or feel the breeze. (Bond, 1988: 22)

Cinema has brought the evocation of sensations such as these much closer. One of the things that most astonished the viewers of the first

Lumière films, according to journalists at the time, was seeing the complex movement of leaves on trees and waves in the sea. The movement of human beings was apparently less astonishing because viewers were used to seeing this in the theatre, but having the intricate movements of nature captured was something entirely new (Sadoul, 1962: 24). Early viewers even had the mistaken impression they had seen colours in the Lumière films, although it would be months before Georges Méliès began to tint his films and years before Léon Gaumont introduced Chronochrome, one of the first colour processes (Jeanne, 1965: 11–12). If the Ruskin Bond story gives us any clue, the excitement that early audiences felt when viewing moving leaves was perhaps due to a process of double authentication. The leaves were made to seem more real by the breeze moving them, but their very movement gave evidence of the existence of the breeze. As the French film theorist Edgar Morin noted, 'movement restores to forms brought to life on the screen the autonomy and the corporeality that they had lost (or almost lost) in the [still] photographic image' (2005 [1956]: 118).[2]

Some of our responses to films are automatic and innate, as when we dodge a lion apparently leaping at us from the screen. (*Bwana Devil*, one of the first 3D movies of the 1950s, made much of this.) But innate responses are reinforced by responses that originate at a higher level of consciousness, in our thoughts and imagination. The sight of a person's face on the screen is often enough to create an intuitive bond. As well, films intentionally link us to the perspectives of their protagonists through their shot construction and narratives. We follow characters through different landscapes and, as often as not, see what they see. We experience their dramas and share their aims and desires. Psychologically and by technical means, we are drawn into their emotional and sensory worlds.

Many of these responses work only if they connect, either directly or by analogy, with events in the viewer's life. The references need not be explicit; it is enough if viewers can put associated experiences together in new combinations. You may never have eaten a mango, but to see it being eaten is to call forth the experience of eating other fruits. You may never have experienced a certain kind of violence, but violence in any form speaks a common language. The cinema recycles familiar settings, many of them created by the cinema itself in earlier films: the atmosphere of a railway station or a city street. Scenes such as these, whether repeated in life or in art, imprint themselves deeply on our subconscious.

Other responses seem to depend more upon the ways in which, as infants, we learn the qualities of objects by handling and observing them. It is often hard to separate these learned responses from innate ones – for example, our fixation with the human face, which every new-born baby seems to possess. The dominance of the face in the cinema of almost every country seems more closely related to this innate response than to cultural patterns.

Even our ability to recognise certain emotions in facial expressions seems to have some universality, although subject to cultural variation. Such deep-seated human responses appear to include a visual grasp of physical spaces, including judgements about depth and the size and solidity of objects. This was once thought to be learned but is increasingly viewed as something we are born with. A famous experiment in developmental psychology in the 1950s called the 'visual cliff' suggested that babies crawling across a sheet of glass understood when there was a drop-off beneath them and refused to go on (Gibson and Walk, 1960).

Despite our biological inheritance, it is clear that there is also an aesthetic basis to many of our sensory responses, and these are carried over into film. Aesthetic valuations vary with culture, even producing some nearly opposite reactions. In many parts of the world cow dung plays an important part in the construction of houses, and in those societies where it is routinely used as a building material or as fuel it does not provoke the sort of disgust a European city-dweller might feel when encountering it on a country outing. In Nilotic pastoral societies, where cattle are the focus of the highest aesthetic appreciation, cow dung is positively associated with utility and beauty. The idea of beauty itself is variable and subject to fashion, influencing how people in different societies judge everything from food to personal attractiveness to works of art. Within a family, one person's music may be another's noise. It seems that individual sensory responses ultimately reflect a mix of the innate, the idiosyncratic and the learned, just as each person's emotional life is shaped both by experiences that are common to most of us and by those that are exceptional. Perhaps because of the sensory immediacy of cinema, viewers' reactions to films are more extreme than their reactions to other works of art. A scene that most viewers simply enjoy may in other viewers trigger feelings of abhorrence or deep emotion, and this can easily spill over into a judgement of the film as a whole.

There is great potential in cinema for heightening normal sensory perception through framing, camera angles, lighting, use of sound effects and, especially, the use of close-ups. Close-ups not only intensify by magnifying objects or parts of the body but by segregating them from their surroundings, an effect of decontextualisation that parallels the more general sensory deprivation of cinema viewing. Films are quite cavalier in their disregard for the niceties of social distance. They are able to examine things in close detail that no actual observer would be able to look at without causing offence, such as the shape of one person's nose or another's dirty fingernails. They can dwell on the pleasant or the unpleasant, on a freshly made cake or a filthy toilet. Films may need to make up for what they lack in sensory range by using more intense kinds of evocation and a more intimate treatment of personal space.

Although these methods contribute much to the beauty and power of cinema, they also have a coercive side. There are things we don't like to look at, such as injuries to the human body, but films frequently make us do so. The close-up is a particularly probing kind of 'directed looking', converting what might in life be a brief sighting into what often feels like an extended examination. Films not only control the things we see but also when we see them and for how long. And although we can close our eyes, there is always the temptation to catch a glimpse of what we are missing. Sometimes what we are shown simply bores us or makes us uncomfortable, but other scenes seem perversely to have been made almost unwatchable – not only the images of violence in many feature films but also scenes we may feel some obligation to watch, such as images of famine or disaster.

Thus films not only have the capacity to challenge our physical vision, but also our moral and cultural vision. They can intentionally address our prejudices and narrowness. Many would argue that because films are able to show us things we don't normally see, or are unable to see, or don't wish to see, this is precisely why they should do so. It is what they were made for. Films can transcend our cultural taboos and show us the realities of how other people live. Filmmakers may also, for similar reasons, choose to show what is improper, indecent or distressing, to break us out of the provincialism of our own time and place.

One of the consequences of the coercive power of films is the underlying anxiety and excitement of knowing that we may be shown almost anything. Certain films arouse the fear of an assault on our senses and emotions even when they don't follow through with it. The mere suggestion is enough to put us in an apprehensive state. This can lead to misunderstandings. Some scholars such as Moore (1988) and Parry (1988) complained about the number of corpses shown in Robert Gardner's film about death in Benares, *Forest of Bliss* (1985). In fact, very few corpses were shown; it was the fear of seeing them that apparently led to this conclusion. It perhaps didn't help that, overall, Gardner's film was deeply immersed in other details of physical existence. It contained scenes of dying people, dead animals and excrement; but also of marigolds, smoke and incense, and the healthy bodies of boatmen on the river (figure 6.2).

Such an intense focus on the senses is often part of an effort by filmmakers to compensate for the ways in which films fail to convey what they have experienced themselves. They are right about some of the limitations – films do not allow us to smell the flowers, or the garbage. But by emphasising other aspects of these objects, such as their texture, they can sometimes fill the sensory gap.[3] Another approach is to make use of the reactions of people we see on the screen. Images showing others enjoying good food or a glass of cold beer can convey some of the pleasure they are feeling, a point not lost on advertisers. Equally, someone's disgust can intensify the viewer's disgust, as in the scene from *The 400 Blows*. In considering the aesthetics of films, taking the term in its broadest sense, it is also important to consider their

6.2 A boatman on the Ganges in *Forest of Bliss*

anaesthetic potential. For all their sensory power, films have the capacity to dull the senses, not only through their failure to convey some experiences but through their overexposure of others. This is obvious in horror films and pornography, but even well meaning cinematic techniques can inadvertently have an alienating effect on viewers. Trite and overused formulas can easily distance the viewer from the subject. If filmmakers try to negate these problems by overstating their case, the result is often just more distance. Films of advocacy tend to produce this effect when they repeatedly show victims and atrocities out of context.

The technical properties of film are responsible for some of the difficulties filmmakers face in conveying what they have seen. Colours tend to appear brighter, dirt disappears and people and objects often emerge oversimplified, as if already tagged and categorised. Even the dreadful conditions of some people's lives can acquire a deceptive simplicity and romance. Apart from the technical limitations of film and video images, this loss of immediacy can be put down to the inherent miniaturisation and reduction of cinema – its compression of months of experience into an hour or two, its clarifying effect of framing reality in neat segments, eliminating all but the essential. To this must be added the medium's predisposition for balance, composition and beauty. To filmmakers, something else is often missing too: not just the surrounding ambience of sights and sounds, since this is often well captured, but the sense of their own presence, the memory of physically being there. This chiefly applies to documentary films, but the artificiality of many fiction films shows they are not immune to it, despite their strivings for realism.

In practice, most of a documentary filmmaker's attention is focused on making sense of the events taking place before the camera and giving them cinematic shape. This means finding a position from which to see them, framing them in certain ways, and thinking about the connections that can be made by moving the camera or creating a succession of shots. Moulding the images in this way is not unlike moulding reality itself. There is a prevailing sense of urgency. 'This is important ... and this too!' Undoubtedly, the filming process also includes a sense of acquisition, of capturing some piece of reality, yet this is just as often tempered and exceeded by a feeling of humility at what the filmmaker has been able to film. Far from being a taker, the filmmaker is often the grateful receiver of gifts, which are to be cherished and preserved for others. There may well be an erotic element in this intensity, highly attuned to sensory awareness. Ordinary objects become aesthetically charged, and the slightest expressions and gestures of the people being filmed become objects of wonder. Even when feelings are less intense, the filmmaker may still experience a sense of awe in the face of reality.

The act of filming produces a convergence of the sensations of sight, sound and touch. The technical side of filming is partly responsible for this. A camera looks with a clarity that opens up its subjects to inspection. It can bring them artificially close, allowing them to be seen as they would otherwise be seen only in moments of great intimacy. The ability to see textures in fine detail, often exaggerated by oblique lighting, becomes equivalent to feeling their surfaces, the eye rather than the hand passing over them. Being touched and observing touching can become closely associated if the viewer and filmmaker identify with a person on the screen. In terms of brain activity, the two can be, in certain circumstances, indistinguishable.[4] This effect can be intensified by sounds that evoke the qualities of surfaces – their roughness, pliability or softness. A footstep echoing in a church or sounding on a wooden floor often says more about the place filmed than the person walking there. For the filmmaker, a camera is thus more than a recording instrument: it may be a means of reaching out to the world and receiving a reply. The sensations that the filmmaker experiences while filming are channelled back into the process of filming, reinforcing and redirecting the filmmaker's choices. Decisions about what, and how long, to film are clearly tied to stimuli that the filmmaker invites but is also subject to.

More and more often in contemporary documentary films, the filmmaker is also the cinematographer, and the film is in a sense *inscribed* rather than produced. The use of digital video rather than film has made this increasingly feasible. The idea of the *caméra-stylo*, first expressed by Alexandre Astruc (1948), was adopted by French critics to assert that the authorship of a film could be like that of a book, with the camera its writing instrument. In this kind of film, the filmmaker's feelings become intimately connected to the recording process and profoundly influence the look and atmosphere of the result. Having such experiences can also be of major importance in the life of the filmmaker.

During the making of a film, the filmmaker and subjects occupy a shared sensory space, although they may respond to it in different ways. For the filmmaker this experience often becomes highly charged. Jean Rouch compared filming at its most intense to being in a trance. Richard Leacock said it was like falling in love. John Marshall called it a kind of intoxication. Robert Gardner described it as erotic. Others have characterised it variously as magical, contemplative and religious.[5] The camera seems to act as a lens above and beyond its optical properties, concentrating physical sensations and emotions. The two may be hard to tell apart: a hair-raising experience is both physical and emotional. Emotions themselves have direct effects on the body – increasing blood pressure and heart rate and so on – but for the filmmaker these are intensified by the physical effort required to change one's position to reframe images with the camera. On top of this there is an acute consciousness of the stream of images being recorded, an anxiety about what will happen next, and quite often an intense identification with the people being filmed. This last emotion may overshadow all others.

One can think of a film as a sensory field in which the experiences of the filmmaker, film subject and film viewer cross and sometimes coincide. If the area of coincidence is great, then the film is likely to be accounted a success. The task is at its most complex when the filmmaker's intention is to convey the sensory and social experiences of others. The strategy of some filmmakers has been to expose themselves to the same conditions as their subjects, thus reproducing as closely as possible the situations their subjects encounter. This means observing, in Philip Roth's words, a 'scrupulous fidelity' to 'specific data', neither filtering nor adjusting what they film by standards outside the subject's frame of reference.[6] This is a responsibility felt by ethnographers and documentary filmmakers as well as novelists. It means putting aside personal inhibitions that have little relevance to the subjects' lives. It may also mean filming scenes they would acknowledge to be true but find difficult to confront.

Combining images with sounds has made it possible to convey human experiences that go well beyond the visible and auditory. The sensations that are evoked can play an important part in our understanding of the weave of physical and social forces in people's lives. But many of these sensations are, in a sense, free signifiers, advancing our understanding only when attached to particular situations. A film that elicits the feeling of walking across a wooden floor tells us little in the absence of knowing who is walking there and why. Physical sensations can also carry varied or nearly opposite connotations – eating for pleasure as opposed to eating from hunger, touching a body that is loved or one that is frightening or repulsive. Sensations by themselves do not necessarily create new understanding, however much they may be intense in their own right and function as instruments of cinematic power. In films, as in life, the senses exist within the context of other relations. Only in those circumstances can they continue to play a significant part in the art of cinema and produce what, with caution, we may call sensory knowledge.

Notes

1 Some animals have additional senses, such as a shark's ability, called electroreception, to detect weak electrical fields generated by other creatures in the water nearby, and the ability of some insects to sense the Earth's magnetic field and navigate by it.

2 Morin cites A. Michotte van den Berck in making this comment. He prefaces it by saying: 'The photograph was frozen in an eternal moment. *Movement brought the dimension of time: film unfolds, it lasts. At the same time, things in motion produce the space that they measure and traverse, and, above all, become real within space*' (original emphasis).

3 Among the more humorous and absurd instances of overcompensation have been the attempts to introduce smells into films, as a sort of third sensory track. Hans Laube's Scentovision of 1939 was followed by AromaRama in Carlo Lizzani's *Behind the Great Wall* (1958) and Smell-O-Vision in *Scent of Mystery* (1960), directed by Jack Cardiff. These methods blew scents into the cinemas where the films were being shown. Other methods included the Odorama process, based on scratch-and-smell cards, used in John Waters' film *Polyester* (1981), and Aroma-Scope, used in *Spy Kids 4: All the Time in the World* (2011), directed by Robert Rodriguez. Les Blank, the maker of *Garlic Is as Good as Ten Mothers* (1980), advocated heating garlic so that its scent permeated the cinema during projection

4 V. S. Ramachandran writes: 'Mirror neurons have also been found for touch; that is, sensory touch mirror neurons fire in a person when she is touched and also when she watches another person being stroked' (2010: 421).

5 Basil Wright described the making of *The Song of Ceylon* (1934) as a 'unique experience in my life. It's the only film I've made that I really loved, and it was in fact a religious experience' (see Levin, 1971: 53).

6 Roth's exact words were: 'It is from a scrupulous fidelity to the blizzard of specific data that is a personal life, it is from the force of its uncompromising particularity, from its *physicalness*, that the realistic novel, the insatiable realistic novel with its multitude of realities derives its ruthless intimacy.' They were part of a speech given by Roth at a celebration for his eightieth birthday in 2013 and are reprinted in *Why Write? Collected Nonfiction 1960–2013* (Roth, 2017).

7

The experience of colour

COLOUR is but one of several aspects of vision, and only one of the many strands that make up our perception of the social and material world. It nevertheless plays an important part in the aesthetics of everyday life. Here I mean not the beauty-aesthetics of fine art or Kantian philosophy, but something closer to the classical Greek concept of *aisthesis*, or sense experience, and what A. G. Baumgarten meant when he introduced the term into philosophy in the eighteenth century as 'the science of sensory cognition'. Aesthetics from this perspective has less to do with artistic expression and the exercise of taste than with the more mundane and pervasive forms of sensory patterning to be found in society, and the ways in which human beings experience and respond to them. It may even denote a particular set of attitudes towards how to live one's life – in Foucault's phrase, an 'aesthetics of existence'.

One place in which to study the social aesthetics of colour is in the highly controlled environments of schools, where colours frequently become important signifiers. In many schools, colour is used for coding and identification, as it is by political parties, religious groups and sporting teams. These uses may or may not reflect national or cultural associations, such as the colours used in flags or linked to religions. In India, for example, colours carry culturally specific meanings that have both a political and a religious significance: white is associated with mourning, purity and abstinence; green with Islam; blue with Brahmanism; and saffron with Hinduism – or latterly, Hindutva religiosity.

There are other uses to be considered. Schools use colours to focus the emotions of students and to set themselves apart from other schools. A pair of colours is often chosen because the number of available possibilities is thereby greatly increased. Students may not in fact identify with either colour when it is used by itself but only when it is combined with the other. It is this binary that becomes meaningful, as in Eisenstein's theory of cinematic montage, where it is the juxtaposition of two shots that generates the meaning. If either colour were paired off with a different colour, it would take on quite different associations. This principle applies to the co-presence of colours generally, allowing them to become closely associated in some contexts but to be used in opposition in others.

This is colour coding at a very rudimentary level, even though such uses may have powerful psychological effects. Equally important, however, are the less obvious effects of colour, involving deeper cultural resonances, the effects of certain dominant colours and the inclusion of colour itself in a broader range of sensory experiences. Some individuals are known to experience synaesthetic associations between sounds, physical shapes and specific colours. It is therefore not unlikely that the reverse is true: that for some people colours may correspond to certain qualities of sound, such as its timbre, or to certain physical forms, or even to certain textures and odours. In any case, colours do not exist in isolation but in relation to objects, events and other colours – and, sometimes, in relation to the absence of colour. Colour is a property of objects – or, more accurately, an effect of light. Objects project their other qualities into the colours with which they are clothed. Colour becomes 'colour' in the abstract only when we begin to see it as a quality cutting across different contexts and binding together different objects. Colours may possess properties that have a direct impact on our bodily responses, but our sensing of colour also takes place within the context of our emotions and social relationships. Colours rarely possess only a single symbolic value: they are multivalent, appearing in different circumstances and creating correspondingly complex and ambiguous feelings in those who experience them. How we respond to colour is thus intimately linked to our activities, our language, our cultural associations and the events in our lives.

BLUE, GREY AND THE SKIN

Doon School, in northern India, is an elite boys' boarding school renowned for the greenness of its campus, the Chandbagh Estate. Until 1933 this formed the grounds of the Forest Research Institute and College. The students of the school inherited an extraordinary botanical garden of some seventy acres, containing several hundred species of trees as well as beds filled with flowers and shrubs. Greenness was the dominant impression I had of the school when I first visited it, in 1996. This occurred during a mid-term break, when the students were away on excursions. I remember seeing massive trees of all kinds and at the heart of the school a broad green playing field bordered by dormitories and other buildings. When I returned to the school the following April, I began to see flickerings of blue through the foliage. This was the blue of the students' games uniforms, which consisted of shorts of a deep blue colour and shirts with a pattern of blue and grey panels (figures 7.1 and 7.2). Inescapable green was now succeeded by inescapable blue.

It was the shirt of the games uniform that produced one of the more memorable statements of the school's first headmaster, A. E. Foot. Addressing the assembled boys in 1936, he said:

89

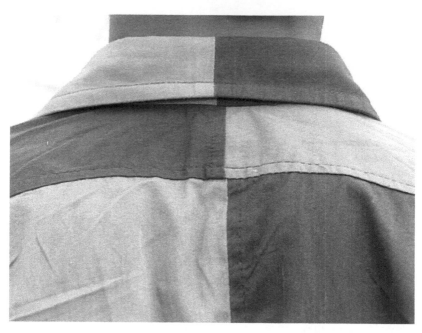

7.1 The Doon School games uniform from the back

7.2 The Doon School games uniform from the front

You can think of yourselves as a pack of cards all with the same pattern of
blue and grey on your backs; on the other side is each boy's special character.

Foot was fond of such metaphors and their implications. In referring to the
school's two official colours, he was underlining several important distinctions. His use of the metaphor of the back and the front may be taken in two
senses. His main point is to draw a line between the school as an institution
and as a collection of living human beings. In the image of the pack of cards,
he suggests the potential for conflict between individuality and uniformity, as
though to stress the boys' need to guard their special qualities.[1] At the same
time, he does not deny the value of seeing oneself as a member of a social
unit. The student thus bears a dual relation to the school, on the one hand as
an autonomous personality, on the other as a responsible citizen. This duality
is reinforced by the way in which the design of the games shirt both unifies
and effectively splits the boy down the middle. More concretely, a distinction
may be drawn between the actual cloth of the uniforms and the boys' faces
and bodies, that is to say, between inert matter and flesh, the incorporeal
and corporeal – and, one might add, between manufactured goods produced
by human beings and human beings themselves. There is one thing more.
In relating the school colours to positive and negative (or neutral) qualities,
Foot may be alluding to the difference between colour and non-colour, for
according to some definitions grey is not a colour at all but an absence of
colour.[2] This has implications for how the school handles colour generally
and the selective use of colour and non-colour throughout the school.[3]

One further consideration is implicit in Foot's statement. Blue and grey
both stand in direct opposition to the varieties of skin colour of north
Indians. This would be much less the case if the Doon School uniforms
included yellow or red, often considered 'warm' colours, unlike blue.[4] And
indeed, among the *ganas* – the Hindu categories of human behaviour and
natural phenomena (literally, 'strings' or 'strands') – the *rajas gana*, or red, is
the *gana* of passion and energy. Could blue and grey, a 'cool' colour paired
with a non-colour, have been chosen to make precisely this contrast with the
warmer colour of the boys' skins? If boys were blue, would their uniforms
have been orange or pink? Or is the contrast merely a fortuitous under-
pinning of Foot's main point? This is not an entirely idle matter, for if one
of the uses of uniforms and colour is to contain and control the body, then
in this context blue becomes the colour of maximum control.

Consciousness of the skin, and skin colour in particular, are matters of
some importance and complexity in Indian society, a fact that must at some
level influence the attitudes of students and staff at the school. Considerable
attention is paid to the perfection of the skin. The smoothness, glow and
well-being of the skin are considered a significant part of looking attractive. I
noticed that even pre-adolescent boys at Doon School spent a large amount

of time on grooming. For many of them this included, along with assiduously brushing their teeth and combing their hair, rubbing their skin with creams and oils several times a day. In India these practices are not confined to the middle class but are found at all levels of society. Allied to this, the lightness or darkness of the skin is part of the subtext of Indian attitudes towards caste. There is no strict correlation between skin colour and caste, but there is often assumed to be a connection. This is complicated by the fact that people from the south are generally darker than people from the north, regardless of caste. In the matrimonial advertisements in Indian newspapers, young women are often described as 'fair', the currently most common term for light skin colour. (A few years ago, 'wheatish' was the popular term.) Although I never heard skin colour discussed openly at Doon, it is reasonable to assume that the colour of the skin is an element in the complex of body and uniform that defines boys individually and arrayed in groups.

Green, as I have already noted, is the dominant colour of the school's surroundings, the colour of foliage, playing fields and even the local parrots. It is so omnipresent as to form an unconscious background to all school activities. It is the colour of nature, not of human intervention, and indeed appears to stand in opposition to the field of human order, which is represented by the school's buildings and walls. Against the towering trees, the students, dressed in blue and grey, seem small units of another order when massed together in sports or school rituals. As if to counter the green, the school's buildings are of warmer colours, some of them, including the original Forest Research Institute building, of red brick. A number of other brick buildings are also painted red, as if to intensify this colour. [5] Most of the buildings have red roofs. Low walls bordering the pathways are painted red, as are the arches of a viaduct that once brought water to the estate. The school's outdoor theatre, the Rose Bowl, is reddish in colour as well as in name. Green and red thus constitute a pair of opposites at the school, but one that seems confined to the physical setting.

It is also apparent that green stands in contrast to the three elements of the triad: blue–grey–skin colour. One would therefore expect a general avoidance of green in most aspects of the school's social life. However, this proves not to be the case. The athletics singlets worn by the students of Jaipur House, and used in inter-house competitions, are in fact dark green. At first sight, this could be put down to the simple need to colour-code the five main residential houses of the school, although the school's general inclination seems to be toward blue in its uniforms. (When a fifth house, Oberoi House, was added to the original four, the colour chosen for its singlet was a kind of turquoise or peacock blue – a shade sufficiently different to distinguish it from the dark blue of Hyderabad House.) But if the green of the Jaipur House singlets is an exception, it is an odd one, since other colours were available when the choice was made. That it is not an exception is further supported by the fact that in the school's dormitories the bedcovers are either green or blue. In fact, blue and green seem to be closely allied here, as they are in the colour spectrum. We may posit that this is so because they serve equally well to provide a contrast to human life. Thus green is treated in two distinct ways, depending on its context. In the broader sphere of the built environment, such as the exteriors of buildings, it is avoided. In more intimate circumstances, such as the boys' sleeping arrangements or clothing seen next to their skin, it becomes acceptable, and perhaps even a desirable counterpoint.

Colour and identity

The importance of colour at Doon, and its controlled use in clothing, may be cause for some puzzlement, particularly at a school with a strong if sometimes paradoxical ethic of individual worth. However, this very ethic may be one of the reasons behind it. The complete absence of variegated colour, in contrast to the clothes worn by students at home, makes the presence of colour, and the selective use of colours, particularly striking.

Terence Turner has argued that external signs of social identity, such as colour, may be more important in non-exchange societies than in societies in which material exchange is highly developed.

> Societies in which social identity is not constituted primarily through the exchange of goods (valuables, gifts, or commodities) nevertheless depend on the public circulation of symbolic tokens of valued aspects of personal identity, such as marks of status, appropriate role performance, and the values associated with them. In the absence of concrete objects that might serve as embodiments of such values or tokens of status, a society may make use of other modes of circulation that do not rely on the exchange of objects. [...] [One] mode of circulation is through visual display. In the case of circulating tokens of personal identity and value, such display typically involves specialised forms of bodily appearance. (Turner, 1995: 147)

An elite boarding school such as Doon could be considered a non-exchange society. Students are there to study and build up knowledge and merit, not commodities. The commodities, it is hoped, will come later, assured by a Doon education. Tokens of wealth are few, and a boy from a very modest background may sleep next to a boy from one of the richest families in the country. There would be little visibly to distinguish them. Boys in their first year are forbidden to wear watches, partly to discourage a show of wealth. Pocket money is limited and doled out by means of coupons from a 'Boys' Bank'. One of the few areas in which boys can display wealth is in the wearing of expensive track shoes, but this is a fairly recent phenomenon.

Turner gives as an illustration of his argument the highly coded use of colour in body painting among the Kayapo of the Amazon basin. At Doon, variations in colour and uniforms, as extensions of the body, also become important indicators of status and affiliation. Variations in uniform, some obvious, some subtle, indicate a boy's house, seniority and personal achievements. Doon's system of dressing its boys is thus perhaps no less elaborate than the painting of Kayapo bodies. There are different uniforms for different occasions in which both colour and the lack of colour carry significance. The use of colour and its absence become part of the students' everyday experience at the school.

After spending several weeks at Doon School, my overall impression was not so much one of varied uses of colour as of monochromes. Where colours are evident, they tend to appear in isolation, or in association with grey. They stand out in their simplicity. This creates a kind of stripping-down of sensory experience in school life. It is in many ways restful in comparison to the chaotic medley of colour on the streets beyond the gates. Monochrome provides an ordered background to life and a suppression of difference, but also, paradoxically, a background against which individual differences – in faces, bodily appearance and manner – may stand out all the more strongly. In the long-standing debate about school uniforms, this difference of emphasis is a recurrent theme. Uniforms, it is argued by some, encourage conformity and suppress individuality; they are inherently authoritarian and undemocratic. Others argue, to the contrary, that uniforms are egalitarian. They iron out differences in wealth and provide a common ground against which the merits of the individual can shine. This is the view implicit in Foot's pack-of-cards metaphor.

Doon School's monochromes are evident in its uniforms, its interior spaces and its natural setting. Here, green is the monochrome of nature, the environment in which social life goes on. The school uniforms are studies in monochrome. They vary throughout the day, the changes determined by school activities, the seniority of the boys wearing them and the seasons. Changes in activities establish a repetitive temporal sequence. A typical day involves five changes of uniform, or possibly even more if a boy is being punished.[6] Upon waking, the boys go immediately for PT (physical training), a set of exercises on the playing field supervised by staff members and other students. For this activity they change from their nightwear into a white singlet, dark blue shorts and white gym shoes with white socks. (In winter they may be allowed a white pullover or a grey and blue tracksuit.) After PT they change into their classroom uniform. In winter this is a grey woollen suit, white shirt, sometimes a school tie (grey with narrow blue stripes), grey school stockings and black shoes. Except on formal occasions, a grey pullover may be substituted for the suit jacket, and a blue shirt for the white one. Junior boys are allowed to wear grey shorts instead of long trousers. In summer, junior boys wear grey shorts and a sleeveless light blue shirt, with or without a grey pullover.[7] Senior boys are allowed long white trousers. Footwear is either black shoes with school stockings or black leather sandals, called *peshawaris*, with no stockings.[8] The turbans of Sikh boys must be either light or dark blue. The dominant 'colours' so far (three of which, in fact, are non-colours) are blue, grey, black and white. After classes there is a change into the games uniform. This uniform has already been described – deep blue shorts with a grey and blue shirt. It is followed by a change into evening clothing (white kurta-pyjamas or white shirt and white trousers, with an optional grey pullover). Finally, there is a change back into nightwear.

What is consistent throughout these many changes is the restriction to non-colours (grey, black, white) and blue. A certain logic may be observed in the amount of blue permitted. Blue, and especially the more saturated blue of the games uniform, is more closely associated with sports than with studies, where the non-colours prevail. The warmer colours make an appearance only in the red, yellow, green and blue singlets worn during some inter-house competitions. This suggests a more general link between colour itself, the human body and physical activity. Colour and skin colour are thus offset against grey, the expression of mind and spirit. When the boys from all the different houses appear at athletics events, and at the annual PT competition, the effect is of a bursting out of colour and animal energy.

We can construct a list of contrasts from some of the foregoing distinctions:

uniformity	individuality
institution	inhabitants
cloth	flesh
grey	blue
non-colour	colour
grey/blue	skin colour
'cool' colours	'warm' colours
studies	sports
mind	body

Colour is a major variable in the clothing worn at different times of day. It thus has an important role in the ordering of time, activities and age groups. If skin colour represents the human body at its most natural, individual and vulnerable, then clothing is what covers it and contains it, expressing the forces of social and institutional control. Perhaps significantly, when the boys remove their uniforms for the evening bath, they appear to remove many of the inhibitions and stresses of school along with them. At Doon this is a time of relaxation and sociability, no doubt enhanced, especially in winter, by the warm atmosphere of steam, soap and running water.[9] At the school, what a boy wears indicates the activities he is permitted to do, just as what he does dictates what uniform he must wear. Clothing thus provides a set of signs about appropriate behaviour and status. Secondary modifications of the uniforms restore a degree of individuality to the students by rewarding them with emblems of personal merit. A dark blue blazer is awarded for prowess in sport, a black blazer for high academic achievement, and house or school 'colours' for related achievements, allowing students to wear various neckties, neck scarves and badges. The school delegates considerable power to prefects and house captains, who are allowed further variations of uniform and are given other privileges, such as rooms to themselves.

SPACE, TIME AND RITUAL

The attention I have given to colour and uniforms would, I think, be disproportionate and unsustainable if these existed in isolation. However, the aesthetic principles of order and restraint that define the school's uniforms are consistent with a broader aesthetics to be found in other aspects of school life – its rituals, its living arrangements, its organisation of time, and the character of its buildings and grounds. The appeal to, and conditioning of, the senses can hardly account for the full shaping of the individual in all matters of taste, outlook and behaviour, but by the same token it cannot be wholly separated from the rituals, manners and expectations that are part of a coherent and instrumental social system. And in some instances it is difficult to escape observing a close connection between, for example, an austere material existence, a subdued colour scheme and a de-emphasising of wealth and ostentation.

As with uniforms, the colours used inside school buildings are restricted. Floors are of cement or grey flagstones, walls are whitewashed, unrelieved by colour except for the dark woodwork of the desks in the classrooms and coloured bedcovers in the dormitories. In some rooms the bedcovers are green, in others blue, but the two are never mixed. The dormitories thus present an image of single colours offset against much larger areas of colourlessness. The use of green and blue maintains the contrast between cool and warm colours contained in Foot's distinction between the institution and the body. In the restricted, even grim, colour scheme of the dormitories, skin colour stands out as the chief sign of human vitality. But once asleep, the boys become encased in the green and blue bed linen of the institution.[10] In parallel with the many changes of uniform required, the student's day is subdivided and highly regulated, leaving little time for unscheduled activities. This is not only meant to keep the boys out of trouble; there is a general sense that time not used in some activity of self-improvement is time wasted. Indeed, the timetable is so crowded that students quite often find themselves required to attend two activities that meet at the same time. The regime was apparently more relaxed in the early days of the school, but even then the efficient use of time was pursued with characteristic thoroughness. In 1941 the headmaster observed:

> While at school, [a boy] will sleep for nine hours in every twenty-four; he will work at his books for six hours; he will exercise his muscles for one and a half hours; he will eat for one and a half hours; he will wash for half an hour; he can allow half an hour for dressing and still there are five hours in each day. (Chopra, 1996: 152)

Several other features of school life reflect a similar quasi-scientific attitude to numbers and measurement. It has been a long-standing practice to record the height and weight of each boy twice a year, although there no longer appears to be much practical application of this to health or diet. Each student is given a number upon joining the school. The numbers are used administratively for recording marks and keeping track of school clothing, but they are also used in daily life to call groups of students together. This is not to say that students' names are avoided, or that students feel depersonalised by their numbers, but that the numbering of students is accepted and perhaps even respected as a feature of modernity. Students take a certain pride in their numbers, which they sometimes incorporate into their email addresses and remember long after they have left the school.

At assembly, students are grouped by age and size and stand in parallel rows along the edges of an open rectangular space. This symmetry and geometry of straight lines and right angles is carried over into the dormitories, where beds are arranged in parallel or in squares of four. Such an arrangement is not unusual in boarding schools, but it represents an aesthetic choice. At some other Indian schools, the students sit on the floor in concentric circles during assembly, and their beds are arranged unevenly around the walls of the dormitories.[11] At meals, Doon School students sit at tables arranged in parallel lines. They are grouped in the first instance by house, and secondarily by age. The tables are white and the stainless-steel plates and eating utensils produce a monotone of silver-grey not unlike the school uniforms. Team sports such as football and hockey – rituals played out in rectangular spaces – occupy a great deal of time at the school, as does cricket, with its calculus of wickets, runs and overs. Physical training at the school culminates in a competition at which houses vie for perfection in the formal arrangement of bodies. Although the school's preference for square geometry appears to be based partly on an admiration for science, it also has military precedents. A former headmaster of the school, John Mason, observed:

> The aesthetic of the school has been a very male ... somewhat physically dominated aesthetic, or culture. I don't know if I'm being wildly sacrilegious in suggesting that this was an early-twentieth-century recipe for the

ideal schoolboy. It may also have something to do with the imperial view
of leadership and ideal growth, and the mould that a society that looked at
militancy as a way of expression expected its men to grow and behave.[12]

As this suggests, the expressive forms of an institution are not only a matter
of cultural style or functionality but are closely linked to its history and
ideological foundations. At Doon School, many of the aesthetic features
that are observable on the surface of everyday life are mirrored in its most
basic structures. Students joining the school enter a social system that differs
in important respects from the Indian middle-class family life they have left
behind. Distinctions of class, caste, religion and wealth are to a large extent
suppressed, even if not altogether forgotten. Power is not so clearly exercised
from above as it is in government; it is delegated to students in a system that
sometimes resembles the British colonial strategy of 'indirect rule'. Each
year, the headmaster and teachers appoint new prefects and house captains.
This produces a hierarchy determined partly by seniority, partly by perceived
leadership qualities and partly by the practice of 'scoping', in which year-11
students seek to win approval (and rank) by making themselves conspicu-
ously useful.

As they progress towards such rewards, the students are divided into two
main age groups. In the first three years (in D, B and C forms) they are
juniors. During the last three years (A, S and Sc forms) they are seniors.
As we have seen, this change is registered in their clothing. Younger boys
wear shorts for more activities, and their bodies are therefore generally more
exposed than those of older boys. Older boys, perhaps in keeping with their
social advancement, must appear in more fully institutional dress. The shift
in status and uniform, which occurs approximately when a boy turns fifteen,
underlines one of the school's most obvious but least acknowledged facts –
that the single category of student has been stretched to include everything
from small boys to near men.

The transformation of boys into men is part of the school's purpose, but it
also poses a threat. Differences in uniforms for juniors and seniors recognise
the changes taking place in the boys' bodies, but there is at the same time a
certain resistance to this process on the part of the school authorities. One
of the major problems facing boarding schools has resulted from the gradual
prolongation of childhood. Its span has been extended with the advance of
higher education and the delayed onset of work. Doon School's students
range in age from eleven to eighteen. New boys entering the school are often
described as 'timid mice' by older students, but by the time they leave, many
are essentially adults, with the physical strength and sense of independence
of grown men.[13] In what is already a hierarchical system, the most senior
boys often compete for power and influence with their teachers. To maintain
its control, the school attempts to de-emphasise the process of maturation

or, rather, to condense it, by encouraging younger students to behave more like men and often restricting older students to the status and appearance of young boys. This is achieved partly by limiting the privileges of older students, partly by applying the school rules more or less universally to all, and partly through clothing. For although older students sometimes wear the long trousers of adults, during games they must wear the same childish uniforms as the youngest boys. Conversely, the youngest boys are made to struggle into the woollen suits of the winter uniform, which are often too big for them.

As may now be apparent, Doon School's social structure involves three overlapping classificatory systems. Students are differentiated according to age, house affiliation and authority. To begin with, a boy is either a junior or a senior, depending upon which form he is in. Seniors can demand 'favours' of juniors, a practice inherited from the fagging system of British public schools. Next comes his house affiliation. There are five main houses, and although students in the first year live in special 'holding houses', their future house affiliation has already been assigned. The third system distinguishes between those who, in their final year, hold positions of authority (as prefects and house captains) and those who do not. Prefects and house captains are given rooms to themselves, or 'studies'. They can order a punishment for almost anyone junior to them in the school. There is considerable competition for these positions, and disgruntled students who are not appointed sometimes joke about belonging to NAPU, the mythical Non-Appointed Prefects Union. Prefects and house captains in fact provide much of the day-to-day labour of administering the houses and supervising other activities in the school.

This system is essentially the one created by the founders of the school, although it is constantly being re-endorsed and subtly modified by the students themselves – by older students, who have already been initiated into the system, and new students eager to fit in. Age, house affiliation and rank form a complex that is reflected visually and tactilely in many of the features of the school, such as its uniforms. These features form a sensory world that students are exposed to day after day. It is evident that the aesthetics of this system exerts an influence at several levels. If social structures dictate appearances, appearances also deepen and naturalise social structures, making the alternatives appear foreign and 'unnatural'. How a boy behaves, and what he approves of, may thus be determined as much by aesthetic concerns – by the desire to preserve the living patterns and sensations he has become habituated to – as by functions that may by now have become outdated or even indefensible, such as 'favours' and bullying. A boy's social and physical surroundings become increasingly expressive of their own existential properties and the associations that have been built up around them over time. In the process, a transferral of emotive power from the signified to the signifier takes place, sometimes even a reversal of meaning, as familiar stimuli take on a life of their own. Something disagreeable may become agreeable through its association with positive emotions of comradeship or belonging. In certain respects this is not unlike the hypothesis put forward by Darwin, and later by William James, that the expressive forms of the emotions, such as crying or smiling, may actually feed back into the subject and generate these emotions themselves. One ex-student told me that while he was at Doon some of his fellow students complained that the school was losing its boarding school identity and becoming more like a day school because bullying was on the decline!

THE CHARACTER OF A SCHOOL

When it was founded in the 1930s, Doon School reflected many of the underlying and contradictory complexities of British–Indian colonial relations. The school had been conceived as a British-style public school for upper-middle-class Indian boys, in contrast to the existing boarding schools in India such as Bishop Cotton School in Simla, which catered primarily to British families, and the 'Chiefs' Colleges', such as Mayo College in Rajasthan, which were for boys from Indian princely families. A number of the school's founders and supporters, including its guiding spirit, Satish Ranjan Das, had attended public schools in England, and their aim was to provide an equivalent form of education for the future leaders of an in-dependent India. However, instead of studying Greek and Latin, the boys would study Sanskrit and Urdu. The school would be open to students of all castes, classes and religions. Doon students would be treated alike, living a simple, even Spartan life in communal dormitories, unlike students at the Chiefs' Colleges, where some of the young princes lived in mini-palaces surrounded by their servants. Vegetarians and non-vegetarians would eat together. Corporal punishment was banned, a progressive step at that time. An ethic of service to the nation and the local community was promoted. Education was to be based on scientific thought, free of ancient prejudices. The boys' minds and bodies would be trained to develop the qualities of endurance, leadership and fair play.

It is not entirely clear how Doon School came to adopt blue and grey as its colours but, as we have seen, that choice came to play a part in the school's conceptions of mind and body.[14] One theory, not confirmed, is that Mrs Foot, the wife of the first headmaster, chose the school colours, a choice possibly determined by what cloth was readily available. In the case of grey, an obvious advantage was that it did not show the dirt. It is also possible that for the school's Indian founders, grey at some level stood for Britain – its weather, its churches and public buildings, and its elite educational institu-tions. Blue, on the other hand, was the colour associated with the Hindu deities, especially Lord Krishna, and with the Brahman caste from which many of the school's founders came.[15] These men belonged to a professional class who admired what they saw as the British values of egalitarianism, self-discipline and scientific thought. They were, at the same time, anxious to assert their Indian (and, more specifically, Hindu) cultural heritage, and in fact many saw themselves as the restorers and custodians of a more en-lightened Indian tradition, stripping away its layers of superstition and caste prejudice. This outlook characterised the 'Bengal renaissance', inspired by Raja Rammohan Roy and the Hindu reformist organisation the Brahmo Samaj, by artists and literary figures such as Tagore, and religious leaders such as Ramakrishna and Vivekananda. In one sense, then, blue and grey were not opposed but complementary. Each suggested distance from the unruly passions – blue as a colour at the cooler end of the spectrum and grey as the repudiation of all colour. Both would have been seen as appropriate to the future character of the school.

Although Doon School's specific combination of features may be unique and immediately recognisable to present students and old boys, it is hardly original. It has developed out of practices established in other schools and their institutional predecessors: seminaries, monasteries, military barracks, guilds and artisans' workshops. When it was created, Doon School was regarded as a novel experiment. Its founders had taken the British public school and refashioned it as an instrument of modern Indian identity. In many respects the school was meant to provide an answer to those who saw the colonial subject as backward-looking, passive and enfeebled. Doon School's emphasis on science and the disciplining of the body was part of the response and became part of its aesthetic orientation. Boys may have been dressed so as to organise and control them, but their uniforms were also meant to show them off. The blue games uniform, made of rough cotton cloth, provided a contrasting frame for shining, healthy bodies. Identical uniforms emphasised the orderliness of the boys when they were massed in formation for assemblies, meals, physical training or 'callover' (rollcall). Such images were the visual correlatives of the school's ideal of a rational existence.

The school's strategy for teaching manners, character and citizenship became evident in the first few years. The intention was to create the conditions in which certain values would flourish and be gradually absorbed by the boys. The study of science was believed to have pervasive effects on character. As the Chief Guest at the Founder's Day celebrations of 1948 put it, 'It is wrong to think that science teaches only science. Science brings about a change in the whole attitude of boys. It brings about correct judgment, alertness and obedience to laws.'[16] Environment, example and peer pressure were considered more effective than discipline, and indeed Foot wrote that 'we believe that character-training is more a matter of organisation than instruction [...]. The purpose is achieved not by precept or instruction, but by creating an environment in which a boy is led to do things for himself.'[17] Nevertheless, Foot was not above issuing advice and homilies to reinforce the principle of environmental learning. Boys were expected to monitor their own progress and make the necessary corrections. The school's programme thus implied a double imperative: first, to mould the individual through exposure to a carefully constructed social aesthetic; and second, to encourage among students the conscious perfection of the self.

Although Doon School, when it opened, may have appeared to be the culmination of an evolutionary process, it soon became the first step in a new one. As time went on, more and more Indian schools were patterned on Doon or gradually adopted its practices. This came about partly by example and partly through the dispersal of Doon teachers to other schools, as masters and headmasters. It also reflected the underlying ties of power and ideology. The values that the school espoused in its early years became institutionalised in the politics of the post-colonial period, especially in the Congress party. The connections are not hard to find. A Doon School boy, Rajiv Gandhi, was later to become prime minister. The Doon School song, Tagore's 'Jana Gana Mana', was to become India's national anthem.

AESTHETICS IN SOCIETY

It is difficult to know precisely how exposure to a particular colour or set of colours over six years might influence a student, either at the time or later in life. It is reasonable to assume that exposure to any sensory environment, apart from making it increasingly familiar, is closely tied to other experiences, either pleasant or unpleasant. If someone had been unhappy at Doon, blue and grey might evoke all the things he feared and hated; it might trigger a nasty reaction in the pit of his stomach. If, though, he had enjoyed his school days there, it might lift his spirits and recall moments of comradeship and triumph. One student told me that his father, a Doon graduate, had a decided preference for blue shirts. A more recent graduate said that he felt an aversion to blue but was attracted to grey, a clue, perhaps, that he was drawn more to the ethos of studies than to sports. But the quality of such responses is not necessarily the most important thing about them. Even if one suffers, emblems of past suffering may become valuable as points of reference, preserving links between one's history and the person one has become.

I have written selectively about certain features of Doon School life, colour being among the most abstract of these. However, focusing on a single feature always runs the risk of placing it in an unrealistically prominent light. When experiencing sensations such as colour, one does not ordinarily isolate them from the broader tapestry of objects and activities in which they are enmeshed. The surroundings of a chosen detail or quality tend to reassert themselves.

How, then, can one single out some quality for attention without depriving it of the connections and, precisely, the unremarked features that it possesses in daily life? Unless one isolates the detail, one cannot see it properly; but one cannot see it properly if one isolates it. An exclusive focus on one aspect of life begins to erode its normality, its connectedness.

And yet it is through the study of such discrete aspects of life in their varied contexts that we are likely to learn the most about the socially generated systems that structure our sensory experience and ultimately influence our attitudes and actions. Examining the role of colour in a number of communities is one way in which we might begin to search for a more general theory of social aesthetics. Although we acknowledge major differences in the ways in which societies deal with sensory experience, we tend to regard these as the concomitant effects of material conditions and patterns of cultural diffusion. And although it is true that these factors may underlie the variations in aesthetic systems, they do not explain why these systems exist in the first place, nor indeed how they evolve, how they influence political and economic decisions, and how they bear upon the personal lives of individuals.

In acknowledging that aesthetics plays a role in society, we must also accept that it may have more profound effects, both culturally and historically. Certain combinations of sensory stimuli appear to play a significant part in reinforcing patriotic and other mass sentiments. One need only recall here the use of colour and ritual in 1930s Germany, which, although replete with ascribed symbolic meanings (e.g. red and black representing blood and soil), clearly exerted a more generalised power. A fuller understanding of the social role of aesthetics may thus benefit studies of nationalism, ethnicity, warfare, religion and sectarian politics. Current studies in body praxis and 'rhetoric culture' may eventually be seen as closely allied to the study of social aesthetics.

A number of questions deserve our attention. Can sensory environments be categorised in any systematic way, and if so by what criteria? To what extent do these environments operate as systems; that is to say, do they have an ecology? In studying them, should we look first for their dominant effects, for their structures, or for the senses to which they appeal? What are the forms of response to specific aesthetic patterns? What are the prolonged effects of these patterns on individuals and populations, and how do they change over time? What are the processes by which they are modified through internal agency or external pressures? Do particular combinations of features emerge through chance, or natural selection, or conscious choice? When we begin to address such questions we may be closer to realising what Baumgarten envisaged as a 'science of sensory cognition'.

Notes

My thanks to David Howes, Judith MacDougall, Howard Morphy, Nicolas Peterson, Lucien Castaing-Taylor and Diana Young for reading earlier drafts of this essay and providing helpful comments.

1 Dai Vaughan (2005: 458) notes that this image may also imply concealment and competition: 'We may reflect that the back of a playing card is the side held towards others until the decisive moment of win-or-lose'.

2 A distinction is often made between chromatic and achromatic colours, the latter consisting of black, white and grey. Chromatic colours are considered to have three components: hue (referring to their wavelength in the light spectrum); value (their lightness or darkness, or luminance); and chroma (the intensity of their hue). Within this system, a colour without hue will appear grey and thus may not be considered a colour in the fullest sense. All languages possess a name for at least one of the achromatic colours, along with varying numbers of names for the chromatic colours. For a detailed study of these cultural variations, see Berlin and Kay's influential *Basic Colour Terms* (1969).

3 For the purposes of this essay, a colour without hue will be characterised as a non-colour.

4 John Gage (1999: 22), citing the colour of gas flames in heaters, observes that, contrary to the popular belief that the colour red signals heat, 'the short-wave, high-frequency energy of the blue–violet end of the spectrum signals the greatest capacity to heat, and the long-wave, low-frequency red end, the least'. However, cultural associations of colour with temperature are not entirely unconnected, for the wavelengths of red and yellow light do lie closer to the infra-red end of the spectrum, the wavelength of heat. And although associations of temperature with colour vary considerably across cultures, there is a general consensus among them that supports a subjective or physiological connection. Values for the wavelengths of the 'standard' colours vary from one source to another, but they are typically given (in nanometres, nm) as follows: red, 780–622 nm; orange, 622–597 nm; yellow, 597–577 nm; green, 577–492 nm; blue, 492–455 nm; violet, 455–390 nm.

5 The school's first two residential dormitories to be built, Kashmir House and Hyderabad House, are of whitish stone with red arches, red detailing and red roofs. When Foot House and Martyn House, the school's original 'holding houses' for first-year students, were recently demolished and rebuilt, the new buildings were of red brick with red roofs.

6 Clothing is used in the school as a means of punishment. The most common punishment is the 'change-in-break'. It is given for minor infractions, such as making a bed badly or having unpolished shoes. If caught, the boy is given a chit and must run back to his house during the mid-morning break and change into his PT (physical training) uniform. He must then run back to the main building to have the chit signed, return to the house, change into his school clothes again, and return to have the chit signed a second time. If he lives in a nearby house he may have to change into his games clothes as well and run two more times, with one more signing.

7 Doon School shorts are quite long, in the British colonial fashion, reaching to just above the knee.

8 *Peshawaris* have recently been replaced by high-tech sandals.

9 Communal bathing with other boys has been the norm at the school from the beginning, perhaps to underline the school's values of openness and equality. Although it runs counter to prevailing Indian notions of modesty, and indeed may be an importation from British public schools, most boys seem to accept and enjoy it after overcoming their initial shyness. However, one boy reported to me his feeling of shock at seeing a sexually mature boy naked for the first time. When, at a meeting of the school council, one student suggested converting the open showers into cubicles, the minutes read: 'The Chairman felt that it was a tradition that had never been

questioned. Moreover, open showering enhanced hygiene and maturity. The cost of maintaining cubicles would be enormous and they wouldn't be hygienic either. It was decided to remain with the present system' (school council minutes, 14 April 2006).

10 One of Berlin and Kay's observations was that the number of colour terms used in small or medium-scale societies was more limited than in larger and more technically complex ones. Is it possible that Doon School, as a small-scale (and, in Turner's terms, non-exchange) society observes a similar limitation, but in its colour usage rather than its terminology?

11 I observed more circular arrangements at both the Centre for Learning near Bangalore and at Rishi Valley School, a Krishnamurti Foundation school in Andhra Pradesh.

12 Quoted from the film *Doon School Chronicles* (2000), scenes 58–60.

13 As might be expected, the usual sorts of early-adolescent sexual activity occur between boys at the school, but, as in other boarding schools, there have also been cases of sexual abuse practised by older boys on younger ones.

14 Headmaster Foot favoured cotton cloth of Indian manufacture for toughness, hygiene and the support of local industries. The choice of colours would also have been influenced by the need to avoid colours already in use at nearby schools.

15 Sanjay Srivastava (1998: 116) maintains that a strong Hindu aesthetic persists at Doon School, in its rituals and emblems, despite its professed secularism. He argues that such emblems retain an indelible aura of their history. While he only discusses the religious connotations of white in school rituals, a similar argument could be made for the uses of blue. He observes: 'It is crucial, then, to understand that the process of the ensconcement of the School's official ideology of secularism within the contours of a Hindu system of meanings [...] was initiated in its earliest days' (Srivastava, 1998: 123).

16 The Governor General of the United Provinces, Shri Rajagopalachari, quoted in *The Doon School Weekly*, 30 October 1948.

17 *The Doon School Book*, 1949, reprinted in Chopra (1996: 40).

8

Notes on cinematic space

THE problem of cinematic space was never a problem of depth. In some of the early films of the Lumière Company we look across vast distances and see things happening simultaneously on several different planes (figure 8.1). There are films that combine foreground objects and distant background ones – sometimes when people inadvertently walk in front of the camera, but also possibly when planned that way by the cinematographer. Many of the films are shot at an oblique angle, along streets and railway platforms. We look along lines of increasing distance and diminishing size, approximating the way we perceive distance in everyday life. In other films the camera moves forward, mounted on a boat or carriage, giving a sense of objects shifting in relation to one another

8.1 Action on three planes in a Lumière film of 1897, *Laveuses sur la rivière*

and the camera. In all these films, we see in depth, and the world seems to open out before us.

The problem of cinematic space was therefore never one of depth. Rather, it was a problem of where we might imagine ourselves to be when watching a film, for we were always simultaneously in the film and somewhere else. In watching films there was never a definitive 'here', only a 'there'. There was, of course, the position the cinematographer had occupied, and there was also the hall or cinema where we were watching the film. But neither of these fully resolved our sense of being both in and out of the film, of failing to find our own position. The cinema has searched for answers to this problem ever since.

Even before films were invented, stereo photography had provided a partial answer. Stereo view cards were enormously popular at the end of the nineteenth century. Seen through a viewer, a well photographed stereo view produced an extraordinary illusion of place and spaciousness. The three-dimensional image helped locate the photographer's viewing position, but, more than this, it suggested a succession of other possible viewing positions within the scene as the spectator's eyes wandered from foreground to middle ground to background. Although none of these points of reference actually produced a new perspective, the sense of being present in the scene was extremely powerful compared with viewing a two-dimensional photograph. Alternative points of view were suggested in the spectator's mind, each of them an imaginary 'here'.

Much of the difficulty in creating a coherent sense of spatial geography in films results from the projection of a three-dimensional scene on to a two-dimensional surface. There is no adequate viewing position for making sense of the image, despite the technical innovations of Renaissance perspectival art. Most of the context is also missing: the frame cuts off everything to the left and right, top and bottom. A moving camera is sometimes thought to show more, indeed show everything, and so enlarge the context. But, unfortunately, this only increases the confusion. What might seem to a filmmaker to convey a logical representation of space, panning in an arc from a fixed point, in fact looks on the screen like a flat, moving façade with no beginning or end.

Early cinematographers apparently believed in a 'long shot' solution, for their films generally take a broad view and cram as much detail into the image as possible. There are a few notable exceptions, including a closer shot in one of the first Lumière films showing Auguste Lumière and his wife feeding their baby, Andrée; and another of a young girl feeding a cat. In reality, though, this was only a provisional solution, although it has become a standby of films and filmmakers ever since. The long shot does indeed include more, but on a smaller scale. It certainly gives us more to look at than most close-ups, yet in a sense it merely distracts us from the problem by directing our thoughts and attention into the distance. The basic, unsettling lack of a solid 'here' remains.

What the early films had not quite achieved, and what remained un-discovered by filmmakers for some decades, was what might be called, as distinct from the long-shot solution, the deep-focus solution. By placing the camera close to objects in the foreground and at the same time achieving a great depth of field, the feeling could be generated of a subjective associa-tion with objects nearby, a sort of substitute for the 'here'. Orson Welles is perhaps best known for this approach, in one instance making us privy to a glass, a spoon and a bottle of the sleeping draught that Susan Kane has just taken, intent on suicide (figure 8.2). This way of creating a sense of depth, with a feeling of closeness to nearby objects, gradually became more common in feature films and documentaries, as film emulsions grew more sensitive (allowing for smaller lens apertures and greater depth of field) and as more wide-angle lenses came on the market. Instead of filming a dialogue scene by alternating between shots of the two speakers, filmmakers could frame their shots more obliquely, so that one speaker's back or profile loomed large in the foreground and the interlocutor appeared farther away in the shot. Provided the foreground speaker had been clearly established in previous shots, the audience could imagine that person without needing to

8.2 Susan Kane's attempted suicide in *Citizen Kane*

see a frontal view. Since documentary scenes were now less often staged, as had been standard practice in the past, this shooting strategy was not only preferable for its simplicity but was necessary if a conversation was to be filmed without any cuts.

There were thus practical reasons for adopting the deep-focus solution, which included shooting whole scenes in single takes to preserve a sense of real time and occasion, a strategy that filmmakers like F. W. Murnau (in *Nosferatu*, 1922) and Jean Renoir (in *Toni*, 1935) had begun exploring before images with extreme depth of field became possible. Today the approach seems to be practised as well for its affective linking of the spectator's perspective with that of the filmmaker. In Donn Pennebaker's film about Bob Dylan *Don't Look Back* (1966) there is a claustrophobic intensity about the offstage scenes in which Dylan's friends and hangers-on crowd around the camera, moving in and out of the frame (figure 8.3). Their proximity to us and to the camera merges into a single overwhelming sensation of being present. 'There' and 'here' begin to merge.

For early cinema the problem remained of how to create a sense of the three dimensionality of a scene, not just in front of the camera but around and even behind it. Stereo cinematography, inspired by stereo photography, although invented quite early (as early as 1915, with patents even earlier), did

8.3 Bob Dylan offstage in *Don't Look Back*

not accomplish this; it merely gave added depth to the scene in front of the viewer. Several key methods began to emerge that relied on the audience identifying, both psychologically and visually, with someone in the film. This tactic was not altogether new, however. It was already well established in literature, providing a precedent for cinema. There are passages in Tolstoy, like the horse race scene in *Anna Karenina*, that clearly anticipate this kind of filmmaking.

The first method involved filming close enough to a person to associate the camera with that person's point of view, although, importantly, not to simulate it. The effect paralleled the 'third person' narration frequently used in fiction, in sentences such as 'She looked at him and wondered why he seemed sad'. By reporting an action as if standing next to a character, the author enters the personal space, and sometimes the mind, of the character as an omniscient, behind-the-scenes observer. In a film, the camera may similarly take up a position closely allied to one of the characters, or several characters in succession. Typically this occurs in dialogue scenes in which the camera alternates between two characters, literally looking over their shoulders. Neither character looks directly into the lens but instead just to the side of it, where the other person is located. The effect for the spectator is of shifting between the two character positions, creating a spatial envelope encompassing both. When we look at one of the characters, the other is always in our imagination, just off screen.

In such cases, where is the 'here'? It may still be nebulous, but it is no longer quite absent. It now lies somewhere in the intersection of the two bodily spaces, in the imaginary geography that the film creates around us, which would not exist without our participation. To a degree not experienced when we simply observe two people talking, we feel physically present within the scene.

The other approach goes a step further, not simply allying us to the characters and their perspectives but inducing us to adopt their exact viewpoints, at least briefly. Again, literature provided the precedent. The first approach would have been 'He looked into the distance and saw a car passing'. The second approach leaps the gap: 'He looked into the distance. A car was passing.' In this case, who is doing the seeing? The author, possibly, but also, by the author's sleight of hand, the character. One of the earliest attempts at this kind of subjectivity occurs in Edwin S. Porter's *Dream of a Rarebit Fiend* (1906), in which the main character is beset by hallucinations and distorted visions that are shared directly with the audience.

In Alfred Hitchcock's *The Birds* (1963) there is an extended scene incorporating the viewer into someone else's perspective, a *tour de force* of cinematic technique. Tippi Hedron is shown in a boat crossing a harbour. As she approaches the other side she slows her outboard motor and allows the boat to drift towards the dock. We begin to see the classic alternation of seer and seen: a close-up of Tippi Hedron's face looking towards the shore, followed by a shot of what she sees, in this case made more convincing by the camera gently moving forward as if from her position in the moving boat. For several minutes more, the alternation continues as she gets out of the boat, walks towards a house, the point-of-view shot also moving, and enters it. At one point, from inside, she furtively looks out of the window, and it's no surprise that the following shot is through the window panes. The process is then repeated in reverse as she leaves the house, gets into the boat, and recrosses the harbour, looking back all the while at the diminishing shoreline.

These methods were probably the outgrowth of another necessity that appeared early in cinema. As soon as film directors began using several shots to create a scene, the question arose of how to convince the audience that they represented different views of the same place. To an untrained audience they might simply seem to be a series of disconnected shots of different places. It was important to link the images to each other. Several methods were developed to establish a coherent cinematic geography. The look of the sets had to be continuous. An object such as a chair seen from one angle could be shown from another angle in a different shot. Gradually the impression could be built up of a single space. The actor became another important linking device. A scene might cut from the actor doing one thing to doing another, or even continuing the same action seen from a different position. Eventually this produced the so-called matched cut, so that an actor stepping out of one frame would be seen stepping into another in perfect synchrony.

Although the sense of continuity was constantly being reinforced by these methods, any notion of 'here' – that is, where the viewer might be – was simultaneously being undermined. The camera could in fact be anywhere in the scene, wielded by an invisible presence that moved from one position to another, from one person to another, from long shot to close-up, and so on. Covering these shots there was usually continuous sound, 'atmosphere' or music, reinforcing the impression of an unbroken passage of time. The mechanics of the process, although never concealed, were meant to pass by unnoticed, so that the action became less like an event actually witnessed than one seen in the mind.

In one respect this kind of cinema, in documentaries as well as in fiction films, brought films closer to literature, in that it provided a series of fragments that the viewer pieced together as a whole. The difference was in the concreteness of the fragments, which in cinema generally refer to something actually photographed, in a studio or outside it. To prevent disturbing questions arising in viewers' minds about the provenance of shots, filmmakers became adept at a subtle kind of distraction. Shots would be kept on the screen just long enough for their primary meaning to be grasped and were then replaced by others. Film construction became a matter of creating questions and satisfying them at the right psychological moment, as in the shot–countershot technique described in chapter 5. The answers were provided by the editing, underpinned by the dynamics of the plot. A wide shot of someone would be followed by a closer shot revealing what they were doing. In the grip of such a powerful system, viewers could be forgiven for not worrying too much about where they were situated in the film or how they got there.

In Japan, Yasujiro Ozu found a different solution to the problem of cinematic space, creating what might be called a 'cinema of familiarity'. By confining his scenes to a few essential places – the home, the bar, the office – he made these into known environments to which his characters repeatedly returned. Filming consistently from a low camera position added another degree of familiarity. Spectators were not so much incorporated into the scenes through structural techniques as made to feel that they were at home, and knew intuitively where they were. With each return they looked through the same doorway, saw the same *shoji* screens and recognised the same people. Ozu's cast was as circumscribed as his settings, in that he used the same actors as similar characters in many films. To his Japanese critics, this sense of place and person tended to brand him as old-fashioned. And his films do in fact underscore traditional values of duty and family, but at the same time, for all their constraints, they release us into a known world that seems to exist independently of the filmmaker. Questions about the exact location become secondary to more enduring questions of sentiment and character.

For many viewers, Ozu's 'here' is more cultural than material. In a sense, there is no 'here' at all, for it is everywhere. Somewhat the same principle is found in certain other kinds of films. The 'here' of genre films (the Western, the gangster movie) is already established and exists beyond the boundaries of any individual film. 'Here' comes with the territory. It is the ground of the fairy tale, the crime story and the gothic romance, each of which clings to a particular aesthetic. One might draw a parallel between the aesthetic forms created by powerful institutions – the military, the church, even banking or advertising culture – and the conventions of classical works of art. The rules, although rarely enunciated, are pervasive and, like a grammar, are so deeply ingrained as to go unnoticed. In the aesthetics of these dramas the viewer's attention tends to focus on details: the amount of gold braid on a uniform, the way the light falls through Venetian blinds, the way a cowboy pulls a gun from a holster. If you were imagining these scenes you would probably include significant close-ups; and it is indeed the close-up that, in one further group of films, provides an analogous solution to the problem of the missing 'here'.

It hardly needs pointing out that bringing an object close to the camera brings it subjectively closer to the viewer's position. Susan Kane's bottle of sleeping draught is disclosed to the viewer like a secret, as is the 'snowstorm' falling from Kane's hand, or the flames consuming his childhood sled. 'Maybe Rosebud was something he couldn't get or lost', says Thompson, the reporter. 'I don't think any word explains a man's life.' But to the audience Rosebud means a great deal. By being close, behind the scenes, as it were, we find a physical and mental space within the film we can call our own. The possession of a secret gives us a new viewing position. This may be why the titles of so many films imply a secret, or why so many films emphasise the importance of objects close to the camera: *The Maltese Falcon* (1941), *The Locket* (1946), the door key in *Dial M for Murder* (1954), the attaché case in *No Country for Old Men* (2007). An object viewed in close-up proves to be the turning point in many films. The audience clings to it while the characters flounder.

Apart from the use of such objects as plot devices, by showing them in close-up they acquire a quality of belonging to the viewer. This is the way we see our own possessions – our keys, our letters, our hands. These glimpses recall the familiar experience of being here and present. In *The Gleaners and I* (2000), Agnès Varda holds her hand in front of the camera, seeing in it the signs of her advancing age. The close-up in films, although frequently a somewhat artificial device, mimics an important form of human perception and lends an aura of intimacy to whatever it touches. The object, separated from its surroundings, presses forward, inviting us to touch and hold it.

At the opposite extreme are films that abandon the physical connections between film viewer and film subject altogether. Their aim is not to convey a particular reality, either fictional or nonfictional. Rather, it is to provide a report on reality at second or third hand. In these films, which include most educational, scientific, public affairs and cultural films, there is no expectation on the part of viewers of having a close relationship with any object, but rather to be instructed about it. The effect is to erase their own position and make it irrelevant. The viewers are in a sense reduced to children, absorbed in an adult's narrative. These films typically draw upon a fund of pre-existing and pre-digested material: archival footage, interviews, artefacts, landscapes and a didactic text, which may either be spoken as a voice-over commentary or delivered by an onscreen presenter. Kenneth Clark's television series of 1969, *Civilisation*, created the prototype for many of the programmes that followed, offering a kind of proxy for the viewer's own intellectual life.

The soundtracks of these films differ significantly from earlier forms of narrated documentaries, which had a long prehistory in the public lecture and slide show. In a programme with an onscreen presenter, the sound comes from an identifiable source, even when, as frequently happens, it shifts between onscreen presentation and voice-over commentary. In the classic narrated documentary, such as Pare Lorentz's *The River* (1938), there is only the disembodied voice, accompanied by music and sound effects. Yet this voice, in its very anonymity, has a kind of dedicated presence – dedicated to us – which that of the television presenter can never quite attain. In a sense it belongs on 'our' side of the film. It may be sound only, but its timbre has a character independent of the images on the screen. Just so, the voices of certain screen actors become more memorable than their faces.

Many techniques that are intended to create a sense of immediacy – the familiarity of a voice, a setting, an object placed close to the camera – suggest that at least some filmmakers feel regret over the divide that separates their own contact with the subject from that possible for the audience. The audience stands on the other side, the blind side, of the film. Since the 1960s one more method has emerged to try to cross the divide. Surprisingly, it was an idea that had occurred to relatively few people before. Among those to whom it had was Dziga Vertov, in his 1929 film *Man with a Movie Camera*, a film about filmmaking. The film plays with the production process – shooting, editing and so on – as though inviting the audience to go backstage at a theatre. It breaks the rule that the filmmaking process should remain invisible, although it is also curiously evasive, referring more to filmmaking in general than to its own production. Despite this, the film inspired later filmmakers such as Jean Rouch, Federico Fellini, François Truffaut and Nanni Moretti to begin referring to themselves and the film they were making within their films.

In nonfiction films, the impetus for this kind of self-reflexivity came from a source quite different from the autobiographical interests of fiction film directors. Many documentary makers of the 1960s realised that the audience's sense of being present at the events they had filmed would be strengthened if these were shown in the context of being filmed, as events being witnessed *now* rather than later, as professionally distanced narratives. To try to show this context with a second camera was obviously impractical and pretentious. There were, however, other ways of indicating the circumstances of filming. The subject's open acknowledgement of the process was one of them. The manner of filming, making clear the physical limitations of the filmmaker's position, was another. Shifting the perspective of the film outwards to embrace the filmmaking encounter thus gave the viewer a greater sense of participating in the event. Although some theorists believed this would increase the objective truth of documentary films by making the filmmaker's bias clear, theirs was essentially a futile desire for certainty. The presence of authorship at a deeper level – that is to say, throughout the filmmaking process – made one realise that knowledge is always provisional and incomplete, dependent on the position the filmmaker occupies.

Although filming in this way created a little more space for the viewer, it was not a complete solution to the problem of cinematic space. Films necessarily continued to present recorded fragments of life, at a distance from those who would eventually see them. There could finally be no resting place in a film for the viewer except by way of the imagination. This did not mean that films were little more than magicians' illusions, however. Filmmakers could still establish a contract with the audience, taking them into their confidence, as indeed most of the Lumière camera operators did implicitly at the very beginning. The terms of this contract were simple enough: to undertake to show what they had seen, not a simulation; to acknowledge the limits of their view rather than claiming omniscience; and, above all, to give the audience something deserving of their attention.

Part III: Film, anthropology and the documentary tradition

9

Observation in the cinema

THERE is a lot of observation in the cinema, certainly in fiction films. Hitchcock's *Rear Window* (1954) is all about what happens when city dwellers watch each other's activities in neighbouring apartments. René Clair, in his light-hearted film *And Then There Were None* (1945), spies on weekend guests at a house party as they spy on one another through keyholes. Most of Abbas Kiarostami's film *The Wind Will Carry Us* (1999) is about villagers observing the antics of a social scientist from the city who has come to observe them. Then there are the numerous films about covert observation and surveillance, such as Michael Powell's *Peeping Tom* (1960) and Florian Henckel von Donnersmarck's *The Lives of Others* (2006).

'Observational cinema' has now become a familiar term for a particular subgenre of documentary film. 'Observational', however, has always seemed to me a curious word to apply to it. Whatever form documentary takes, it is generally a more interactive process than the word implies. In 'observational' there is also, for some people, an implication of covertness, as if the person doing the observing were somehow in a superior position to the person being observed. This is no doubt true of surveillance films (the fictional and the clandestine) but it has not been my experience of nonfiction filmmaking. I have usually been the novice, trying to follow events that evaded me, to learn about customs that were not my own and to understand people who knew each other much better than I knew them. To make films at all, I have had to rely on the people I filmed in countless personal and practical ways. And if I was observing, I was also being observed. 'Participant observation', long a watchword of anthropologists in the field, would seem to be the better term. But we are stuck with 'observational cinema', so let it stand.

We are all in fact born observers. From infancy, observation is how we learn. We are never apart from the world we observe. To deny that we constantly observe others, and that they have little access to our thoughts, is to deny our everyday experience. Some people may use this as a weapon against others, but most do not, nor do I think most writers or filmmakers who record their observations in words and images.

Observational filmmaking, unlike Direct Cinema and *cinéma vérité*, is a more recent designation and has close ties to anthropology. The first use of the term is often attributed to Colin Young (1975: 66), although in an interview in

1970 Richard Leacock was already speaking of 'observational, observing films' (see Levin, 1971: 215) and as early as 1938 John Grierson wrote of 'this fresh new art of observation and reality' (1938: 138). In 'Observational Cinema', published as part of a collection of articles on visual anthropology in 1975, Young sought to distinguish films made to provide entertainment or instruction from those that looked at the world from the more modest position of an observer with a camera, sharing this perspective with the viewer. Young saw this as the most obvious and logical use of a motion picture camera: to bring viewers close to actual events by recording them. And far from viewing the camera as an instrument of total recall or authority, Young stressed its restricted point of view in the hands of the individual observer.

Although observational cinema emerged as a recognisable style of filmmaking in the 1960s and 1970s, it owed much to earlier developments in both cinema and social science. Young's ideal of a cinema that allowed others to see what the filmmaker had seen was clearly the motivation behind some of the earliest films ever made, such as those of the Lumière brothers in the 1890s and cinematograph records made by social scientists such as Alfred Cort Haddon and Walter Baldwin Spencer. Even earlier, anthropologists had attached great importance to the visible aspects of culture, using drawings and photographs extensively in their books and articles. Although this interest declined during the inter-war period as anthropology turned towards more abstract features of culture, such as kinship and religious belief, cinematography continued to be used as a way of making records of rituals and technology. Gregory Bateson and Margaret Mead took it a step further in their study of child-rearing and personality development in Bali and New Guinea in the 1930s, using film and still photography to study the psychological effects of interactions between mothers and their children (Bateson and Mead, 1942). Mead's main interest in using films and photographs was to substantiate and document her findings, but Bateson viewed it as a more investigative mode of research in which the very act of filming could unearth new knowledge.

It is often suggested that the changes in documentary that occurred in the 1960s resulted from changes in film technology. New cameras developed during the Second World War eventually made it possible to shoot films with synchronous sound under almost any conditions, using relatively cheap 16mm film stock. Older-style news cameras could also be adapted for the purpose. An alternative view is that certain young filmmakers, impatient with traditional styles of documentary, initiated the technological changes so they could make the films they wanted to make. The new generation, which included Richard Leacock, Michel Brault, Jean Rouch, D. A. Pennebaker, and David and Albert Maysles, all played a part in promoting the innovations, supported by mechanical wizards like André Coutant, Stefan Kudelski and Jean-Pierre Beauviala.

Both views have merit, but they leave out an important factor: television. Television may have killed off the Hollywood studio system, and perhaps even killed off the new documentary cinema at a later stage – or at least left no place for it beside archival compilations, talking heads and celebrity presenters. But for all its sins, broadcast television nevertheless created new possibilities and fuelled a desire for change among documentary filmmakers.

In 1964 a film appeared that seems to sum up both the impulses and the contradictions of this period in documentary film history. *Point of Order!* was both a clear demonstration of what live television had achieved and a presentiment of what the new documentary cinema might accomplish. It put together in more or less chronological order a selection of raw kinescopes (filmed copies of live television coverage) from the Army–McCarthy hearings of 1954 (figure 9.1), in which Senator Joseph McCarthy's claim to any political or personal integrity was finally demolished. By selecting from hours of live television, it revealed to an extraordinary degree the special qualities of the medium and its sheer power to observe human behaviour. In one sense, it only demonstrated what everyone already knew about television, that which made it superior to all other forms of visual communication except face-to-face encounters. But it also made it clear that filming spontaneous events with their accompanying sound had a potential that had been vastly underestimated by both the film and the television industries.

9.1 Senator Joseph McCarthy and Roy Cohn in *Point of Order!*

Upon its invention in the 1920s, television was envisaged as a means of live communication, rather like the dreams of video telephones in science fiction. It would provide an instantaneous visual link between one place and another. Before video recording and before kinescopes, live television offered immediacy and the promise of the unpredictable, however much television producers tried to guard against the latter. Everything was done by means of multiple cameras and selective feeds to lessen the chances of embarrass-ment, yet live television also thrived on that possibility, perhaps best reflected in Groucho Marx's aggressive treatment of his unwary guests in his 1950s show *You Bet Your Life*. What was enticing about live television was in fact the spontaneity of human beings rather than the mannered performances of professionals, whether this spontaneity occurred during sports broadcasts, interview programmes, quiz shows or press conferences.

I believe that it was the decade of exposure to live television in the 1940s and 1950s that chiefly inspired the new documentary cinema of the 1960s. One reason for thinking this is that one of the first memorable examples of it, *Primary* (1960), was an attempt to make something like live television where live television had never been able to go. With its smaller and more manoeuvrable cameras, Direct Cinema, as it was soon called, could gain access to previously unfilmable events, such as candidate John Kennedy listening to the election results in his hotel headquarters during the night of the 1960 Wisconsin primary. It would do what television, with its studio-bound equipment, could not. The underlying desire for this kind of access, even within network television itself, is suggested by the invention of the primitive 'creepy-peepy' mobile television cameras first used at the Democratic national convention in Los Angeles in 1960.

What was direct about Direct Cinema and truthful about *cinéma vérité* was the uncontrived nature of the recording. In part this was a consequence of the reduced scale of this kind of filmmaking, in that it typically required only two persons: a cinematographer and a sound recordist. Among the various attempts to find a name for this approach, 'observational' was no surprise. 'Observational cinema', however, carried a slightly different implication than the other terms. It not only acknowledged that an observer was present but that the observer had some personal responsibility to the people filmed. This emphasis was significant, because without it such films could simply have been made by a professionally indifferent cameraman, or even automatically with a surveillance camera. In *Primary* the roughness of the camera work left no doubt that what we were seeing was the result of human intention and error. But as documentary cinematography became more settled and free of wobbles and zooms, some critics believed that these films might be mistaken by viewers for definitive and impartial accounts of the events filmed. They should have given the viewers more credit. The films that emerged – by Leacock, Brault, Wiseman, the Maysles brothers – couldn't have been more personal. They were signed as clearly as a painting by Edward Hopper or a photograph by Henri Cartier-Bresson.

The emergence of observational cinema was encouraged by changes in fiction filmmaking in the post-war era. Probably the most significant influence was that of Italian Neorealist directors such as Roberto Rossellini and Vittorio De Sica. Neorealism rejected the froth and artifice of much previous Italian film production, especially the melodramatic 'white telephone' films, which ignored the lives of ordinary Italians, particularly the underprivileged. Neorealist films focused instead on the details and undramatic incidents of everyday life, often allowing actions to play out in extended scenes and avoiding the multiple camera set-ups and composite editing (the *découpage classique*) of other fiction films. Neorealist films also looked at the mean streets and urban interiors of everyday life that had previously been largely invisible in mainstream cinema. Non-professionals were often cast instead of actors, and the opportunity to observe unaffected aspects of their behaviour instead of a performance was integral to the new Realist aesthetic. In Vittorio De Sica's *Umberto D.* (1952) there is a long scene, unusual in a fiction film, of a servant girl working unhurriedly in the kitchen (figure 9.2), making coffee and dealing with an infestation of ants. In Roberto Rossellini's *Germany, Year Zero* (1947), a young boy tries to carry on a normal life, ultimately unsuccessfully, in the surreal landscapes

9.2 The kitchen scene in *Umberto D.*

of bombed-out Berlin. Scenes such as these were celebrated by the French film critic André Bazin, who advocated a 'cinema of duration' (1967: 76) that would permit a different kind of engagement on the part of the audience. Rather than tightly controlling their responses, viewers were to be given more space to watch events unfolding and to interpret what they saw.

Most documentary films until the 1960s were either heavily didactic, with a voice-over commentary supported by representative images, or they were poetic evocations of human society, exemplified by the British documentaries of the 1930s and 1940s. Both approaches employed images as symbols or illustrations rather than as accounts of particular events. Both tended to treat people as human types or in the mass, and were more about general social forces than the life of individuals. The possibility of making films that were more focused on specific human beings, although rarely taken up, was at least implied by some documentaries, including one of the first, Robert Flaherty's *Nanook of the North* of 1922. For all his tendency to romanticise people in other societies, Flaherty was also capable of paying close attention to the events of their everyday lives.

The most striking feature of observational cinema, and what set it apart from most other approaches to documentary, was the sense it gave of a sustained encounter between filmmaker and subject. *Primary* and other films produced by Robert Drew at Time, Inc. tended to deal with news stories or subjects of public concern, such as capital punishment in *The Chair* (1963) and racial segregation in *Crisis* (1963). Films such as *Lonely Boy* (1963), by Wolf Koenig and Roman Kroitor about the rising pop star Paul Anka, and David and Albert Maysles's *Salesman* (1969) came closer to the more intimate style of filmmaking that would come to define observational cinema in the 1970s. In their book *Observational Cinema*, Anna Grimshaw and Amanda Ravetz (2009: 55) stress Colin Young's influence in encouraging this approach among some of his film students at the University of California at Los Angeles (UCLA) in the 1960s. Among early works of observational cinema they note David Hancock and Herb Di Gioia's four-part *Vermont People* series (1971–5) and their more explicitly ethnographic film *Naim and Jabar* (1974). My own involvement, and Judith MacDougall's (both of us Colin Young's students), began in UCLA's Ethnographic Film Program and resulted in *To Live with Herds*, filmed in Uganda in 1968, and the *Turkana Conversations* trilogy, filmed in Kenya in 1973–4. Where ethnography and observational filmmaking came together in these projects was in their exploration of the social experience of individuals in societies where the filmmakers had spent extended periods of time. Their other distinguishing feature was that they positioned the filmmakers at the centre of the film as investigators and invited the audience to share this perspective.

Apart from manoeuvrability, the most significant asset of the new camera equipment was its ability to record sound synchronously, especially speech.

Some practitioners of Direct Cinema insisted on recording only the spontaneous conversations of their subjects, whereas observational filmmakers were
more willing to include their interactions with them. Sometimes these took
the form of interviews, but often they were less formal, with the subjects
speaking casually to the filmmakers. In some films the two kinds of speech
are inextricably mixed, as in Gary Kildea's *Celso and Cora* (1983), in which
the protagonists talk alternately to the filmmaker and to each other. A few
such films came to be dominated by one person. They turned into virtual
monologues, as in Tanya Ballantyne's *The Things I Cannot Change* (1967).
Despite the variations, the emphasis of all these films was on immediacy and
informality. It was only when documentary films began to be composed
more abstractly of formal interviews and archival footage that they veered
significantly away from the observational style – for example, Emile de
Antonio's *In the Year of the Pig* (1968), one of the first films to pioneer an
amalgam of interviews and archival footage.

Most observational films focused on one person or a group of persons and
followed a succession of events in their lives. This involved the audience in a
way resembling that of fiction films. But in abandoning the editing structures
of fiction films and their heavy reliance on melodrama, observational films
nevertheless often retained, like the Italian Neorealist films before them, the
forward movement of narrative cinema. And like fiction films, this approach
allowed viewers to identify with characters who were often caught between
contradictory social forces, just the sorts of 'double binds' that Bill Nichols
(1981: 96–103) has identified as a key driver of fiction.

Because of their focus on the filmmaker's viewpoint, observational films
have often been regarded as the creations of one person, generally the person
holding the camera. A documentary film made in this way clearly represents
a conjunction of visual and intellectual perspectives, and quite a number
of films have been made by one person working alone, especially since the
mid-1990s, following the introduction of digital video. Many other observational films, however, have been made by a cinematographer and sound
recordist working closely together, sharing the direction. Such combinations
include Albert and David Maysles; David Hancock and Herbert Di Gioia;
D. A. Pennebaker and Chris Hegedus; Judith MacDougall and myself; Bob
Connolly and Robin Anderson; and the team of Nick Broomfield and Joan
Churchill. Frederick Wiseman forged a long-term working relationship with
the cinematographer William Brayne on such films as *Hospital* (1970), *Essene*
(1972) and *Juvenile Court* (1973). Wiseman directed, edited and recorded the
sound but, in a significant departure from most observational films, tended
to adopt an episodic theme-and-variations structure rather than follow one
person or group throughout. As a result, although his films are perhaps
technically observational, they don't give the sense of there being a close
relationship between filmmaker and subject.

When I wrote about observational cinema in the 1970s, one of my aims was to caution filmmakers against thinking they could remain detached from their subjects, as had been advocated by some social scientists in the interests of scientific objectivity (MacDougall, 1975, 1998). Nor, I said, should they fail to acknowledge their role in the making of their films. Otherwise, a filmmaker might retreat into an isolated position and become what some critics were already calling a 'fly on the wall'. In practice, as observational filmmaking developed, it almost always reflected a personal commitment on the part of the filmmaker, going well beyond mere recording. In underlining this participatory aspect of the process I was only emphasising what I felt was already fundamental to the observational approach.

Another misconception is that observational cinema observes situations but makes no attempt to analyse them. This can perhaps be put down to the fact that, unlike older documentary and educational films and much cultural and public affairs television, these films don't express the filmmaker's views explicitly in a voice-over commentary. But in selecting what and how to film, filmmakers invariably make an analysis, and this is implicit in the structure and content of their films. They expect the viewer to grasp this fact and interpret the film much as they would interpret a fiction film, by following its development as it unfolds. When commentary is used, it is usually spoken by the filmmaker and represents a personal rather than an institutional position. This tends to run against the grain of those who expect to be given explanations, or who prefer clear-cut statements to the ambiguities and complexities of real-life situations. These films generally do not make statements, except possibly for the statement that what they refer to exists. Their strength lies in pointing to the multiple strands of their subjects' existence, not by separating the strands from one another in the abstract but by showing them in their co-presence and interdependence. The best of these films reveal a complex mix of actions, thoughts, feelings and physical settings.

One further misconception is that observation means prolonged and unbroken viewing of a subject. From this it is often concluded that observational cinema must be made up of long camera takes. It is true that many documentary filmmakers of the 1960s discovered the value of allowing events to unwind within a single shot, much as fiction filmmakers like Jean Renoir and F. W. Murnau had done earlier in fiction films, but I would argue that the long take is not the defining characteristic of observational cinema: first, because it is not true in practice; and second, because it is not the way we actually observe things in daily life. An analysis of observational films makes it clear that although many contain long takes, these are frequently combined with shorter ones. What defines these films is not that the shots are long but rather that the stance of the film is one of exploring situations over a period of time. It is the view of someone present, witnessing events, rather than

126

a collage of fragments assembled to make a point. Observational cinema is better defined by its characteristic perspective than by a camera style.

The long take preserves certain continuities of time and space, which is part of its appeal to those seeking an unbroken view from a single viewpoint. But that viewpoint is also limited in its ability to explore details more intimately. A more flexible approach to filming tries to see as we see in everyday life, sometimes looking at the wider scene, sometimes looking more closely at a person's expression or an object that for some reason catches our attention. The shorter shots in such scenes are often just such registrations of significant details. The idea that a camera should be left running in a single wide shot harks back to the view that this can somehow become a substitute for being present, allowing access to anything we might wish to know about a subject. But to observe intelligently with a camera requires more strategy and enterprise. As Gregory Bateson once remarked, 'putting a dead camera on top of a bloody tripod [...] it sees nothing' (Bateson and Mead, 1977: 79).

It may be that the visual precision of film has led some scholars to assume that it resembles writing and is only more comprehensive in its technical powers. There are certainly some similarities between filmmaking and writing in the shaping of the material and the thought that goes into them. In films, as in texts, there can be cross-references and resonances, and films can be metaphorical like poems. But writing a text is very different from filming an event, because the material that one works with is so different. Words can be changed, but once shots have been made they become fixed. They can be combined and edited in various ways, but they cannot be rewritten. The images framed and recorded at the moment of contact with the subject become the fabric of the finished work and will always carry the imprint of that encounter. This means that the processes of selection and construction must be brought into play at an earlier stage than in writing, when the filmmaker's choices become crucial to what the viewer will eventually see. The film becomes physical evidence of those choices. More than in fiction filmmaking, and in many other forms of documentary, observational cinema exposes the contingency and provisional nature of the processes that produce it.

Documentary films in the 1960s gradually altered earlier ideas of the proper relation between the filmmaker, film subject and film viewer. In the typical documentary film of the 1930s and 1940s, the filmmaker was essentially invisible and the film's production was cloaked in professional secrecy. Bill Nichols (1991: 125–33) has observed that even today most documentary films are organised around the structure of an argument. The audience is presented with statements which it can accept or reject, but there is little room for independent interpretation. A voice-over commentary usually dominates the images, but even if not, the images are used to advance the argument rather than act as evidence for it. Observational documentaries depart from this primarily by a more sustained focus on events, drawing the viewer more fully into the ambit of the filmmaker's experience. In minimising the use of disconnected images, an observational film also seeks to give the viewer a greater sense of time and space. The film is no longer a set of propositions about a subject constructed as a lesson, but a more modest view of the filmmaking encounter.

Unlike filmmakers whose purpose is to argue a case or bring about social change, observational filmmakers are more likely to focus on the simple existence of things in their own right. In some cases they may wish to draw attention to a dire situation, or alter how people look at it. But in others they may wish to do no more than to reveal the complexities of life and how we experience them. This turn towards the world itself often means turning away from forming theories about it or proposing plans for changing it. There is also, I suspect, a more personal motive. Observational filmmakers may be looking for ways to link their own sensibilities to those of others, using film to reach out to them. This is not just a matter of giving the world its due, but of searching for what binds us together in it.

One consequence of observational filmmaking is that it has made us think in a more nuanced way about what it means to observe. We can look casually or with a heightened sense of awareness. We can learn by watching or simply impose our preconceptions on what we see. Observation can be a way of registering facts or, alternatively, of entering into a more intimate relation with the world. In achieving that perspective, filmmakers sometimes risk losing something of themselves in the unfamiliar regions they enter.

As filmmakers, we take away certain images and then, with the particular framing we have given them, return them to the stream of life. The film has created a trace of what we have seen. And because film is recursive, what we have filmed creates a kind of loop in our consciousness which we can go back to again and again. At the same time, it leaves a small mark on the surface of reality. For when a film is lost – and all that it contains – that mark is smoothed over and disappears forever.

10

Anthropology and the cinematic imagination

S OME years ago George Marcus (1990) wrote a paper on the cinematic imagination and its emergence in contemporary ethnographic writing. Marcus was referring to the cinematic technique of montage – not *montage* as the French use the term, referring to film editing in general, but montage as defined by Soviet theorists and filmmakers such as Kuleshov, Eisenstein and Pudovkin. For them, montage meant the juxtaposition of shots to produce a specific effect. The effect could be kinaesthetic, psychological or intellectual. Eisenstein described a whole range of effects involving the juxtaposition of graphic and dynamic elements and symbols, for which he borrowed musical terms such as metric montage, rhythmic montage, tonal montage, overtonal montage and contrapuntal montage. Marcus's point was that anthropologists had begun to employ the principle of montage in their writing and that juxtaposition was itself a feature of the modernist sensibility. One of the things that interested him was the potential of montage for creating effects of simultaneity in narratives. Another was its challenge to nineteenth-century certainties of place, space and time, and the authority of the grand narratives of history and science. Today we might also see montage as an analogue for the fragmented consciousness produced by rapid travel and globalisation.

Here I want to discuss a similar instance of the emergence of the cinematic imagination in anthropology, but in a form very different from montage. I shall also argue that this appears in anthropology before, and probably independently of, its appearance in anthropological filmmaking.

Indeed, I would argue that this expression of the cinematic imagination predates the cinema itself, in that it represents a way of thinking that was already being prepared for cinema in nineteenth century literature and photography. Unlike Soviet montage, which often sought to shock the viewer with the disjunctions between shots, this cinematic approach aimed to direct the psychological processes of the viewer in a gentler and more indirect way. Through the experiments of directors such as D. W. Griffith, Fritz Lang and Alfred Hitchcock it was to become the dominant way of putting shots together, adopted wholeheartedly by Hollywood and often called 'continuity editing'. Here the aim was not so much to exploit the dynamic or intellectual effects of juxtaposition as to create an impression of smooth continuity from one shot to another, even though the shots might be taken from different positions and bridge major gaps in time and space. The objective was to create from a set of fragments a seemingly whole imagined world. Looking at a sequence constructed in this way, viewers feel they are witnessing a coherent event, and they are generally unaware of the cuts between the shots. In some respects, this approach was designed, perhaps unconsciously, to imitate the way in which our perception is already fragmented, and how we reassemble the fragments of experience in our minds to create what we call 'reality'. Similar techniques had already been developed by novelists from Stendahl to Flaubert, turning the reader into a virtual spectator within the narrative. In cinema, continuity editing created comparable constructed worlds. What was perhaps most important about this was that cinema constructed these not in front of the viewer, as one might assume when thinking of a flat movie screen, but in three dimensions around the viewer.

The ground for this was prepared by the new technologies of the late nineteenth century – the telephone, gramophone, motor car, stereo photograph and of course the cinematograph – all of which posed a challenge to familiar ways of experiencing the world. You have only to read Proust or look at the photographs of Lartigue to sense the impact of these inventions. Telephones brought voices from distant places, robbed of the presence of the speaker. Motor cars allowed people to see the landscape at ever increasing speeds. Photographs and films suggested the movement of people and objects, but movement largely divorced from the accompanying sensations of pressure, sound, touch and colour.

One of the most important of these inventions was the stereograph. I would suggest that the stereographic imagination was a necessary precursor to the development of the cinematic imagination. What distinguished stereo photography from ordinary photography – or, for that matter, from painting – was both technical and aesthetic. It produced a distinct break from single-plane monocular photography and from the conventions of perspective, which had involved the projection of a three-dimensional image on to a two-dimensional surface. Instead, the eyes and the brain converted the two images presented to them into a simulation of everyday binocular vision. Along with this, stereo photography created a new aesthetic in which the subjects of the photograph, as well as the viewing subject, became fragmented and decentred. Single objects became part of an integrated complex of objects that receded from, and invaded, the space of the viewer. Different points in the stereograph could each function as a new locus of perception. Indeed, when looking at a stereo photograph, your eyes shift from one plane to another, creating a number of different viewing positions and virtual photographs within the frame. The stereograph produces a sort of 'surround sight'. The spectator is positioned three dimensionally in relation to every other object and becomes physically implicated in the photograph.

Today, stereo photography is an almost vanished technology, but in some ways this may actually help us to imagine its power at the end of the nineteenth century. People today are amazed when they look at stereo view-cards through one of the simple hand-held viewers designed by Oliver Wendell Holmes. They are no longer inspecting an object. These pictures seem to enfold them physically, turning them into imaginary participants. Just in this way, stereo viewing prepared both anthropologists and filmmakers for the new imaginary spaces of cinema.

People often wonder why anthropologists, who were so excited by photography and motion pictures in the nineteenth century, gradually lost interest in them in the twentieth. We could rightly call the first half of the twentieth century the 'dark age' of visual anthropology. At some point – perhaps even before the First World War – the curtain seems to have come down on vision as far as anthropologists were concerned. Some years ago Luc de Heusch (1962: 12) pointed out that anthropologists had become reluctant to publish photographs in their monographs. Ethnographic filmmaking, which A. C. Haddon had recommended so enthusiastically to his colleagues, had become a sideline of anthropology, practised more by amateurs, adventurers, missionaries, journalists and travel lecturers than by anthropologists. A number of explanations have been given for this. One is that photography and cinematography were considered too difficult and costly. Another is that anthropologists had lost faith in vision as a source of knowledge, perhaps as part of the undermining of all verities by the First World War. Another is that the photographic media had been contaminated by popular entertainment: they were considered vulgar and exuded the aura of the music hall. Another is that the research methods of anthropologists had changed. As more and more of the world's indigenous societies were disrupted, anthropologists had become increasingly dependent on the testimony of a few informants, reinforcing anthropology as a 'discipline of words' (Mead, 1975: 5).

Perhaps the most plausible explanation is that anthropological knowledge itself was changing, shifting away from the visible world of human beings and their material possessions towards the invisible world of abstract relations such as kinship, political organisation and social values. But if this is so, the result is still perplexing. For this was also the period of the rise of participant observation as the new cornerstone of anthropology. If observation was so important, you would think that filming people in their daily interactions would have become increasingly useful. Yet it was just at this time, when filming people became possible, that anthropologists began to drift away from it. The human body, which had excited so much interest in the nineteenth century, when it was constantly being measured and photographed, had ceased to be a site of meaning.

The loss of interest can also be ascribed to the primitive state of cinema at this time, despite the excitement it aroused. Early in the century, when anthropology was becoming institutionalised as a discipline, cinema could do few of the things we now consider central to it. It was still too crude to be of much use in examining social relationships, and by the time it was able to do so, anthropologists had consigned it to the narrower roles of note-taking and public education. Few if any anthropologists at that time could have imagined how a film could report on a society in the way that a journal article could, much less theorise and make statements about it. Films and photographs were more like objects put in a showcase or a diorama at a museum. They had gravitated to the margins of anthropology – to the earliest stages, where they had some limited utility in producing notes upon which anthropological conclusions could be based, and to the end, where those conclusions were already formed and ready to be popularised.

There was not much change in this situation until after the Second World War – with a slight hiccup, or perhaps a glimmer of hope, with the Balinese Project of Margaret Mead and Gregory Bateson in the 1930s. I have made no mention here of Robert Flaherty, nor of Walter Baldwin Spencer, nor of Merian C. Cooper and Ernest B. Schoedsack, and their film *Grass* (1925). Nor have I mentioned Basil Wright's *The Song of Ceylon* (1934) or Georges Rouquier's *Farrebique* (1946). I admire the films made by these anthropologists and non-anthropologists, but I believe they had little impact on anthropology.

One must really wait until the appearance of Jean Rouch to pick up this story. He once said he was lucky to have lost his tripod in the Niger River, because he was then forced to see what he could achieve with a hand-held camera. In 1951 we find him in a dugout canoe, up the Niger without a tripod, participating in a hippopotamus hunt, the spray from the oars around him, shouting to us on the soundtrack about what is happening. The film was one of his first, *Bataille sur le grand fleuve* (1952). Jean-Luc Godard once said that Rouch was the father of the French New Wave, because he had invented a new form of cinema, using a lightweight camera as a kind of personal writing instrument (Piault, 2000: 207). In 1961 Rouch and Edgar Morin released *Chronique d'un été*, a film that would forever change people's thinking about documentary. It was also destined to have a tremendous impact on fiction films. In *Chronique*, Rouch and Morin borrowed fictional devices from feature films and applied them freely to documentary, often blurring the line between fiction and nonfiction. But very soon filmmakers like Godard and Truffaut were borrowing devices from documentary and applying them just as freely to fiction. Rouch was quite happy to break the rules of cinema. Godard once said, 'Rouch doesn't give a damn anyway. He never listens' (1972: 134).

The years 2004 and 2005 brought the deaths of Jean Rouch and John Marshall. Together they had probably done more than all their predecessors to reinvent ethnographic film and revive interest in the possibilities of visual anthropology. Beginning in the 1950s they began to demonstrate that cinema had more to offer anthropology than a technology of note-taking or a means of popularisation. Their films tried to enter into the thoughts and feelings of their subjects and the physical spaces in which they lived. Few if any anthropological films had attempted this before, and the attempt was long overdue. However, this step was assured by a transformation of consciousness that had begun much earlier in the century.

When photography was being developed in the 1830s and 1840s it seems to have accorded remarkably well with the scientific perspectives of the time. Astonishing as photography must have seemed at first, it was soon accepted as a confirmation of the power of seeing. Sight at this time appears to have been valued far more highly as an avenue to knowledge than in later periods. It was felt that through photography, reality could be grasped and inspected at leisure – grasped, however, at arm's length, as though separated from the scientist by a pane of glass. The relation of the scientist to the scientific object was thus characterised by a certain perceptual and conceptual 'flatness'. One of the first natural objects to be photographed was the moon, in 1840. There could hardly have been a more suitable emblem for the separation between observer and observed. When anthropologists began photographing people, the resulting photographs positioned their subjects in a similar manner. Anthropometric photographs of human 'types' were typically a pair of frontal and profile views made on a flat plane in front of the camera. Looking at them today, they suggest medical cross-sections of the human body and police 'mug shots'.

This flatness was also typical of early motion pictures. The films made by Edison, the Lumières, Demenÿ and others at this time generally viewed events as if they were framed pictures – or theatrical performances on a stage, with people making entrances and exits from the wings. This was also true of early fiction films, such as *Le Voyage dans la lune* (1902), by Georges Méliès. Although it was extremely inventive visually, what it presented to the viewer was a series of flat, cut-out figures and effects. The flatness of such films was as much intellectual as it was visual. Reality was an object to be looked at. Films did not yet aim to recreate the actual experience of living in a three-dimensional world. Yet this is quite understandable given that a motion picture was still conceived as a still photograph to which motion had been added. It would have required a great conceptual leap to imagine it as a way of restructuring the viewer's consciousness. To do that, it was not enough simply to invent the cinematograph. It required the invention of cinema.

This began to happen with great speed in the decade between 1910 and 1920, coincidentally or not the decade of the First World War. At this same time, a parallel shift was taking place in anthropology, towards the more cinema-like perspective of 'participant observation' – although not, I think, with any direct connection to the cinema. Still, 'participant observation' could just as easily have been the mantra of the newly emerging art of cinema as it was of anthropology. Filmmakers such as D. W. Griffith began to construct their images not in front of the viewer, but around the viewer, who was treated as an invisible participant within the scene. This was accomplished by methods that are now so familiar that we hardly notice them: the alternation of over-the-shoulder shots during a conversation; the shot of someone looking at something immediately followed by a shot of what they are looking at; or the reverse of this, the shot of a person reacting to an object or event we have just seen. Through these means we as viewers are 'inserted' into the action, so that we know the positions of all the characters around us, and often what is happening to them even when they are off screen. Unlike Soviet montage, this was an editing system based not on dramatic contrasts but rather on an illusion of smoothly flowing time and space. The aim was to guide us into the midst of a physical setting and control our perceptions of what was going on there. This was usually done in such a way that each new shot came at the psychologically right moment, just when the filmmaker judged that we wanted to see it.

Also at this time, similar moves were being made by anthropologists to try to describe the world as a person of another society saw and understood it – indeed, was 'inserted' into it. This change owed much to developments in linguistics and represented a major shift in scientific purpose. It was not a renunciation of the precision that an analytical stance requires, but an effort to add to anthropology an understanding of other societies in cognitive and psychological terms, and visual terms as well. Here the shift from a figuratively 'flat' observational stance to a multidimensional one could well stand as a metaphor for the more profound multidimensionality of the individual's complex social experience. Anna Grimshaw (2001: 35–7) has made the point that Rivers' invention of the kinship diagram was not simply a schematic representation of kinship structure as seen from the outside, but a way of representing human relationships from the multiple and contingent perspectives of those inside them. Towards the end of his career, Bronislaw Malinowski (1935: 45) was to write: 'Throughout our enquiry we are trying to overcome the limitations of [the] ethnographic apparatus and get beyond the fieldworker's notebook to the reality of native life.' For Malinowski, combining an analysis of linguistic terms with a description of the contexts in which they were used would provide what he called a 'double account' and, as he put it, 'the material thus illuminated will stand out, so to speak, stereoscopically' (1935: 3).

The shifts in anthropological writing at this time were not in the direction of montage – that would come later – but towards forms that would draw the reader imaginatively into the material realities and thought processes of the inhabitants. Ethnographies of the 1920s began to do this through the visual imagery of prose descriptions and accounts of the anthropologist's first-hand experiences. These should perhaps be seen as an interim measure that would eventually lead to the incorporation of the accounts of the informants themselves. But there were other techniques too. The language of anthropology had begun to shift away from a style modelled on the natural scientist's report to a professional society. As well as drawing the reader more fully into the fieldwork experience, the writing began to report the indigenous view of things in a way that implicated the reader subjectively, much as continuity editing in films created subjective identification with the characters. The impersonal 'he, she, or they do that' began to be written 'one does that' and, finally, in E. E. Evans-Pritchard's writing, 'you do that' – for example in his book on the Azande, where he writes 'If you suffer a serious misfortune you will immediately suspect witchcraft' (1937: 29).

I am attempting here to stitch together two ideas: first, that anthropologists and filmmakers invented, more or less independently, a way of looking at the world that involved repositioning themselves and their audiences imaginatively in relation to their subjects; and second, that as far as visual anthropology was concerned, these two inventions remained almost completely isolated from one another for a long period, until they began to converge after the Second World War.

Which brings us back to Jean Rouch on the Niger. In his film of the hippopotamus hunt, he attempts to recreate both the physical and the psychological involvement of the hunt. The psychological state of social actors was to become for him an increasingly important subject in his many films on performance and spirit possession. But equally, in films such as *Moi, un noir* (1958) and *Jaguar* (1967), he is as much concerned with the mental world of his subjects as with their participation in the objective processes of urbanisation and labour migration. For Rouch, anthropology was as much about culture as an interior state as it was about the world of social institutions.

In many ways, this is unremarkable. Rouch's interests are completely consistent with those of many other anthropologists of the same period. What is remarkable is that prior to this there is hardly a trace of these interests apparent in visual anthropology or ethnographic film. I can think of just a few exceptions – one or two of the films of Flaherty, a non-anthropologist, and those of Bateson, an anthropological outsider like Rouch. In his penchant for filmmaking, Rouch was arguably even more of an outsider than in his intellectual orientation.

The other great pioneer of visual anthropology in the 1950s was another outsider, John Marshall. Despite their different temperaments and backgrounds, Rouch and Marshall shared two important characteristics. Both were interested in using the camera to explore interpersonal relationships, and both recognised, or came to recognise, the value of cinematic techniques for doing so. The techniques they employed were very similar to those invented by Griffith and others some three decades earlier. Rouch once said: 'Making a film, for me, means writing it with your eyes, with your ears, with your body' (Rouch, 2003: 147). In his films Rouch becomes, as he often remarked, the 'first audience' for the events he films, recreating for the viewer the physical environment in which they occur. The viewer participates by being drawn into Rouch's experience. Rouch's films, perhaps more vividly than any others, convey a sense of the life that surrounds the filmmaker – even what lies behind his back.

John Marshall often claimed that he was ignorant of formal cinematic techniques when he started filming and had to reinvent many of them from scratch. But like many of his generation and class, he cannot have escaped exposure to the cinema, and I think this is evident in his filming style. In many ways he is more systematic than Rouch in his visual analysis of events and his manner of reconstructing them in edited sequences. He once wrote:

> When a family was sitting and talking, I would get my camera close to the person listening while I filmed the person speaking. Rather than standing back to take a middle shot, or choosing angles and distances that reflected my ideas and projections, I would pretend to be different members of the group while I shot the other participants. (Marshall, 1993: 42)

Marshall's crucial discovery was that 'the relationship between what is happening on and off the screen is what film language is all about' (1993: 127n3).

> I began to learn how little we see of the reality around us through the window of a camera, and that most of the content in a film is either unseen or invisible. [...] Invisible content is most of the reality that surrounds the camera. (Marshall, 1993: 39)

Rouch and Marshall believed that visual anthropology could and should do more than simply record what is in front of the camera. They were after the invisible content of the scenes they filmed, in terms of both the sense of space they conveyed and the experience of individuals. They respected the film viewer's ability to grasp the fact that life goes on even when the camera is not actually showing it. Their achievement was to build on this understanding and provide the clues from which we, as viewers, can reimagine the world in which their subjects lived and breathed.

Anthropological filmmaking: an empirical art

THEORETICAL CONSIDERATIONS

Anthropological filmmaking is necessarily defined by what is considered anthropological at any particular time. But because there is no unanimity about the definition of anthropology, either today or historically, there are many different conceptions of what constitutes an anthropological film. These range from using film (or video) as a simple recording technology, to films made according to specific rules or principles (designed to yield certain categories of knowledge), to audio-visual illustrations of written texts, to films combining these approaches with more interpretive accounts of social and cultural life. Anthropological films have also followed changes in what has technically been possible. Films from the silent era relied on images and inter-titles. Sound films added speech and natural sounds, with increasing flexibility as this became more feasible. The first anthropological sound films added soundtracks of commentary, natural sounds and music to film footage previously shot, because recording image and sound simultaneously required massive and expensive equipment. When this became easier in the 1960s, anthropological films were able to incorporate spoken dialogue (translated in subtitles) in the way fiction films had done since the 1930s, although this still required manual synchronisation in the editing room. With the advent of video, synchronous sound recording became essentially an integral part of the filming process, so that introducing non-synchronous sound actually became the greater challenge.

The ideas, subject matter and methods of anthropology are always changing, and anthropological filmmaking has both influenced and reflected this process. Many of the recent concerns of anthropology – the agency of individuals, their subjective experience, social performance, built environments – are well served by the expressive potential of film, which was perhaps less well suited to the study of social structures and religious beliefs in an earlier anthropological era. Because of this, there has been a renewal of anthropological interest in the visual, reminiscent of the intense interest in visual knowledge among nineteenth-century anthropologists, travellers and the general public.

Today's scientific interest in the visual (and audio-visual), however, has a markedly different character from that of the nineteenth century, when the technical and expressive range of film and photography was more limited and the focus was more strictly on material culture, technology and human physiology. Anthropological filmmaking now is as much concerned with the non-visual as the visual. Audio-visual recording has evolved to become a means of exploring the full gamut of human social experience, including ideas, feelings, verbal and non-verbal expression, aesthetics, the role of the senses, and the formal and informal interactions of everyday life.

Visual anthropology and writing

It is important to understand that this has created a tension between conventional ways of doing anthropology and the possibilities opened up by visual anthropology. Anthropology, as a discipline of words, developed specific methods of research and forms of discourse that were both challenged and complemented by anthropological filmmaking. As anthropology aspired to be a science, with systems of data collection equivalent to those of the laboratory sciences, it produced ways of summarising and testing its knowledge that could, in theory, be reproduced by other researchers, even if this occurred rather rarely. Anthropological knowledge came to be understood as that which could be expressed in writing or in the schemata of diagrams and tables. Films, by comparison, do things in a very different way, and anthropological films, partly as a consequence of this, have often failed to live up to anthropological expectations. In considering the potential of filmmaking for anthropological research, we need to look more closely at the sorts of knowledge films can create and how they create it.

Much learning is visual but, in the processes of codification and communication knowledge tends to become verbal. To a great extent films bypass this unless they are built around a verbal text, such as a spoken commentary or interviews with informants. The viewer of a film is exposed to scenes recorded by the camera, and these are organised in the editing to suggest a certain way of interpreting them. But there is always much more detail in the scenes than is governed by the interpretation, and viewers may derive knowledge from this material independently. Thus, despite the differences between human vision and photographic reproduction, and the many choices made in filming and editing, viewing a film is closer in character to the visual and auditory experience of an anthropologist in the field than to that of the readers of an anthropological text, where much of the detail must be reconstructed in the reader's imagination. This materialist basis of film stands in sharp contrast to the verbal codes of written anthropology.

Because film and writing are such different modes of communication, filmmaking is not just a way of communicating the same kinds of knowledge that can be conveyed by an anthropological text: it is a way of creating different knowledge. For many, this has been both its greatest drawback and its greatest promise. The problem has been how to identify what is anthropological in the knowledge that film uniquely makes possible, and to have this recognised by anthropologists generally. The promise has been to introduce methods of research and publication that add to what anthropology has already achieved, and ultimately to expand the depth and range of the discipline. But to do so, anthropological filmmaking must make the best use of its specific properties, rather than attempt to copy anthropological writing. Anthropological filmmaking can thus be seen as a parallel stream of anthropology, with its own areas of interest and its own distinctive ways of creating meaning.

Filming and writing each have certain advantages and are subject to certain limitations in portraying and interpreting human societies. Recognising the limitations and utilising the advantages of film are therefore important in deciding how to employ it. Anthropological film obviously has advantages in visual description. Every image is specific to a time and place, with all its particularities as well as its general features. But this is also a limitation, in that it makes anthropological film an anthropology of the particular. Films can summarise by presenting a set of different cases for comparison, but they cannot make general statements and draw overall conclusions in the way writing can. This inability to state abstract propositions about society is, however, offset by the potential of film to explore the individual case in detail, not only visually but also in its temporal, physical and emotional dimensions. Visual research using film is capable of investigating a wide range of elements, individually and in their combinations: movement, speech, the visual, the auditory, the material, the corporeal and so on. There are thus certain areas of social research that are particularly accessible to filmmaking and in which it can make significant contributions, both as a method of enquiry and as a means of communicating knowledge to others. These areas include, at the very least, formal and informal interactions among people, their relationships with their physical environment, the social experience and agency of individuals, and the performative aspects of social life.

Anthropological filmmaking as a process

What also makes anthropological filmmaking deserving of special attention today is its relevance to many of the other current concerns of anthropology: globalisation, migration, gender, emotion, individual and group identity, and visual culture. Yet it is important not to regard visual anthropology just as a method of reporting on these phenomena. Filmmaking is also a research process. Film has often been seen as a way of presenting knowledge previously gained by other means, a medium of publication and popularisation. Conversely, it has also often been seen simply as a recording method, to extract data for later analysis. But the process of filming can be much more than this, a means of interacting with a subject and exploring it in new ways. Filmmaking is a way of looking, sometimes motivated by intellectual objectives and sometimes anticipating thought. Often what is learned by filming is only an intermediate step towards quite different knowledge, or an indicator of what deserves closer attention. Thus, filming can become an integral part of the fieldwork process, shifting the position from which the anthropologist sees.

A major difference between anthropological filmmaking and most other modes of anthropological research is that it is collapses the distance between enquiry and publication. The visual recording – that is, the research data – becomes the fabric of the finished work. What is filmed cannot be rewritten, although it can be edited and presented in different ways. This is in marked contrast to conventional anthropology, which is the result of gathering data, reflecting on it and then presenting conclusions in a written form. This means that much of what the audience eventually sees, and how they see it, will have been inalterably determined at the time of filming. The expressive strategies of an anthropological film must therefore be ever present in the mind of the filmmaker as it is actually being shot.

Cinema and social science

Several recurring theoretical debates have bedevilled anthropological filmmaking since its origins, concerning the relation of the filmmaker to the work and the relation of cinematic art to science. In both cases the debate has become polarised, creating an impression of incompatible opposites when in fact more complex interrelationships are involved. In general, these debates run parallel to historical shifts in anthropological thought, although films, perhaps because they are judged to have more public influence, sometimes throw the issues into sharper relief.

Anthropological films take many forms and reflect different strategies for achieving an understanding of culture and society. One cause of anthropological disquiet over film has been the assumption by some of its advocates that anthropological filmmakers should adopt a single correct approach, and that approach only. Other approaches are dismissed as biased, naïve or un-anthropological. A further suspicion surrounds the field as a whole, stemming from its uncomfortable position between cinema and social science, and the suggestion that films are essentially forms of popularisation and entertainment. This is compounded by the different communicative systems of filming and writing, and what they actually communicate. But knowledge of society is not independent of how it is pursued, and using the creative potential of cinema can be a legitimate way of enlarging previously unexamined subjects and increasing anthropological understanding. Art and science therefore need not be opposed if the art is in the service of more accurate description and analysis. Each filmmaker must decide at what point the means of expression employed begin to obscure rather than clarify the subject – in short, at what point aesthetic choices begin to undermine the creation of new knowledge. In the past, the development of clearly recognisable genres, and the specific contexts in which texts have been used (such as teaching, or publication in journals), have provided the discipline with its guidelines as to what kinds of discourse are anthropological. But these genres and contexts remain less clearly defined for anthropological film.

Positioning, bias and truth

Another source of uncertainty, fuelling much debate, has been how anthropological filmmakers have positioned themselves in relation to their subjects and audiences. This positioning is crucial to understanding what any work represents; it provides a set of indicators on how to interpret it. Certain genres carry this information with them. We know, for example, that a Western will be a kind of morality play. In anthropological film, assumptions range from trusting that the work will explain itself to believing that a meta-commentary outside the work is necessary. The points at issue are how the author regards the subject and audience and how, in turn, the subject regards each of these. In films, these relationships are reflected in the camerawork, editing and the content of images. Does the filmmaker stand aloof or record his or her interactions with the people in the film? Are the conditions of filming made evident? Is the filmic language familiar, relying on established conventions from fiction or documentary, or is it more personal, reflecting a particular sensibility? How much is assumed about what the audience already knows? Does the filmmaker expect the viewer to understand the situation or make explicit efforts to guide them? Each of these possibilities expresses an ideological position, a theory of knowledge, and expectations about how the film will be used.

One of the dominant debates in visual anthropology has centred on the reliability of the filmed record. Since the invention of photography and film, they have been regarded by many social scientists as ways of overcoming the inaccuracies of written description and the biases of the individual observer. It was thought that they might become a substitute for direct observation, allowing others to see accurately what the first observer had seen. To some extent this has proven true. Film has allowed anthropologists to inspect certain aspects of human behaviour in minute detail, leading to a better understanding of facial expression, posture and gesture, technological processes, rituals, child-rearing practices, the social uses of space, and so on. But beyond questions of the accuracy of photographic reproduction lie more complex questions of scientific truth and interpretation.

Anthropological films should be distinguished from raw anthropological film footage: they are constructed works, making use of cinematic conventions and the selective potential of the camera and editing. Like written ethnographies, they are authored works, influenced by the particular interests and circumstances of the anthropologist. This fact has run up against the ideal of a transparent work in which authorship is effectively erased or bracketed, whether by means of scientific rigour, self-restraint or self-explanation. Thus anthropological films are caught in a bind. They are expected to be objective and yet interpretive, and are criticised if they fail in either respect. Perhaps more than written works, they are also often accused of being misleading for leaving things out, as if films must be comprehensive, even though this is not expected of anthropological writing. There is in this position what might be called a 'primitive' view of what an anthropological film can or should be.

The participant observer

The problem has often come down to questioning the objectivity of the filmmaker, underpinned by the supposed neutrality of science. But the anthropological filmmaker can never present reality as a single objective fact (assuming this even existed), just as he or she can never avoid the selectivity involved in filming from a specific camera position, or having certain interests, or being part of a particular historical and intellectual generation. What, for example, is the objective reality of a ritual? Is it the structure of the event, the symbolic meanings it encodes, or the thoughts and feelings of those performing it? It is all of these, but every film must choose which aspects to explore. Subjectivity and objectivity are not alternatives – they are elements to be balanced in the work, and each filmmaker will balance them differently.

This argument applies to whether, while filming, the filmmaker should remain apart from the people being filmed or interact with them. A stance apart is sometimes founded on the ideal of capturing an unmediated reality, but it may also simply reflect a strategy of learning through observation rather than employing more invasive means. Anthropological research typically utilises a variety of methods: observation, participation in daily life, interviews with informants, statistical surveys and so on. Filmmakers choose from similar possibilities. Malinowski's 'participant observation' was never meant to suggest opposed approaches, but rather the two combined: the participant as observer. Interaction with the researcher's subjects is a quintessential part of fieldwork. The questions facing anthropological filmmakers, therefore, become how much to interact and how much of this interaction to include in the film. I shall have more to say about this in relation to uses of the camera (see 'Camera modes', below).

METHODOLOGICAL CONSIDERATIONS

Anthropological filmmaking involves both filming methods and research methods, although in practice the two are closely intertwined. When filming is itself a form of investigation, the two become almost synonymous. 'Visual research' may suggest the recording of images for later analysis, and it has meant this for many anthropologists; but it can also be a primary means of investigation. Research of the first kind views anthropological filmmaking primarily as a technology; research of the second kind as a practice, a way of actively exploring social phenomena.

Prospective uses

How one makes an anthropological film depends largely on how one hopes it will be seen. (There may also be an eye on posterity: creating a historical record for uses unknown today.) The prospective use is generally clear already, but it is as well for the filmmaker to give it a second thought. This does not mean identifying a 'target audience', as educators and television producers like to do, because a film may have several quite legitimate audiences. Rather, it means trying to imagine how it will be received, for without this it is unlikely to emerge as a coherent work. Will it be viewed as scientific data to be studied, or will it provide an experience from which viewers can gain insights into other people's lives? There are a range of possibilities in between. A filmmaker may want to illustrate a particular topic, create a case study, present a set of variations on a theme, or construct a narrative of events. Filming a craftsperson making an object, for example, could be: (1) to show the technological process, (2) to show the craftsperson's knowledge and skill, (3) to make a point about labour, (4) to reveal the craftsperson's character, (5) to reflect a passage of time, (6) to recreate a sensory environment, (7) to describe a cultural function or artistic tradition, and so on. The context in which the material appears will direct different readings, and it will also influence the manner of filming.

What is filmed will also be determined by what it is possible to film. What is the best strategy for filming kinship? Should the anthropologist even try to use film for this? Clearly, a diagram is a better means of representing the abstract structural relations of kinship. But film may be better at expressing situations of dominance, affection or such special relationships as avoidance or 'joking relationships'. How parents treat their children, and vice versa, can be described through written accounts and oral histories, but filming provides a further level of understanding by conveying postures, facial expressions and records of actual incidents.

It was once thought by many anthropologists that film offered anthropology only a way of sketching in the background of anthropological study – the natural setting, the appearance of dwellings, how individuals exemplified certain social roles and so on. Film was considered useful for illustration in teaching but not intellectually important to anthropology. It is now increasingly believed that appearance is in fact a significant locus of meaning for anthropology. The physical body, material culture, the performance of social roles, the aesthetic systems of societies, the agency of individuals – all these are now part of the mainstream of anthropological theory. This has provided new and productive opportunities for anthropological filmmakers.

Crews and collaborations

Approaching the task of filming in the field, the anthropologist will be faced with the question of whether to film alone or seek the help of one or more other persons. In the past, in order to film with 16 mm film and synchronous sound, a second person was usually essential to handle the tape recorder and microphone. Today, equipped with a video camera and smaller microphones, one person can achieve almost as much. But the choice also has important consequences for the resulting film material.

A film crew, even as small as two people, creates a quite different relationship of rapport with the people filmed than a single filmmaker. Two people form a social unit from which it is possible to feel excluded, whereas the anthropologist filming alone is always in a more exposed relationship with others. This can have benefits, in that people may be more likely to treat the filmmaker as a member of their social group, or as an intimate to whom information and feelings can be confided. The equipment carried by a single filmmaker is also less likely to appear threatening. Another difference, from the filmmaker's point of view, is that most decisions can be made immediately, without requiring consultation or pre-arrangement with an assistant or collaborator.

One of the advantages of filming with another person or with a crew, however, is that the people being filmed may feel better able to establish an understanding about what will be filmed: that the whole process can in effect be more public and regulated. This may be particularly important when restricted knowledge is involved or the situation is politically sensitive. A crew of filmmakers may be seen as less likely to form allegiances with a particular faction. If the filmmaker's assistant is from the group being filmed, there may also be greater trust (but, it should be noted, sometimes quite the opposite). Two filmmakers may also have access to a wider range of events if they differ from one another, for example if they are a married couple, or persons of different ages. Sometimes people will fully accept one of the two filmmakers because of gender or ethnicity and allow the other to be present in a supporting or honorary capacity. Working with another person also has the advantage of giving the filmmaker someone to talk to about the film, in ways not possible with the people being filmed. A second person can contribute new ideas and throw things into better perspective.

Collaboration between a filmmaker and an anthropologist is often put forward as the ideal formula for successful anthropological filmmaking. Each, it is supposed, will complement the skills of the other, the assumption being that anthropologists are untrained in filmmaking and filmmakers are ignorant of anthropology. This may once have been true but, increasingly, anthropologists are eager to add filmmaking to their traditional methods of note-taking and writing. In this, anthropologist filmmakers like Jean Rouch have led the way. Filmmakers trained in anthropology are also more common, and indeed the separation of the two domains is beginning to look outdated. Younger anthropologists increasingly regard filming skills as a necessary part of their research repertoire.

In any case, collaboration of any kind can be difficult, and it is all the more so if the collaborators have different interests and ways of doing things. A common pitfall when an anthropologist and filmmaker collaborate is that the anthropologist wants the film to be all-inclusive, believing that leaving anything out will distort the result. The error here lies in assuming that a film must cover everything and avoid pursuing specific interests, and that the viewer has no recourse to other sources of information. The anthropologist may therefore come armed with an encyclopaedic list of topics and become upset when they cannot all be dealt with. A variant of this, also meant to guard against misinterpretation, is to want to load the film with a complex superstructure of verbal explanation, under which the film eventually sinks. Filmmakers, for their part, may be too eager to give the film a conventional dramatic structure, feeling that without this the audience will lose interest. They may become increasingly anxious if that structure doesn't emerge on its own, and be tempted to interfere with events to make it happen. An obsessive fixation on 'story' is a weakness of many filmmakers. There are many other ways of structuring a film effectively.

Another form of collaboration can be between filmmakers and their subjects, with the purpose of producing a film that includes an interior per-spective or gives a larger voice to the people filmed. A common weakness of this approach, however, is that it may be difficult to know whose view of the situation the film finally represents. Because of the different interests and objectives involved, the result may be a compromise that avoids exploring anything very deeply. Related to this is another potential problem. One of the underlying principles of an anthropological or cross-cultural perspec-tive is that cultural specificities are best understood in relation to cultural difference. In theory, therefore, a cross-cultural collaboration should develop just such a comparative perspective. But if a film contains too many compromises between the collaborators, it tends to lose its cross-cultural edge. In recent years, a better alternative seems to have emerged: the simultaneous encouragement of both indigenous and cross-cultural filmmaking. This allows cultural differences to be observed from both positions. Increasingly, too, films are being made that are not only cross-cultural but also cross the divides of gender, age, class and ideology.

Research relationships

This may be an appropriate point to introduce another problem often faced by filmmakers: resolving the tension between trying to present an honest analysis of a situation and avoiding giving offence to those who are part of it. Frequently, the very things that are most revealing of underlying social forces are precisely the things that people do not want shown or discussed. And yet to tailor one's analysis to what will not disturb anyone amounts to self-censorship. But this formulation perhaps represents a false dichotomy, for it suggests that people will always prefer silence to the truth, or will be intolerant of others' views, and that the filmmaker and subjects cannot work through such differences together. Often, too, with the passage of time, a film takes on a new ambiance. It begins to be viewed as a historical document, and even an object of nostalgia. Depending on the time taken between the filming and the film's completion, people's attitudes towards it may shift markedly. Thus, a situation that originally aroused controversy may later be regarded more dispassionately, and people may be quite happy for it to be shown.

Sometimes, however, this doesn't happen, and then the filmmaker must make a moral judgement about whether it is more important for the material to be seen, or to protect people's sensibilities. And it is a matter not only of sensibilities, but of rights. The understanding under which the film was made is crucial to this decision. But rights are not always clear cut and the right course is not always obvious. Who has the right to speak for a community, or defend it? When there has been an injustice, does anyone have the right to prevent it being discussed? And there is the reverse situation, in which the filmmaker realises that even though people may allow something to be filmed, including it in the film may cause distress or damage to some individual. In that case, the filmmaker might decide to leave it out. There are even cases in which someone's life may be endangered by a film. Ethics committees attempt to cover all the eventualities, but they cannot. There are some situations in which a legalistic interpretation of rights is useless, and the filmmaker must ultimately be guided by his or her own conscience and understanding.

The relationship between a filmmaker and those filmed is clearly not a simple one, and it is important to realise that it evolves over time during the making of a film. For that reason, the understanding struck when the filming began will also change, for better or worse. Usually it is for the better, as filmmaker and subjects get to know each other, but tensions can also arise. Having a filmmaker around may look enjoyable at the beginning, but it can wear thin. Filmmakers must judge how not to overstay their welcome. Furthermore, the shift is not always in one direction; there will inevitably be ups and downs in the relationship. Both filmmaker and film subjects should feel they are deriving some benefit from the making of the film even if, as is usually the case, the reasons differ for each of them.

Fieldwork and filming

One question that frequently arises is about how soon filming should begin. Is it better to conduct a period of research and familiarisation before beginning to film, or to begin filming immediately? This is both a practical matter and a matter of principle. The conventional wisdom, based on the typical pattern of anthropological fieldwork followed much later by publication, holds that filming should be introduced only after a period of preliminary research. How can one film what one does not know anything about? This is also the common formula for successful documentary filmmaking: that the research should precede the filming. For one thing it reassures the producers that they won't lose their money. But one consequence of this is that the filmmaker may film no more than what has already been established by the research, so that the filming simply becomes a way of illustrating it. In effect, the filming has contributed nothing in the way of new knowledge. One might well ask: if one makes a film based on what one already knows, what is the point of making it?

A different approach, based on the idea that filming is an integral part of the research process, is that it should begin quite soon, as the filmmaker begins to explore the film's subject matter. Often when this is done the filmmaker realises that the ideas that initially appeared so crucial are of less importance than the new ones they lead to. In this case the act of filming has served as a catalyst to understanding. But if the film is made according to a prefabricated script or treatment, it will tend to be frozen at that earlier stage. There are other reasons too for filming from the start. As first observations become more familiar, they are often taken for granted. They may become so familiar that the filmmaker loses sight of them altogether, discovering the loss only when it is too late. Filming when observations are fresh can cause the filmmaker to film them more perceptively.

Filming from the start can also be a matter of principle. If one introduces a camera after a long period of fieldwork, it tends to alter and even disrupt the nature of the relationships that one has built up, for the filming process necessarily introduces a different mode of behaviour on the part of the filmmaker. One must focus more on one's job and may find it impossible to interact with people as before. Furthermore, filming inevitably means placing a piece of alien equipment between oneself and one's subjects. It may thus be thought preferable, from both a moral and a practical point of view, to introduce the camera early, showing one's subjects straightforwardly what one is doing and allowing the relationships to grow around that.

Filmmaking behaviour

These relationships are also crucially affected by the methods and character of the filming. In the days when filmmaking required massive pieces of equipment, and even later, when it became somewhat less intrusive, the filming process tended to dominate any situation. No wonder documentary filmmakers had to direct people to play their parts like actors. Today, with small video cameras, when technically excellent films can be made by even one person, the intrusion of the technology and the filmmaker can be much reduced. But it is less the technology itself and more the approach of the filmmaker that makes the primary difference. If the filmmaker is constantly calling attention to the filming process, or constantly interfering in things for technical or other reasons, the camera will naturally remain the centre of attention. But if the object is to make films that reflect people's normal lives, it is wise to learn how to work more unobtrusively.

How filmmakers comport themselves is the first consideration. A low-key approach to filming requires an ability to treat the camera not as a problem, but as a trusted companion. This means learning to operate it with a minimum of fuss. It is a little like mastering a musical instrument. Holding the camera steady, for example, is a skill that can be learned by almost anyone. The more experienced one becomes, the more one can operate the controls without thinking, and the more the camera becomes an extension of a way of looking at things and interacting with others. The more comfortable you are with the camera, the more open you can be to what is going on around you.

There are other factors involved in filming that affect how people respond to the camera and that shape the resulting film material. These have partly to do with the filmmaker's individual personality and partly with larger matters of method and style. Is the filmmaker working alone or with others? Does the filmmaker work close to the people being filmed or stand farther back? Is the filming done with a tripod or a hand-held camera? Many of these factors are determined by the genre of the film, its anthropological objectives, or the culture from which the filmmaker comes. But they are also open to choice. For example, to film people's informal interactions and conversations may require staying close to them, hand-holding the camera in order to move easily with them, and using a wide-angle lens so that they don't constantly go out of frame. But this can also be a matter of personal stylistic choice, the filmmaker's own preferred way of seeing the world. Another approach, more interested in relations to space, or to the surrounding environment, might call for a camera on a tripod, framing the world in more formal ways. In both cases it may be difficult to separate the subject matter from the aesthetics of representing it.

Camera modes

The choice of camera style is personal in another sense. It has to do with how the filmmaker relates to other people and what sort of relationship with them the film will ultimately express. This is an integral part of a larger strategy of how the film explores its subject. There are various ways of employing a camera, which could be described as responsive, interactive and constructive. Each has its uses, and each represents not only a different mode of enquiry but a different way of addressing the viewer.

A responsive camera (figure 11.1) is largely reactive, responding to what is occurring in front of it. It looks, explores, but does not interfere, even

11.1 Responsive camera style in *With Morning Hearts*

11.2 Interactive camera style in *The New Boys*

though the filmmaker may be on intimate terms with the subjects. The viewer's perspective here resembles that of the filmmaker, who watches but does not otherwise enter into the event.

An interactive camera (figure 11.2) is quite the reverse. It does intervene, and records its own interaction with the subject. The filmmaker, even if not actually seen, is now pushed more into the forefront of the film, along with the subjects. Such interactions often take the form of conversations or interviews. Clearly, such events would not occur unless provoked or invited by the filmmaker. In a figurative sense, the viewer is now situated farther outside the film, watching the filmmaker at work.

A constructive camera (figure 11.3) presents the viewer with an intervention of a different kind, focused this time on the film images themselves. Through the style of camera work and editing, the images are reprocessed to produce an explicitly interpretive work, based on a concept of the subject or a set of formal conventions. The manipulation of images by the filmmaker is made very obvious. This is a far cry from the realist mode of the other approaches, for here the filmmaker disassembles the subject and reassembles it according to some external logic. In effect, the filming is used not to report on an event but to report on the filmmaker's interpretation or impressions of it. The viewer's position is thus shifted still farther away from the original event and closer to that of the filmmaker's particular consciousness.

11.3 Constructive camera style in *Doon School Chronicles*

One of these modes of camera use may dominate a film, but often a single film employs several modes for different purposes, sometimes with modes merging into one another. It may be difficult, for example, to identify the point at which people who have previously been absorbed in their own affairs begin to involve the filmmaker in their conversations, or at which the filmmaker starts introducing formal elements into the film that will become increasingly pronounced. It may also be difficult to distinguish between formal elements that are part of generic conventions and those that are idiosyncratically those of the filmmaker. For example, if the filmmaker films always from a position close to ground level, is this a cultural choice or a personal one? In the hands of a great filmmaker like Yasujiro Ozu it is evidently both.

There is no good reason why several camera modes may not be used in a single film, provided they appear justified and are not sprung unexpectedly on the audience. For if this happens, the filmmaker will be judged to have lost control of the material or to be indulging personal whims at the expense of the subject and the viewer. Stylistic consistency has much to be said for it, as a guarantee of the coherence of the filmmaker's vision. If there are to be shifts of method, it is wise for the filmmaker to establish these possibilities early in the film. If film viewers do not know the ground rules of the film, they will have difficulty interpreting what they see.

Filming strategies

Anthropological filmmaking can centre on an event such as a ritual, a social institution such as marriage, or even an abstraction such as identity or masculinity. It may look at the role of an individual or the experiences of a large group. In some cases the structure of an event provides the framework for the film to follow. This can lend a degree of predictability to the filming, although sometimes even the people involved are unsure of what will happen next. It is not unusual to go to a place where something is supposed to happen only to be told that it is happening elsewhere, or happened yesterday. The best the filmmaker can do is to get the most reliable information from knowledgeable people and be prepared for other possibilities. Patience and flexibility are both necessary assets in these situations. The filmmaker who is too rigid in his or her expectations is likely to face frustrations and resort to hasty decisions. All too often, filmmakers refuse to film something because it doesn't fit into their plans, only to realise later that something of importance has happened right under their noses. Sometimes an unexpected scene contributes far more to the film than the scene the filmmaker originally had in mind.

There are a number of different strategies for anthropological filmmaking in the field. Some filmmakers will look for certain events or individuals to follow. Others will look for tensions or conflicts that appear to be moving towards some kind of crisis, reasoning that discovering what is at stake will reveal the underlying forces at work. These social dramas, like more formalised events, have a certain predictability to them and, as Gregory Bateson, Victor Turner and others have reasoned, reflect the ways in which communities reconcile fundamental structural divisions that threaten to disrupt them.

Still other filmmakers will try to explore social forces by concentrating on particular themes that express them, either symbolically or in everyday events. This theme-and-variations approach can be especially productive when the tensions never rise to the level of a crisis but remain as undercurrents. It can be equally valuable in exploring less volatile aspects of culture, such as the transmission of knowledge from one group or generation to another, or the ways in which cultural traditions evolve and adapt to change.

One tactic in filming a set of related themes is to note down relevant material that may recur. These may be events the filmmaker has witnessed, or other forms of expression. The filmmaker is then attuned to a specified range of possibilities and is prepared to begin filming when something happens that fits one or another of the target items. As the film progresses, new items will be added and old ones removed, either because enough material about them has now been filmed or because they no longer appear relevant. Since the filmmaker is constantly learning more about the subject, it is quite normal for the priorities to change.

Visual anthropology also offers considerable scope for studying visual culture. We live increasingly in a world of visual images. Anthropological filmmaking can make an important contribution to the understanding of visual cultural forms, since it can show how visual images and visible objects are produced and consumed, as well as their physical appearance. There is also a valuable differential perspective to be gained from using one visual medium to explore another, such as film or video to study still photography, religious iconography or advertising. Here, filming offers anthropology and cultural studies a 'language' particularly suited to its objects of research.

The cinematic triangle

Most anthropological films implicitly involve three separate and reciprocal relationships: (1) between the filmmaker and the viewers, (2) between the filmmaker and the subjects, and (3) between the subjects and the viewers. The last of these obviously involves how the viewers see the subjects, but may also be expressed in the way the people in a film imagine the audience will see them, and how, through the film, they attempt to address them. The first is more like a compact between filmmaker and audience that is established by the genre of the film but also by certain more direct signals from the filmmaker. The genre of the film – whether research filming, a television documentary or a film for teaching – tells us partly what to expect. The filmmaker may then tell us more by establishing a particular style, for example by introducing voice-over commentary, subtitles, inter-titles or still images. A camera style will also be established. The filmmaker may prefer long takes or short ones, close shots or wide shots, movement or stillness, or a distinctive combination of these. The film may observe a convention of creative distance or give the viewer an insight into the filmmaking process. The editing will also create a logic and rhythm. Does the filmmaker prefer smooth-flowing continuity or the use of juxtapositions? Do the images progress from the general to the specific, or vice versa? The point is not that one approach is necessarily better than another; what is important is that viewers sense an intention and intelligence behind the work, and feel they are in good hands.

It is also important for a film to establish the filmmaker's relationship to the people being filmed. This may evolve over the course of the film, but we get early evidence of it in people's behaviour before the camera. Do they appear to be aware of the filmmaker's presence, and if so are they comfortable with it? Do they appear to have been directed? Is there interaction with the filmmaker? Does the filmmaker stay close to them or film from far away, as if from an observation post? The manner of filming embodies an attitude towards the subject.

It also embodies the filmmaker's attitude towards the viewer. Earlier styles of documentary encoded a theatrical convention of distance between the work and the audience. The film was a performance prepared for their consumption. How it was produced was a professional secret, and this mystery was part of its power. Like fiction films, most documentaries assumed an Olympian view of their subjects. Human beings were observed and recorded, but the eye observing them remained unacknowledged and unseen, both by the audience and, apparently, by the subjects as well. If someone looked at the camera, that shot was cut out. This was a far cry from the novel, in which authors frequently confided their thoughts and methods to the reader. Documentaries made since the 1960s, however, have begun to treat the camera more like a personal writing instrument, although this shift has yet to affect much television production. In most films, but particularly in anthropological films, the acknowledgement within the film of the filmmaker's situation in the field becomes an important element in allowing us to interpret accurately what we see.

Modes of reflexivity

The disclosure of the filmmaking process is not a single act but may be distributed through many aspects of the film. It need not take the form of overt self-reflexivity – in itself often unreliable, because it can never be wholly disinterested. As filmmaking becomes a more personal and less industrial process, we can learn a great deal from the filmmaker's apparent behaviour. A highly intrusive camera, creating signs of resentment, not only tells us about the insensitivity of the filmmaker but also that what we see is produced under a kind of duress. A camera that moves in certain ways and follows certain details tells us much about the particular interests of the filmmaker. It has often been argued that anthropological films should be accompanied by written notes that describe the field situation and fill in much of the missing ethnographic detail. This may be valuable for teaching, but it should not become a crutch that the film depends upon. For in that case, anthropological filmmakers may take it as an invitation to produce obscure or unintelligible work.

Reflexivity essentially means contextualising the content of a film by revealing aspects of its production. Makers of anthropological films should distinguish between two kinds of reflexivity. One kind is explicit, making the conditions of filming more apparent. This may mean including footage of interactions between filmmaker and subjects, showing the subjects' acknowledgement of the filmmaking situation, providing a voice-over commentary and so on. It also means providing a sufficiently rich context for the events shown to make them understandable in interpersonal and cultural terms. A more implicit kind of reflexivity also permeates most films, to which viewers should be sensitive. It is the stamp of the filmmaker's research interests and personal involvement. It can be read in a multitude of signs in how the film has been made, from the camera work to the editing, to the responses of people on the screen. It is an expression of the filmmaker's living presence in the film.

The experiences of individuals

If the filmmaker's role is embodied in this way, what about that of the film's subjects, and the viewer? The subjects are clearly embodied in a physical sense, because it is their existence that has generated the images on the screen. The camera also registers the outward expression of their emotions and, through their words, signs of their intellectual life. But these signs must be interpreted by viewers and, in a sense, made their own. The viewer becomes a collaborator in the creation of the film's meaning. In anthropological films this can be complicated by cultural differences, since the signs (most obviously of language) may vary from one society to another. Filmmakers then must often rely on the context to clarify these meanings, or provide explanations by other means. But one of the great assets of anthropological film as opposed to writing is its ability to reach across cultural boundaries through those aspects of life that are common to many societies. Viewers may not be able to understand another language, but they can recognise many situations in other people's lives and respond to them. The better the film contextualises these situations, the better the viewer can interpret them in culturally appropriate ways.

Although films cannot get inside another person's mind or emotions, they can, by cinematic means, communicate aspects of their subjective experience. They do this partly by paying close attention to the expressions, movements and responses of individuals, and partly by following narratives in their lives. Viewers, through a process of identification, begin to make connections between the behaviour on the screen and their own past experiences. Films rarely adopt the actual visual perspectives of their protagonists. Rather, figuratively and literally, they look over their shoulders, staying close to them through different events. Viewers come to understand others' feelings not by experiencing them directly but by vicariously sharing their social interactions and physical surroundings.

In the creation of subjective identification, narrative has a central role. Because of this, it has great potential for contributing to anthropological understanding, a potential more often employed in anthropological filmmaking than in anthropological writing. Narratives occur in every culture and provide an important mechanism for cross-cultural understanding. They have explanatory power, for they can demonstrate patterns of cause and effect. By observing how something happens, we can often come to understand why it happens. Perhaps more importantly, narratives of individual lives provide a way of leading us imaginatively through the experiences of others in societies different from our own. In the process we encounter the complexity of social forces and the ways in which individuals are affected by them. Narratives of social interaction also provide a framework for observing how people inhabit their physical environment – how they use it, alter it and experience it in sensory terms.

Lastly, the filmmaker needs to take account of how the people portrayed in an anthropological film see themselves, for they are, by right, its first audience. They are involved in it both personally and as disproportionately exposed representatives of their communities. Films can provoke a wide range of responses, many of them unpredictable. Like still photographs, they can elicit memories, emotions and tacit cultural knowledge. People's responses to the films made about them can also reveal much about how they see themselves. Filmmakers should be sensitive to these reactions, even as they resist making only the films that people would like them to make. The responses will also undoubtedly change over time. Many of the cultural and intellectual assumptions clinging to a film will drop away and it may come to be valued less for its interpretation than for the physical reality it has captured. In a similar way, anthropologists may well make use of old films in new ways. The films we make today become future sources of documentary evidence and evidence of the ideas, prejudices and interests of their times.

Documentary and its doubles

I N his 1991 book *Musical Elaborations* Edward Said argued that the playing of Western classical music had ceased to be connected to ordinary life. It had become an 'extreme occasion' performed almost exclusively by professionals in the concert hall and recording studio. New works by contemporary composers were no longer eagerly awaited by the public. Concerts were now largely frozen in the orchestral and operatic repertoires of the eighteenth and nineteenth centuries. Music education was perfunctory in schools and few people could play a musical instrument. Classical music had been captured, polished and repackaged by the corporate world and disconnected from people's lives.[1]

Said makes no mention of documentary film, but it could be said to have had a similar history. Documentary began by showing ordinary things, looking at what was exotic in the ordinary and, ranging further afield, ordinary in the exotic. This curiosity about the world has gradually been replaced by productions in which even the most arcane subjects are enveloped in a knowing professionalism. Today, perhaps because of the widespread ease with which anyone can make video recordings, directors of documentaries strive increasingly to make films that distance themselves from the ordinary, seeking out the unusual or extreme and marshalling an intimidating repertoire of 'production values'.

The early films of the silent era were essentially pictures of whatever took the camera operator's interest – the *actualités* of the Lumière Company, the chronophotographic films of Otto Anschütz and Georges Demeny, the newsreels of Dziga Vertov, the expedition films of travellers. For audiences they held a fascination similar to that which had greeted still photography some sixty years earlier. But in addition to offering the realism of photography, they offered another, almost unthinkable possibility: that one could capture the experience of observing something happening in some other time and place. The act of looking could now be fixed and endlessly replayed. Although this was astonishing enough in itself, for some it opened up a further possibility. Tolstoy prophesied that it would make the invention of stories unnecessary because stories of people's actual lives could now be recorded on film (Leacock, 1975: 147).

The motion picture emerged as one of the most successful new tech-nologies of the 1890s. It was limited, however, to single shots of less than a minute and was widely considered little more than a commercial novelty. Despite this, the journeying cinematographers of the Lumière Company soon filmed a wide range of subjects from all over the world. In the process, they developed considerable sophistication in selecting and framing events. Although their cameras recorded some notable historical occasions, such as the coronation of Tsar Nicholas II, most of their films were about ordinary people engaged in everyday activities.

Running through most of the Lumière films is an evident interest not only in specific events but also more generally in *how things look*; for it was this phantom vision, seen through film, that was the medium's magical attraction, as had also been true of still photography in its early days. How otherwise to explain the many films made of street scenes, or people playing games, or shots made from moving vehicles, all of which would have been familiar experiences to most people of the time? No particular artistic purpose motivated the Lumière Company in documenting these scenes, although some of the Lumière camera operators may have had higher ambitions. Rather, it was what people would pay to see. And yet many of these films are now profoundly moving glimpses of the past, as well as being important historical records. A typical colonial film made in French Indochina shows two well dressed European women throwing *sapèques* – small coins – to a crowd of children, who scrabble for them in the foreground: a telling image of colonialism. The children are after something manifestly real and desirable, and we must assume that it was something equally attractive in the grain of reality that made audiences want to see scenes like this (figure 12.1).

The early films were neither definitively fiction nor nonfiction. Although some Lumière films recorded public events, many showed acted-out episodes or other activities obviously staged for the camera. In one film, three children busily eat grapes; in another, a man is run down by a car and magically resur-rected. A group of men pretend to play *pétanque* and a gardener is watered by his own hose. Considering the time and effort required to set up a camera, it is not surprising that most of these early scenes were performances specific-ally enacted for the cinematographer.

Yet among them are other films that did not require a performance. These are records of routine matters such as the arrival of a train (the subject of a famous Lumière film, a train arriving at La Ciotat station), scenes of everyday life on city streets, and views of industry and commerce. Even so, it is often difficult to distinguish between their fictional and nonfictional elements, for it depends on how we regard them. Writing of the Lumière film of a boy tricking a gardener into spraying himself with his own hose, the critic Dai Vaughan (1999: 6) asks, 'Is this a fiction film or simply a filmed fiction?' At one level it takes very little imagination to turn almost any film,

12.1 Throwing coins to children in French Indochina c. 1899

including a fiction film, into a documentary record of its own making. One has only to switch from viewing it as signifying something other than what it records to signifying *only* what it records (Vaughan, 1999: 84–6). An unconvincing film forces us almost automatically to regard it from this second, documentary perspective.

Virtually all films, apart from animated films and films with special effects, record events that occurred before a camera, whether acted or not. But it would be oversimplifying matters to say that there are no qualitative differences among them. Even if actors are performing, the landscape behind them is not; nor (as early viewers noticed) are the leaves on the trees, nor probably many of the bystanders. In a number of the Lumière films, two or three events are occurring simultaneously at different distances from the camera, often in different parts of the frame (see figure 8.1).[2] In *Enfants jouant aux billes*, a film of children playing marbles (figure 12.2), a group of boys have clearly been asked, or told, or cajoled, to perform. But standing on a platform behind them are other children, who are fidgeting as they watch and wait. What is their role? Did they simply turn up? They apparently belong to a variety of social classes. One well dressed boy is carrying his satchel, perhaps on his way to school. Another is barefoot and dressed in overalls. In the far

12.2 Children playing marbles in a Lumière film of 1896

distance a woman walks across the scene and turns away, oblivious of the camera and intent on her own affairs.

Thus documentary began. Its attraction lay in the fascination of watching something that had happened in the past as if it were happening freshly in the present. Through film one could travel backwards in time or across the world. Early photography had held a similar attraction, presenting commonly seen things in a new form: buildings, implements, faces, rural and urban scenes, and individuals in all walks of life. One of the early genres of still photography was a cataloguing of 'petits métiers' – images of knife-grinders, chimney sweeps and street vendors. Film added a new dimension to these images. It was not just the effect of motion or the passing of time that made film appear extraordinary but the uncanny emanation of life being lived, however familiar or unfamiliar the locale. It lay in the sensation that, like oneself, people elsewhere were experiencing their own lives. This sense of other realities was perhaps more arresting then than it is now. Somewhere boats were being loaded, children were playing, crowds were gathering and crossing streets, horses and streetcars were passing by. Behind them were their shops and houses, the fields or the sea. It was like a telescope trained on the world, or memories come to life. A spiritual wound had somehow been opened, for films brought to the viewer, with a fresh poignancy, the self-awareness and vulnerability of others.

160

If there was at the beginning something both painful and fascinating in this new intimacy, it would soon be softened and contained by a system of *quotation*. Documentary films would begin to treat images not as scenes of actual events but as cinematic illustrations of them. Documentary films would begin a retreat from the present moment and begin approaching their subjects in increasingly detached, professionalised and symbolic ways. Although claiming to be 'documentary', most nonfiction films demonstrated a shift away from the documentation of events to the construction of reports about them, the characteristic work of educators and journalists. For some years to come, the qualities of immediacy and informality that had once defined documentary films would, ironically, find refuge in fiction films. And if a fiction film came a little too close to reality, it could always be explained away as a work of the imagination.

Science played a part in this process of distancing. The late nineteenth and early twentieth century was a time of scientific heroes. Naturalists, ethnologists, biologists and physicists made forays into the unknown and reported back to their colleagues and the public. Their reports appeared in journal articles and speeches to scientific societies, and increasingly in the popular form of lantern slide lectures. It wasn't long before films replaced the lantern slides. At Melbourne Town Hall in 1902, Sir Walter Baldwin Spencer projected films from his 1901 expedition to Central Australia to raise money for further expeditions. When sound films arrived in 1928, the pattern was already set for the narrated documentary film. Here an authoritative voice delivered a commentary over a series of representative images. Often the images served as little more than a background to the text and provided meagre evidence for what was claimed by the narration. This pattern continues today in cultural television programmes, although today's presenters are more likely to be on the screen than off it.

This oblique use of images had been anticipated by newspapers and popular journals, in which the journalist functioned as an intermediary between a distant event and the public. When engravings and photographs began to be printed along with the text, newspapers and journals were able to illustrate the event pictorially, but only very selectively. By the time newsreels came along, the idea was firmly established that an image was to be taken as a sign of something rather than as a way of seeing it. The narrator's words gave the details, while the image gave the general category it represented. There were some dramatic exceptions – such as the burning of the *Hindenburg* airship in 1937, Joe Louis's knockout of Max Schmeling in 1938, the Kennedy assassination in 1963 – but otherwise the passing parade of news images remained more or less unchanged: a political meeting, a war or train disaster, a sports event. Reporters quickly learned to get the symbolic shot that the story required, since anything more enterprising would probably be discarded.

FLAHERTY AND GRIERSON

Although documentary films had existed for more than two decades, documentary cinema is generally dated from the release of Robert Flaherty's *Nanook of the North*, in 1922. There had been travel films before, and Flaherty himself had made such a film in the Arctic before making *Nanook*. It was destroyed by fire, supposedly from a cigarette that Flaherty dropped in the cutting room. Looking back, Flaherty (1950: 12) described it as an embarrassing series of disconnected shots, not unlike those in other travel films. 'It was utterly inept, simply a scene of this and a scene of that, no relation, no thread of a story or continuity whatever.' He realised he had failed to come to grips with his subject, perhaps assuming that his audience would have only a passing interest in it. His next film would require a closer, more personal approach. He already had ten years of experience travelling and surveying in the Arctic. 'I had learned to explore', he said, but 'I had not learned to reveal'.[3]

The new approach was both more intimate and more rehearsed. It focused on everyday activities but knitted them together in a story of a family confronting a series of daily tasks and hazards. This meant setting up some scenes and devising others, like the famous walrus hunt, which Flaherty filmed in collaboration with his Inuit subjects. If *Nanook* reflected a romantic and essentially late-Victorian world view, it also achieved something new. It produced the first filmic ethno-biography and the first rounded portrait of daily life in a society remote from the viewers' experience. It was based on typical and often routine events in Inuit lives. For all its contrivances, it recorded a broad range of important activities and linked them to personal interactions. Few filmmakers had tried to do anything like this before, and Flaherty had done it far more effectively than they had.[4]

Almost no one tried to imitate Flaherty's working method, although *Nanook* undoubtedly encouraged the production of travel films and the vogue for filming in exotic places. His approach was perhaps too demanding and required too much time. There were the popular films made by the wife and husband team Osa and Martin Johnson in Africa, but these celebrated the filmmakers more than their subjects. In 1925 Ernest Schoedsack and Merian C. Cooper released their film *Grass*, bearing the subtitle *A Nation's Battle for Life*, its slender story-line about a father and son possibly inspired by Flaherty's creation of a family group in *Nanook*.[5] This was tacked on to remarkable footage of a migration by the Bakhtiari of Iran from their winter quarters in the western foothills adjoining the Khuzestan plain to their traditional high summer pastures in the Zagros mountains. According to some accounts, the footage was originally shot to be background material for a film that was never made.[6] But even if so, it produced a document of great power and detail, as the herders – men, women, children and their animals – crossed rivers and climbed through snow-covered passes.

If Cooper and Schoedsack had greater ambitions, one wonders what they were. The answer is perhaps made clearer by their next film, *Chang* (1927). By this time documentaries had begun to sink under the weight of embellishments and extra plot-lines designed to appeal to audiences used to fiction films. Rather than building on the strengths of documentary, producers seemed to be trying to bypass them. The most dramatic event in *Chang*, a conflict between wild elephants and Lao villagers, is obscured by faked scenes and pretentious dialogue.

These excesses were anathema to John Grierson when he founded the British documentary movement a few years later. He had praised Flaherty's early films but found *Man of Aran* (1934) escapist and romantic. As for the more fictional *Elephant Boy* (1937), co-directed by Flaherty and Zoltan Korda, he said, 'the synthetic spectacle of studio camp scenes and West End voices brings the film at every turn to an artificial, different plane' (see Hardy, 1946: 204). Grierson had another conception of documentary and its mission. The movement began with a resounding commitment to put into practice the possibilities that fiction films had long ignored – as Grierson put it, 'to send our creators back to fact' (Hardy, 1946: 142). He declared that the subjects of documentary lay close at hand in 'this English life of ours' – not the Englishness of village greens and country lanes but 'the new fact of industry and commerce and plenty and poverty' (Hardy, 1946: 141–2). 'We have to build on the actual. Our capital comes from those whose only interest is in the actual. The medium itself insists on the actual. There we must build or be damned' (Hardy, 1946: 140).

But for Grierson 'the actual' quickly became secondary. Some years later he wrote: 'The British documentary group began not so much in affection for film *per se* as in affection for national education. If I am to be counted as the founder and leader of the movement, its origins certainly lay in socio-logical rather than aesthetic aims' (Hardy, 1946: 207). Here, as in many of his pronouncements, Grierson was hedging a little. By claiming education and sociology as his beacons, his allegiance to the actual had already slipped a notch. His embracing of sociology was also dubious, for the films that were made under his aegis were more ideological than sociological. The true alter-native to the 'aesthetic' would not have been to produce films for national education but films that looked more extensively at individual people's lives. By this standard – however brilliant many of the Grierson-era films were in other respects – most failed.

What complicates the picture is that Grierson himself seems to have been aware of the trap of 'mistaking the phenomenon for the thing itself' – in other words, mistaking the sign for its referent, the general concept for the concrete instance: what he termed 'the actual' (Hardy, 1946: 201). Yet, in the end, he couldn't resist doing so himself, constantly looking for images to represent universal qualities. He described shooting his film *Drifters* (1929)

12.3 The worker as hero in *Shipyard*, a British film of 1935

in these terms: 'Image for this, image for that. For the settling of darkness, not darkness itself, but flocks of birds silhouetted against the sky. [...] For the long drift in the night, not the ship, not the sea itself, but the dark mystery of the underwater' (Hardy, 1946: 136). This emblematic approach was consistent with his admiration for Sergei Eisenstein's films, in which images were stripped down to their most elemental meanings and deployed like the words in a poem. But although Grierson often praised poetry, he was more moralist than poet. The films made under his influence typically celebrated workers as national and class heroes (figure 12.3).

Grierson's other writings during this period are similarly equivocal, for he skirts around the question of what documentary cinema is. This is understandable when he is trying to praise Flaherty and at the same time scold him for his 'escapism, a wan and distant eye, which tends in lesser hands to sentimentalism' (Hardy, 1946: 148). But when he comes to writing a manifesto for documentary, the most he can come up with is to say, blandly, 'we believe in the cinema's capacity for getting around, for observing and selecting from life itself' (Hardy, 1946: 146). He acknowledges the importance of observing actual events, but this is almost always overlaid by a call for film to convey a message about 'the essentially co-operative or mass nature of society' (Hardy, 1946: 149). In contrast to studio production, all he can claim for documentary is that 'the original (or native) actor, and the original (or native) scene, are better guides to a screen interpretation of the modern world. They give cinema a greater fund of material' (Hardy, 1946: 147).

What have been the consequences of this approach for the development of documentary? Grierson later admitted that, in his view, 'the documentary idea was not basically a film idea at all, and the film treatment it inspired only an incidental aspect of it. The medium happened to be the most convenient and exciting available to us. The idea itself, on the other hand, was a new idea for public education' (Hardy, 1946: 250). For many of the filmmakers who worked with him, the goal was equally tangential, less about exploring actual events than about the aesthetic possibilities of the medium. Films made under Grierson's patronage at the GPO Film Unit were frequently daring in their use of images and sounds. Given the filmmakers' often unexciting assignments, their films perhaps had to be, for whatever else they did, they had to promote in some way the activities of the British postal service. Sometimes this could be stretched to include telecommunications more broadly, as in *Weather Forecast* (1934), or international air services, as in *Air Post* (1934). Other topics were, if anything, even less promising. *The Coming of the Dial* (1933) is about the shift to dial telephones. Unexpectedly, it is one of the most attractive and innovative films of the period.

Grierson gave free rein to his team of young directors to try anything so long as it conveyed important messages with energy and flair. Like Grierson himself, many of the filmmakers were admirers of Soviet avant-garde cinema, especially the films of Eisenstein and Victor Turin, which had been circulated through British cine clubs. Their experiments accordingly made much use of dramatic shot juxtapositions, dynamic camera angles and rhythmic variations in editing. Yet they tended to ignore the fact that there was another side to Soviet cinema, a commitment to observing ordinary people's experiences, particularly in the work of Vertov, who had initiated a more down-to-earth approach under the heading of *Kino-Nedelya* and later *Kino-Pravda*. These films of everyday life were closer in spirit to what the Lumière brothers had called *actualités*. The few Grierson-sponsored films that came close, such as *Housing Problems* (1935), were exceptions.

A further influence on British documentary was the abstract style of the 'city symphonies', a type of film that had begun to be made throughout Europe in the 1920s. Partly inspired by Soviet cinema, these films orchestrated what Vertov called 'fragments of actuality' into impressionistic portraits of city life. Walter Ruttmann's *Berlin: The Symphony of a Great City* (1927) epitomised the genre, which included Alberto Cavalcanti's *Rien que les heures* (1926) and Jean Vigo's *À propos de Nice* (1930). Sound, which Eisenstein had long advocated using in counterpoint to images, became another area of experimentation, and many of the GPO Film Unit productions played with it in novel ways. Grierson had been impressed by Cavalcanti's experiments with sound and soon invited him to England to join his group. GPO productions like *Coal Face* (1935) made use of complex layers of sound; others, such as *Night Mail* (1936), for which Cavalcanti directed the sound, employed a similar mix of spoken verse, standard commentary and music by Benjamin Britten.

Despite the high spirits motivating much of this filmmaking, there remained a stern imperative. The films had to educate and promote, and if possible change attitudes. They also had to show the workers of the postal service (and later, other government and non-government agencies) in the best light. This was not only demanded by the sponsors but coincided with Grierson's eagerness to celebrate the heroism of working people. The result was most often a modernist display of images and sounds overlaid by a more conventional spoken commentary. This was often didactic and condescending in tone, as if addressed to children. At its worst, it had the air of the upper classes instructing the lower, in accents redolent of a public school education.

There were a few significant exceptions, and they were acknowledged by Grierson as important at the time. Cavalcanti's *Coal Face* and Basil Wright's *The Song of Ceylon* (1934) stood out from the rest, not least for challenging the politics of their sponsors. The most radical film was *Housing Problems*, made for the Gas Light and Coke Company. In place of spoken commentary and idealised images, the directors, Edgar Anstey and Arthur Elton, took the unusual step of asking slum-dwellers to speak to the camera in their own homes. This required using lights and synchronous sound – at the time a technically demanding task if attempted outside a film studio. Perhaps predictably, the result is a series of stiff, rehearsed statements, but the film still communicates a vivid sense of being present at a barely controlled event. The very self-consciousness and earnestness of the protagonists reinforces the effect. As Grierson later said, 'It is not so well made [...] but something speaks within it that touches the conscience' (Hardy, 1946: 216).

The brilliance of some of the Grierson-era films tends to obscure a more troubling truth. This is not that they were condescending or propagandistic, nor even that they were fundamentally conservative and romantic in spirit. It is rather that, in order to advance the cause of documentary, the movement had abandoned the one quality that had made the documentary idea extraordinary: the unique opportunity it gave, made possible by film, to witness events unfolding in another time and place. Film technology had produced a completely new experiential phenomenon. It was this that had made the Lumière films and *Nanook of the North* so revolutionary. But in response to the requirements of sponsors, and for his own ideological reasons, Grierson had moved decisively away from documentary films witnessing events towards a new kind of synthesis. He called it 'the creative treatment of actuality' (Hardy, 1946: 13).

The shift took place at two levels. Grierson was always more interested in images as exemplars of values than in their specificity of person or place. He wanted the films to reflect contemporary Britain, but in a general sense.

For their part, many of his directors were more interested in the expressive potential of film than its connection to reality. Basil Wright, one of the younger members of the group, later said in interview, 'We were deeply involved, profoundly involved, in experimenting in the use of the film medium' (Levin, 1971: 52). Grierson drew a line between what he called the realists and the 'aesthetes'. His aim was to harness both groups to 'public instruction'. The realists were useful because they were interested in filming outside the studio. As for the aesthetes, Grierson later wrote: 'We had always the good sense to use the aesthetes. We did so because we liked them and because we needed them' (Hardy, 1946: 249).

In some cases the realist and the aesthete could be found in the same person. This was probably more common among American documentary filmmakers than British. Their films used poetic conventions but made more use of archival material than their British counterparts. They addressed social and conservation issues and, like the British films, were largely produced under government auspices. Pare Lorentz, in both *The Plow That Broke the Plains* (1936) and *The River* (1938), combined new and newsreel footage in a dramatic collage, accompanied by a poetic commentary and the music of Virgil Thomson. *The City* (1939), directed by Ralph Steiner and Willard Van Dyke, which also focused on environmental matters, had a musical score by Aaron Copland. *The March of Time* newsreels, beginning in 1935, used a similar diversity of materials, although for want of documentary footage increasingly resorted to scripted re-enactments.

The technical limitations of filming in the 1930s meant that, in practice, most apparently spontaneous indoor scenes were carefully rehearsed. The techniques for producing them were borrowed from fiction film production – from the 'studio' that Grierson abhorred. Although ordinary people were the subjects, the films required them to become actors. It was decided before each scene what they would say or do, and the director then directed them to do it. If this went badly there would be repeated takes until they performed to the director's satisfaction. Although the recording of synchronous dialogue was standard procedure in fiction films in the 1930s, it was very rare in nonfiction films. Artificial lighting was required in both cases for interior scenes because of the low sensitivity of film stocks. To get the effect of postal workers sorting letters on a moving train in *Night Mail*, the directors had to have the actors sway slightly as they worked in a studio-lit postal carriage. Studio techniques thus gradually invaded documentary films, shifting documentary towards the industrial model of fiction film production, with its separation of duties among producers, directors, editors, lighting experts, cinematographers, sound engineers and other technical staff.

Filmmakers working on their own, like most of the Lumière camera operators – or Flaherty, or even a pair like Schoedsack and Cooper – could no longer, it seemed, produce a documentary film. British documentary production was increasingly conceived as a group effort. When Flaherty made *Man of Aran* (1934), more than ten people were involved in its production. Part of the reason for this was the desire of directors to give their films the look and status of studio productions, with the hope of showing them in cinemas. A number of Grierson-era films such as *Night Mail*, *The Song of Ceylon* and *Man of Aran* did in fact get a theatrical release, although Grierson continued to insist that a much larger audience for documentary existed outside the cinemas, in schools and film clubs and the like.

One of the primary impulses that inspired the Grierson-era documentaries was to generalise human experience in the interests of British self-respect and solidarity. This goal became even more urgent during the Second World War. In a nation divided by class and regional differences, Grierson sought to express common values: modesty, hard work, reliability, decency and heroism. Films that celebrated the ordinary worker, whether blue or white collar, would instil pride and good citizenship. There was also the wider international goal of celebrating the benefits of empire, implied in *The King's Stamp* (1935), about the history of stamps and George V's collection, and in *Air Post*, about intercontinental postal links. Writing in the dark days of the war, Grierson said, 'Our job specifically was to wake the heart and the will' (see Hardy, 1946: 250).

There were attempts to make the films more personal through the introduction of exemplary characters – a prudent clerk in *John Atkins Saves Up* (1934), about the postal savings bank, the two couples of *Pett and Pott* (1934), a genial fisherman in *North Sea* (1938) – but these figures were either composite creations, sometimes played by members of the film crew, or people chosen for their typicality. Whatever individuality they possessed was subordinated to their role as models.

Would it have been possible, given the resources at hand, to follow the lives of individuals more fully and credibly? Undoubtedly the lack of synchronous sound and the cumbersome cameras of the time would have made it difficult, but not impossible. Yet it seems there was little interest in doing so. The precise detail of place and character seen in fiction films was not carried over into documentary, although the studio technology was. Perhaps no 'ordinary' person was considered sufficiently interesting to warrant it. There was also an ideological objection. As Grierson put it, 'we believed, like the Russians, that you should use individuals in your film in a not exactly dehumanised way but a sort of symbolic way' (see Sussex, 1975: 18).

Forty years later, Colin Young was to write:

> In the field of documentation you would think there would be an irresistible urge to do with the camera what only the camera can do, that which even the fastest speed writer or stenographer in the field could never do – record actuality in a form which when replayed, allows a viewer elsewhere to have a sense of experiencing the event. (Young, 1975: 70)

But that was not what British documentary filmmaking was all about. It would take another generation for that idea to re-emerge.

COUNTERPOINTS

British filmmaking in this period established a conception of the documentary that would dominate the genre for decades to come. Its influence can be seen in quite a number of British fiction films of the 1940s and 1950s, such as *A Matter of Life and Death* (1946), *The Blue Lamp* (1950) and *The Galloping Major* (1951). These open with deliberately 'documentary' material that leads into the story. The Griersonian style was apparently pervasive. Yet several earlier nonfiction productions, such as *Nanook of the North*, *Grass* and Vertov's *Kino-Pravda* (1922–5), as well as several films made not much later, such as Humphrey Jennings's *Fires Were Started* (1943) and Georges Rouquier's *Farrebique* (1946), suggest that alternative approaches were available, had the prevailing film culture encouraged them. Paradoxically, it was not documentary filmmakers but fiction film directors like Luchino Visconti, Vittorio De Sica and Roberto Rossellini who would soon be chronicling the lives of ordinary people in a realist style using non-professional actors. Films like *Shoeshine* (1946) and *La Terra Trema* (1948) (figure 5.4, p. 72) came closer to observing the everyday experiences of people than most documentary films had done. Documentaries tended to use fragments of reality to convey general truths; these filmmakers looked to specific human stories to do so.

The idea of the documentary as a compilation of fragments, which had developed with the 'city symphonies' and avant-garde films of the 1920s, was intensified in the war years in numerous propaganda films such as the *Why We Fight* series (1942–5) produced by the US War Department. It was discovered that a fragment of film, put in the right context, could be made to mean almost anything. Even enemy propaganda films were found useful for this and were mined for footage. At the same time, there were stirrings of resistance and dissatisfaction among filmmakers. The more blatant examples of propaganda had made the hollowness of this sort of manipulation apparent. Couldn't documentary footage be used in a different way, as had been done briefly in *Housing Problems*? Instead of heightening reality, couldn't one capture more modestly what an observer would have seen?

There are intimations of this approach in the wartime films of Humphrey Jennings and John Huston. In Jennings's *Fires Were Started* there are informal scenes among the firemen that have the unrehearsed qualities of everyday life. Was it simply that Jennings was more skilled at directing non-professional actors, or did he want something more recognisably spontaneous to break through? Writing about changes that the Industrial Revolution had wrought on English society, Jennings had asked, 'was not this the period of the repression of the clear imaginative vision in ordinary folk?' (see Lovell and Hillier, 1972: 64). His sense of the importance of the individual as well as the mass is a continuing undercurrent in his films. The moments that reveal this are often fleeting but they stand out as unexpected interventions in the cinema of the time, like his avoidance of spoken commentary in many of his films. They are consistent with certain other elements in his treatment of reality: the portrayal of firemen actually fighting the fires and the informal shots of survivors surveying the wreckage. There is little attempt to exaggerate the drama or pathos of what we see. Jennings's fresh approach was picked up by the next generation of British documentary filmmakers in such films as Lindsay Anderson and Guy Brenton's *Thursday's Children* (1954) and the films of the Free Cinema movement, such as Karel Reisz and Tony Richardson's *Momma Don't Allow* (1956) and Karel Reisz's *We Are the Lambeth Boys* (1959).

In the United States, a similar challenge to wartime propaganda appeared in John Huston's *Let There Be Light* (1946). The film was banned by the War Department for showing too explicitly the traumatic effects of warfare on ordinary soldiers, although Huston viewed the film as celebrating their powers of recovery. Huston had recorded the responses of the men during group therapy sessions in an army psychiatric hospital. Their suffering was harrowing. The film was suppressed because it was thought to undermine the war effort, but it is possible to read the reaction as a more deeply held suspicion of documentary itself. Documentary films have the potential to reveal secrets, create official embarrassment and – to some, an equally worrying possibility – introduce ambiguity and doubt.

When a film is troubling or shocking, a predictable response is to withdraw from it, as from the sight of a wound. One solution is to ban the offending film, but this is often made unnecessary by self-censorship. Many producers instinctively avoid looking too closely at their subjects, relying instead on stereotypes and generalities, even though they must, at the same time, balance this caution against the advantages of choosing topics attractive to audiences. The more sensational the topic, the greater is the advantage, but also the risk. There may be other reasons for retreating from reality, such as a romantic attraction to the past or the exotic. This was the accusation that Grierson levelled against Flaherty when he wrote that 'he is of a persuasion that does not easily come to grips with the more modern factors of civilisation' (Hardy, 1946: 142). Yet in the documentary style that Grierson himself fostered, and in his need to win government sponsorship, there was just such a tendency to promote a heroic vision of society.

Most documentary filmmakers experience the pull of opposing forces: the desire to explore a subject honestly against the desire to confirm their preconceptions. They will often trade off some of the former for the latter, avoiding the most unsettling aspects of a subject by idealising it, generalising it or burying it in explanation. The compromise may also be justified on the grounds of propriety or the sponsor's demands. Filmmakers thus frequently find themselves torn between what they actually see and what they are allowed to show.

Very few films actually address the dilemma itself. Two that have done so, by very different means, are Luis Buñuel's *Land without Bread* (1932) and Alain Resnais's *Night and Fog* (1956). *Land without Bread* is a perverse parody of 'educational' and travel films. Instead of providing the expected edifying lecture, it sets out to shock the audience. We see grotesque images of an impoverished Spanish village, accompanied by the sounds of Brahms' Fourth Symphony and an outrageous commentary. Villagers shiver miserably with fever and a donkey is stung to death by a swarm of bees. Buñuel's intention is to goad us into realising that most films do just the opposite. They keep the world at a comfortable distance by reducing it to disconnected images and a litany of words. What is more, they are unreliable as evidence. To underline this, *Land without Bread* is full of demonstrable lies.

Resnais's *Night and Fog* approaches the problem differently. The film is about the Nazi death camps, seen through the double perspective of black and white footage shot in the camps and colour footage shot a decade or more later, with a deserted camp now rusting and overgrown with grass and weeds. The film shows two realities, each equally vivid, suggesting how easily a particular reality can be covered over and forgotten. There is a sinister quality in the way the later camera observes the tranquil scenes of former horror. The film becomes a metaphor for the difficulty of looking at any subject from a single 'true' perspective, and the particular hazards of attempting this on film. In a later film, *Shoah* (1985), Claude Lanzmann takes up the same theme of an elusive reality.

How, then, are we to distinguish documentary films from their doubles, the innumerable films that do little more than circle around their subjects? Since all films are constructions, what disqualifies a film from its claim to documentary value – or to put it another way, as Dai Vaughan (1999: 55) does, at what point does a 'film as record' cease to 'survive its metamorphosis into language'? One answer would be, the point at which it becomes more interested in its own devices than its subject. Another would be, the point at which the balance of the film shifts from trying to show us something to insisting on its meaning. All films have a point of view, so this is not the issue. What matters is their attitude to the audience. How much are we allowed to see? As Colin Young (1975: 74) points out, in some films the filmmaker directs the subject; in others, 'the subject directs the filmmaker'.

The early Lumière film of two women throwing coins to a crowd of children can be read either as colonial largesse or as colonial oppression (figure 12.1). The way in which the film is made does not dictate one reading, however objectionable the scene may appear to modern eyes. One may glimpse the probable intention of a shot if it is framed within the context of a particular sequence of shots, but this shot, standing alone, remains ambiguous. By the same token, a shot stripped of any complexity by its framing or brevity – an arm raised, or seagulls against the sky – easily becomes little more than an instrument of meaning. Documentary begins to stutter and fade when it uses images like this. Grierson provides a further illustration of the process in his description of making *Drifters*: 'By fortune a whale came along side to clean the nets. I used it for more than a whale. I used it for a ponderous symbol of all that tumbled and laboured on that wild morning' (Hardy, 1946: 137).

Few documentaries are as ambiguous as the early Lumière films, nor do we expect them to be. Filmmakers have reasons for addressing certain subjects and for wanting to make films about them. They convey these interests through their choice and arrangement of material. But, ideally, their films provide sufficient evidence to support the analysis they are making, not mere fragments presented out of context. As well, they possess a 'voice' that establishes the filmmaker's position in relation to both the subject and the audience. The best films develop multiple levels of understanding – material, intellectual and emotional. Even when they employ cinematic conventions such as narration, juxtaposition and metaphor, they nevertheless grant the human subjects of the film a certain autonomy, independent of any cinematic effect.

EXPERIMENTS IN DOCUMENTARY

A form must have reached a degree of stability before it is ready for experimentation. By then there is something to experiment on. In the early days of documentary everything was an experiment, but it required an established form such as the Griersonian documentary to provide a baseline against which alternatives could be tried and measured. Experiments are as much rejections of old forms as the creation of new ones. Insofar as experiments in documentary are the latter, they are about the possibilities inherent in the documentary form itself; but motivating this must also be a desire to show something about the world that documentary films have not shown before.

Successful experiments tend to herald the emergence of new styles, although not always immediately. In 1934, A. J. A. Symons published *The Quest for Corvo*, subtitled *An Experiment in Biography*. The book was as much about the process of gathering and presenting biographical information as it was about the life of its subject, the eccentric British writer Frederick Rolfe, also known as Baron Corvo. Instead of following the familiar convention of tracing the subject's life chronologically, it gave instead an account of the biographer's gradual unearthing of clues about him, rather in the manner of a detective story. The book's focus on the provenance and status of biographical knowledge was ahead of its time and foreshadowed many postmodern and poststructuralist approaches to historical and biographical writing.

Several films in the history of documentary have played a similar role, challenging existing forms and opening up new possibilities for future filmmakers. *Nanook of the North* was one, introducing elements of observation, narrative and collaboration with its human subjects that, despite Grierson's protestations, influenced both the Griersonian documentary and such filmmakers as Georges Rouquier and Jean Rouch. Sometimes the influence reappears in forms that are almost unrecognisable. For example, the educational agenda of many Griersonian documentaries can be seen fused with elements of the interview-based films of the 1970s to produce the style of many of today's arts and travel programmes on television.

Two films stand out as experiments in documentary that, whatever their immediate success or lack of it, have had long-term consequences for the genre. These are Jean Rouch and Edgar Morin's *Chronique d'un été* of 1961 and Errol Morris's *The Thin Blue Line* (1988). The first challenged the mystique of the filmmaking process, dissolving the barriers between the filmmaker, subject and audience. The second introduced doubts about the authority of documentary films as evidence and blurred the lines between documentary realism and fiction. It employed a number of devices as provocations that were later taken at face value by other filmmakers, initiating a new trend in documentary film as entertainment. Both films are preoccupied with questions of truth, and both challenge the ways that previous documentary traditions claimed to arrive at it. For Rouch and Morin the target is belief in the authority of filmic conventions; for Morris it is belief in the evidence of film itself. Both employ methods that undercut accepted approaches to nonfiction cinema, even though both seem equally attached to its power and pleasures.

Chronique d'un été presents itself as an experiment in filmmaking, the two directors appearing on screen early in the film (figure 12.4), pondering what it is possible to learn about how people live their lives at a particular moment in history, which in the summer of 1960 happens to be during the closing days of the Algerian war. The film builds on the participatory approach that Rouch had employed in his earlier films *Jaguar* (shot in 1954, released 1967) and *Moi, un noir* (1958). These had explored the dreams and ambitions of young men in West Africa by offering them the chance to act them out on film. *La Pyramide humaine* (shot in 1959, released 1961) was an exploration of race relations among a group of black and white students at a secondary school in Abidjan. It foreshadowed a number of the techniques of provocation and role-playing that Rouch and Morin were soon to employ in *Chronique d'un été*.[7] A famous scene in *Chronique* plays with the conventions of television journalism as some of its protagonists ask people on the street if they are happy. The results are inconclusive and portend a dead end for

12.4 The directors discussing their plans early in the film
Chronique d'un été

this method of arriving at any sort of truth. The rest of the film tries out an array of other means, some conventional, such as extended interviews, others more innovative, such as filming dinner-table conversations or, in still another case, prompting one of the protagonists, Marceline, to give a meditative soliloquy about her return from a concentration camp. The film ends on a note of doubt, the two filmmakers discussing what the film has achieved and concluding that, despite some successes, gaining access to the truth of others' experience remains as elusive as ever. Of one thing they seem more certain, that they have let loose some daunting new problems for documentary. In a curious coda mirroring its opening, the film returns to the streets of Paris, accompanied by music, as if to evoke the mood of a fiction film or even embrace it.

Rouch and Morin cut through the pretences of filmmaking by trying to rewrite the filmmaker's compact with the audience. Instead of presenting their film as a take-it-or-leave-it representation of reality, they present it as a discourse on the problems of filming reality, with all its attendant traps and ambiguities. The audience is taken inside the film, so to speak, and made co-conspirators in the experiment. But this is taken only so far. The ostensible openness of the film is limited, and certain conventions of cinematic omniscience are retained – such as avoiding reference to the filmmaking process itself, despite the ubiquitous but unseen presence of the camera, camera operator and sound recordist.

Chronique d'un été nevertheless led to the opening up of documentary in several new directions. Once the barriers were down, audiences began to be given a new kind of access to the relationship between filmmaker and subject. The frame of the film had been expanded, revealing the filmmaker at its edges, or even as a protagonist within it. The filmmaker's presence was more clearly emphasised as the mind behind the camera – one more social actor in an encounter with the film subject. In a sense, this had been anticipated by the new technologies of film production. Cameras and recorders that could be handled by just one or two people already implied a more intimate form of film authorship.

Chronique d'un été was not the only film, or even the first, to proclaim this shift, but it was perhaps the most explicit. The same ideas were being tested in North America, along with the new technologies that would allow them to be put into practice. There was a fertile exchange between filmmakers in France and Canada, especially between Rouch and Michel Brault, who came to Paris at Rouch's invitation to film *Chronique d'un été*. Their common objective was a documentary cinema that would shed some of the encrustations of pretence and performance that had been built up over the past half century, a desire to return it to something closer to the direct relationship between filmmaker and subject characteristic of documentary in its earliest years. Rouch and Morin were under no illusions that this new documentary would give access to a single, uncontested reality. The very situating of it in the perspectives of fallible individuals militated against this. But they believed that *cinéma vérité* (their nod to Vertov's *Kino-Pravda*) could come closer than documentary had come previously to conveying the elusive qualities of actual experience, what Morin (1962: 4) was later to call 'the emotive fabric of human existence'. The truth was not something cinema could discover outside itself; it had to be found in the interactions of cinema with everyday life.

In the twenty-seven years separating *Chronique d'un été* from Morris's *The Thin Blue Line*, several new elements were added to the various forms of documentary that had continued to evolve concurrently. During the Second World War, Frank Capra and other filmmakers working for the US War Department had rediscovered the principle of collage, building up their films largely out of found materials. In the 1950s the release of wartime footage provided a wealth of new material that could be mined for television programmes like NBC's twenty-six-part series *Victory at Sea* (1952–3). A new subgenre of documentary specific to television was created, consisting of archival footage, music and voice-over commentary, perhaps best exemplified by NBC's *White Paper* (1960–89) and *Project 20* (1954–70) series, the latter including the episode *The Twisted Cross* (1956), narrated by the actor Alexander Scourby. Television had also taken the filmed interview to a new level in such programmes as ABC's *The Mike Wallace Interview* (1957–8), which by the time of the Vietnam War had become an integral element of television documentary. The main innovation of films like Emile de Antonio's *In the Year of the Pig* (1968) was to replace the usual accompaniment of voice-over commentary with fragments of interview, thus removing the authority of the institutional voice and even sometimes undermining the authority of the interviewees, who up until then had generally been presented as infallible witnesses.

All these changes were perhaps necessary preconditions for the emergence of a film like *The Thin Blue Line*. Morris had based his previous films, *Gates of Heaven* (1978) and *Vernon, Florida* (1981), on extensive interviews with subjects whom the audience were invited to assess on the evidence of their own words and demeanour. In *The Thin Blue Line* he wove together interviews, music, atmospheric lighting and dramatic re-enactments around the murder of a policeman in Dallas. For the most part the re-enactments are impressionistic and surrounded by darkness, focusing on small details in extreme close-up, such as a revolver being fired, a milkshake in a paper cup dropped on the road, a policeman's shoes, a stenographer's notebook, a typewriter typing (figures 12.5 and 12.6). The introduction of the re-enactments, none of which gives a clear-cut 'realist' answer to crucial questions about the event and which tend to contradict each other, proceed out of the testimony of witnesses who also prove biased or unreliable. Morris plays with these elements somewhat in the manner of a fiction filmmaker like Alain Resnais, not claiming that there is no objective truth but rather that it is impossible to be certain about it. The film mirrors the perceptions and self-perceptions of the protagonists. Through its use of fiction techniques it evokes the imaginary, shifting perspectives of fiction and its potential for ambiguity and irony. Although the film anchors itself in the factual situation of a man convicted for a murder he probably did not commit – a familiar trope of investigative journalism – the film's purpose seems to be at least partly to tease the viewer's appetite for intrigue and entertainment. This is enhanced by the music, lighting and visual effects drawn from fiction films. Morris thus brings to documentary a range of devices justified by their ironic reference to fiction, but at the same time gains benefit from their appeal to viewers of fiction. In a sense he has his cake and eats it too.

This possibility has clearly not gone unnoticed by many of the less sophisticated documentary filmmakers who have followed him. Rather than using Morris's devices to challenge documentary assumptions of certainty, most of his imitators have simply taken *The Thin Blue Line* as a licence to stage re-enactments, make their interviews more cosmetic and employ music to encourage belief. They thus claim both truth and entertainment value for their productions. Despite Morris's originality, a long procession of crudely

12.5 A dramatic detail recreated in *The Thin Blue Line*

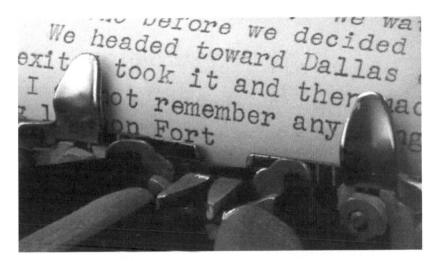

12.6 Typing a suspect's statement in *The Thin Blue Line*

fictionalised and over-decorated documentaries attest to the damage that has been done.[8]

A further addition to documentary was the first-person autobiographical film, of which an early example is Chris Marker's *Letter from Siberia* (1958). It was followed by films exploring a wide range of personal and familial relationships, such as Jonas Mekas's *Lost, Lost, Lost* (1976), Ed Pincus's *Diaries: 1971–76* (1982), Doug Block's *51 Birch Street* (2005), Tomer Heymann's *I Shot My Love* (2009) and Ross McElwee's *Photographic Memory* (2011). In some respects these films were the logical outgrowth of the moves towards first-person authorship in such early *cinéma vérité* and Direct Cinema films as Chris Marker and Pierre Lhomme's *Le Joli Mai* (1963), Pierre Perrault's *Le Règne du jour* (1967) and the Maysles brothers' *Salesman* (1969). They also owe something to American experimental cinema, which emphasised the individual voices of filmmakers like Kenneth Anger, Jack Smith and Bruce Baillie.

A close cousin of the autobiographical film, the documentary portrait, had been around for just as long. It often permitted a similar intimacy and used a confessional framework. Among these films were *Don't Look Back* (1967), *The Things I Cannot Change* (1967), *Portrait of Jason* (1967), *Marjoe* (1972) and, later, *Unknown White Male* (2005). Autobiographical films paralleled the increasing tendency of television companies to design programmes around individuals, whether ordinary citizens, experts in some subject or celebrities, and to turn their news presenters into public personalities. Since then, an increasing number of presenters of travel and adventure programmes, with no particular qualifications beyond youth and bravado, have been pushed into such celebrity roles.

NONFICTION TELEVISION

In 1986 Colin Young put the following propositions to the members of CILECT, the International Liaison Centre for Film and Television Schools:

1. *Documentary* and *fiction* are not the same thing (although they overlap and have much in common).
2. *Documentary* and film or television *journalism* are not the same thing (although they both are aspects of non-fiction).

He continued with these observations:

> Most non-fiction on television comes under the heading of journalism – such programmes are organised on the principle that the narrator or presenter appears as an authority on the subject. This presenter co-ordinates and makes comprehensible, with the help of commentary, a stream of images which often lack any internal coherence, and this illustrates an analysis or argument whose final proof lies outside the images themselves. [...] In [documentaries] coherence and the validity of the images depend entirely on how they are photographed and made clear in the editing. (Young, 1986: 115 17)

Basil Wright, in an interview in 1969, described films and television programmes as completely different forms of the motion picture (Levin, 1971: 41). His own film *The Song of Ceylon* is certainly far from what television programmes became, with their designer formats, decorative titles and talking heads. Looked at critically, television journalism and documentary cinema appear to be two quite separate genres. Nonetheless, it was British and American film documentaries of the 1930s, with their emphasis on music and spoken texts, that laid the foundations for much of the nonfiction television of today.

As nonfiction television has evolved, it has preserved many of the features of Grierson's 'creative treatment of actuality', although often in exaggerated form. The core elements remain: voice-over narration, music, re-enactments and a mix of new and archival footage. As the programmes edged closer to journalism, they added interviews, onscreen presenters and the testimonies of experts from every possible field. Perhaps because interviews can now be conducted anywhere, they have become more dominant than ever. Many films that are today considered documentaries are essentially collages of interview fragments interspersed with archival footage. Two notable variants are based on extensive interviews with one person: Robert McNamara in the case of Errol Morris's *The Fog of War* (2003) and Daniel Ellsberg in Judith Ehrlich and Rick Goldsmith's *The Most Dangerous Man in America* (2009). In watching such films, it becomes obvious that the editing of the spoken texts generally took precedence over the images that accompanied them.

In a narrow sense, the interview-based film is the most 'documentary' form one can imagine. It gives us direct (although often condensed and rearranged) records of people speaking about their experiences and the events of their times. We would give a lot for comparable records of Julius Caesar, Catherine the Great or William Shakespeare, just as today we prize early piano roll recordings of Grieg and Debussy playing their own music. The strengths of this kind of cinema portraiture are obvious. To be able to watch a person speaking extemporaneously, and at length, is a way into their minds and feelings – one might even say, into their souls. We interpret the slightest inflections of voice and facial expression as clues to character, the workings of the mind and truthfulness.[9]

The chief disadvantage of interview-based films, on the other hand, is that they are always retrospective. Their images record people describing past events rather than showing the events themselves. Another liability is the bias, self-interest and faulty memory of interviewees, and the tendency for such testimony to be presented and accepted as accurate. In many documentaries, contemporary history is boiled down to a few first-person accounts, illustrated and bolstered by archival material that may be only vaguely related to it. To illustrate a particular battle, it seems as if almost any war footage will do. In the interests of economy, filmmakers may search no further than the first approximately relevant shot and may even prefer using interviews to buying costly footage of the actual events.

In another sense, documentary films are diminished by being so dependent on the spoken word. Films of people speaking, either to camera or to one another, belong to a specific cinematic register. For all its value, this represents only a fraction of our experience of life or what it is possible for a camera to record. When sound was first introduced to films, critics warned against reducing cinema to photographed stage plays. It has now become clear how impoverished both fiction films and documentary films can be when they exploit only the verbal side of life.

It was perhaps inevitable that television would be dominated by the spoken word, given that for many years its images were of poorer quality than its sound. Yet this does not altogether account for the rapid growth of interview-based films that began in the 1960s. Just a little earlier, nonfiction television series were being given titles like *See It Now* (1951–8), but the trend was increasingly away from seeing. One possible reason for this is that nonfiction films tended to be focused on topical and political issues: films such as *The Selling of the Pentagon* (1971), *The Day after Trinity* (1981) and *With Babies and Banners* (1979). Because these films looked at events in the recent past, they relied heavily on the accounts of the participants. Undoubtedly radio, as a forerunner of television, also played a part in encouraging speech over images, as did the news-gathering habits of journalists. If television crews failed to film something actually happening, they could always film someone talking about it. From the standpoint of producers, events in the recent past were often in fact safer subjects than current ones, being, as it were, more predictable. Programmes could always be made on these subjects, provided there were experts to be interviewed and archival materials to be found. Today, not even these ingredients are thought strictly necessary, as producers resort more and more to fictional re-enactments.[10] Increasingly, too, television exerts a disproportionate influence over other kinds of nonfiction filmmaking. Independent documentary films made outside the broadcasting networks are now routinely shot and edited with television in mind, even if there is little chance of them ever being bought by television.

Few producers like to risk documenting events with an unknown outcome. Sports broadcasts remain one of the last bastions of uncontrolled documentary on television, but even here a win, draw or loss is certain, even if how the game is played is not. For an independent filmmaker to propose making a film on a subject with no prospective resolution is to court incredulity and rejection by commissioning editors. The risk to broadcasters is not only financial but also managerial. Few like conceding so much control to a programme-maker. In less corporate times there were some exceptions, such as Craig Gilbert's *An American Family* series (1973) and the films of Frederick Wiseman, including *High School* (1969) and *Hospital* (1970), made for broadcast on the American PBS network. More recently, Jean-Xavier de Lestrade's series *The Staircase* (2004) succeeded in following a court case with no guarantee that it would ever arrive at the truth, although it did arrive at a verdict. Reality television further reflects broadcast conservatism. Programmes such as *Big Brother* (2000–) and the various versions of *Survivor* (1997–) trade on unpredictability, but in such highly manipulated situations that they more closely resemble game shows. In another of its variants, reality television gives special access to police, customs and airport procedures, filming dramatic incidents and generally padding these out with extensive repetitions and commercial breaks. To their credit, these programmes sometimes provide remarkable insights into actual encounters between ordinary citizens and state authorities but, on the other hand, they are inevitably compromised towards the authorities by the terms of their access. As one might expect, police excesses (such as those revealed in the 1991 Rodney King videotape) are rarely shown and the police come off well enough to ensure the producers have continued cooperation. The ordinary citizens shown are presumably paid for their images, but this side of the production process is never revealed.

Television soon developed another new form, equally distinct from documentary cinema. Beginning as cultural programming, it was not about exploring events but, as Grierson had advocated, providing public education. The first programmes were presented by experts such as Kenneth Clark, discussing Western art in his *Civilisation* series (1969) and Jacob Bronowski discussing the history and philosophy of science in *The Ascent of Man* (1973). Once presenters moved out of the studio they could be found almost anywhere – beside a ruined abbey or, like David Attenborough, among a family of gorillas. These programmes provided viewers with access to authoritative figures through whom they could think about the world. The presenters came increasingly from television itself, and although they were sometimes just as knowledgeable as the academic experts, were often more approachable. Attenborough, in his numerous natural history programmes, provided for his viewers not only information but also vicarious experiences. Yet however personable the presenters were, programmes of this kind still positioned themselves at a professional distance from the ordinary viewer. They did this, and continue to do so, through their production methods, producing magical effects. At one moment the presenter is standing on a mountain in the Andes, the next moment among penguins in Antarctica. Hillsides change from winter to spring in a matter of seconds. The perspective shifts from an aerial view to someone striding across the moors. Chicks are shown hatching in their nests and polar bears are born in caverns beneath the snow.

Concealment of method has long been a feature of professionalism – in the theatre, in magic shows and on television. Television production methods, however, have tended to become more formulaic than magical. Today's experts may be less famous than previously, but they still come to us carefully coached to stride around while talking to the camera, making meaningful gestures with their hands. Sometimes they have to push through bemused crowds as they talk, and they often stride dramatically out of the shot towards the horizon for no apparent reason.

A comparatively recent trend is to find presenters with whom it is believed modern viewers will identify more readily. They tend to be young and adventurous. These young presenters quickly gain status as television celebrities. Among the most familiar are the 'innocents abroad' of travel programmes. They are the televisual counterparts of travel writers like Eric Newby and Paul Theroux, and their programmes owe something to this literary tradition. One of the first such presenters was Michael Palin, in *Pole to Pole* (1992) and similar series. He has been followed by a raft of others prepared to experience exotic places and cultures on the viewer's behalf. These include Simon Reeve of *Equator* (2006–7), *Tropic of Cancer* (2010–11) and *Russia with Simon Reeve* (2017) and the motorcycle duo Ewan McGregor and Charley Boorman in *Long Way Round* (2004) and *Long Way Down* (2007). They set off to see the world, usually accompanied by music. Their *naïveté* becomes a commercial asset. The original image of the carefree traveller, which evoked the backpacker spirit of the 1970s, has evolved into a hybrid form of reality television in which the presenters undergo various types of pain and culture shock in programmes such as *Tribe* (2005–7) with Bruce Parry (figure 12.7), *Man vs. Wild* (2006–11) with Bear Grylls, and *Freddie Flintoff Versus the World* (2011).

Many of these programmes require the sustaining of a complex illusion. In *Tribe, Great Railway Journeys of the World* (1980) and *Great Indian Railway Journeys* (2018; with Michael Portillo) the presenter is portrayed as someone travelling alone. But the traveller's isolation, and the dangers encountered, ultimately have an air of unreality about them, for if one stops to reflect

12.7 Bruce Parry among the Suri, from the television series *Tribe*

(asking, for example, who the presenter is speaking to), it becomes clear that there is always a film crew standing by just a metre or two off screen, even if they are never seen. Yet audiences are not invited to reflect; the convention is to preserve the illusion of solitude. The artificiality of the situation is normalised.

These programmes are marketed as documentaries. Any suggestion that they acknowledge their methods would doubtless be ruled out by the producers as unprofessional. Viewers are persuaded to accept that this is how television documentaries must be. Most series – generally those on cultural and historical subjects – continue to preserve the illusion of the omniscient, invisible camera. Just a few, however, have begun to limit the extent of the artifice. The trials of filmmaking can sometimes become part of the story, and the film crew among its heroes. Some producers have come to realise that there is something to be gained by taking the audience into their confidence. This can even inspire a second programme about the making of the first, as in those about the difficult challenges of nature photography.[11]

DOCUMENTARY EXPECTATIONS

Along with the dominance of public affairs television, a widespread assumption has developed that documentary films concern the public domain rather than the private, and that their primary function is to convey information. If Tolstoy's model for the documentary was the novel, today's model is the newspaper or textbook. Yet there is no fundamental reason why this need be so. In 1974 Ernest Callenbach, the editor of *Film Quarterly*, foreshadowed another kind of documentary, 'in which small events – the tiny and yet compelling patterns of everyday life – [are] given the kind of attention that Virginia Woolf or some such novelist has given them' (see Young, 1982: 7).

Bill Nichols has gone to some lengths to define the documentary film. He sees documentary as a form that is 'basically instrumental or pragmatic', operating in 'terms of problem-solving'. He suggests that:

> a paradigmatic structure for documentary would involve the establishment of an issue or problem, the presentation of the background to the problem, followed by an examination of its current extent or complexity, often including more than one perspective or point of view. This would lead to a concluding section where a solution or path toward a solution is introduced. (Nichols, 1991:18)

As Nichols acknowledges, this description would loosely fit the dramatic structure of most narrative fiction, with its conflicts, crises and resolutions. He contends, however, that documentary is more text-like than dramatic and follows the logic of an argument rather than a story (Nichols, 1991: 19–20).

Although he says there is no absolute test of this difference, the 'constituency of viewers' of documentary expects the genre to deal with social issues in the historical world. Such films will generally construct an argument and give primacy to the soundtrack in the form of commentary and testimony (Nichols, 1991: 24). Documentary films, he says, are 'discourses of sobriety' (Nichols, 1991: 29). Nichols's definition in fact sounds very much like a description of public affairs television, with some allowance for films by independent filmmakers and variants that he calls Observational, Participatory and Performative documentary (Nichols, 2001). But it is hard to reconcile the primary definition with documentary films that, like fiction, deal with private lives rather than public issues. Nor does the characterisation 'discourses of sobriety' easily fit documentary films that are comic or ironic, films such as *A Happy Mother's Day* (1963), *Gates of Heaven* (1978), *Crumb* (1994) and *Catfish* (2010).[12] As these films suggest, a short story, novel or memoir could as easily be the model for a documentary film as an article in a newspaper.

A substantial body of documentary filmmaking further supports this possibility, despite the commanding influence of television. These are films that, like much of fiction, deal with individuals in their daily lives, and that employ narrative and thematic structures rather than expository ones. Although some documentaries of this kind, such as *An American Family*, were made for television, many others are the work of independent filmmakers. The titles reveal their emphasis on persons rather than topics: *Joe Leahy's Neighbours* (1988), *Lonely Boy* (1963), *The Things I Cannot Change* (1967), *La Vie est immense et pleine de dangers* (1995), *A Month in the Life of Ephtim D.* (1999), *A Wife among Wives* (1981) and *KJ: Music and Life* (2008). These films may indeed expose social problems and express political sympathies, but in doing so they have no need to adopt an expository structure, any more than do such socially conscious fiction films as *Bicycle Thieves* (1948), *All the King's Men* (1949) and *On the Waterfront* (1954).

Films about private lives, exploring feelings and relationships, tend to undermine any overarching conception of the documentary as an argument-based genre. Even films built around interviews, such as *Marjoe*, are hard to label categorically as political or social arguments. What point, among many, might that film be making – that religious charlatans exploit the gullible, that parents exploit their children, that religion is part of show business? Instead, the film introduces us to a person caught up in all these questions. A more extreme example would be a film like *The Act of Seeing with one's own eyes* (1971), a silent film about autopsies, which Nichols (1991: 144) describes as 'all evidence, almost entirely bereft of exposition or narrative'.

Unlike television journalism, documentary films about private persons rarely make claims to objectivity. More often, they are presented as personal and subjective. Even when the filmmakers minimise their own presence, this does not mean they are necessarily detached or disengaged from their subjects. Nichols is quite right to remind us that 'a non-intrusive, non-didactic mode of representation does not guarantee any sort of value-free or unambiguous access to situations and events' (1991: 195). What it does do, however, is give priority to an experiential approach to events in preference to second-order commentaries on them. Expository films, by contrast, tend to favour illustration over personal experience. The documentary tradition inaugurated by Lumière and Flaherty takes an empirical stance, preferring what Bertrand Russell (1912: 46–59) called 'knowledge by acquaintance' to 'knowledge by description'. In allowing the spectator to follow the experiences of others, these films make new knowledge *available* to us rather than trying to impart it.

Gary Kildea's film *Celso and Cora* (1983) demonstrates the difference. Its subject is a young couple and their two small children living in the slums of Manila. The setting is one of poverty, but the film is not 'about' poverty. In fact, Kildea has stated that his purpose was to treat his protagonists in such a way as *not* to define them by their poverty. Their lives tell us a lot about the difficulties of the poor – the precariousness of their finances, their vulnerability to illness – but the focus of the film is on their personalities, their marital difficulties, their methods of getting by and the care and affection they bestow on their children. When Celso declares at the end of the film, 'that's really how it is, *pare*, with the life of the poor – it's not equal', it comes as a confirmation of all the complexities we have begun to understand rather than a point the filmmaker is trying to make.

Nicolas Philibert's *Etre et avoir* (2002), which concerns a school teacher and his pupils, and Björn Reinhardt's *The Third Violin* (2010), about a Romanian peasant community, show a similar focus on the intricacies of human relations rather than on making sweeping social statements. Philibert's film documents a specific method of teaching and the emotional bonds that develop between the pupils and their teacher, who is retiring at the end of the year. The background is a French farming community, but the film does not go into the politics of the European Union's farming regulations or the survival of the small-scale farmer, much less the state of French education. Upon its release the film was accused of romanticism for not addressing the problems of violence and disaffection in urban schools, despite this being irrelevant to a film about rural schooling. That response, however, tends to confirm Nichols's point that people expect documentary films to adopt a journalistic perspective.

The Third Violin also looks at rural life, focusing on the transmission of knowledge and skills from one generation to the next in a Romanian village. Although this takes place within a context of rural isolation, economic change, and problems of unemployment and alcoholism – conditions that the film readily acknowledges – the context itself does not become the subject. Instead, we perceive these conditions through the lives of those they directly affect, in a sense gaining a double perspective. At one point we meet a severely disabled man who appears to mix freely in the community and to be accepted without prejudice. This could have been used to make a point about disability, but here it is simply shown as a fact, allowing us to ponder its significance.

Both of these films unfold over extended periods of time, marked by the changing of the seasons. Each is episodic and lacks a central dramatic conflict. Questions are resolved, if they are resolved at all, by fits and starts, and are often left hanging in the background while other matters take precedence. Several events occur unexpectedly – in one case a death, in another an illness – unheralded by what has gone before. These events leave behind an atmosphere of uncertainty which, if anything, is underlined rather than dispelled at the end of the film.

When considering possible models for documentary films, one factor is the density of description and incident. This obviously differs between the novel and the newspaper but also distinguishes the documentary from other forms of nonfiction film, such as news broadcasts. Density in this case does not refer to the number or variety of scenes in a film, which might be the same for any film of a given length. Rather, it is closer to what the anthropologist Clifford Geertz meant by 'thick description', a term borrowed from the philosopher Gilbert Ryle. Density, in this sense, can be understood as the difference between merely stating a fact and conveying it through its significance for those who experience it. In a number of fiction films (such as Antonioni's *Il Grido*, 1957) there is an accumulation of detail and minor incident that has minimal dramatic importance but is highly significant in establishing the existential world in which the protagonists live. These details are filmed so that we experience them in a way analogous to the experience of the characters, as the environmental subtext of their actions. They are conveyed both through their sensory immediacy and by their closeness to the characters' emotional lives. How the filmmaker is positioned – whether figuratively 'inside' or 'outside' the event – determines the nature of our response. Nichols (1991: 193) notes (referring to a passage from Lukacs) that a horse race described by Zola is only 'a piece of verisimilitude, whereas Tolstoy narrates the horse race in *Anna Karenina* as an integral part of his characters' lives'.

The possibility of identifying with others, afforded by the novel and shared by documentary, underpins narrative strategies that allow us to understand how varied and often contradictory social forces bear upon an individual. We understand them in their simultaneous effect, rather than as an enumeration of abstract factors. In the theatre and many fiction films, narrative serves to accentuate dramatic conflict. In documentary films it may be more diffused, resulting in an attenuated or 'weak' narrative. In this case the film relies more on other elements to engage the viewer's attention. As in the novel, where the reader's interest may derive as much from the quality of the writing as the plot, in documentary films the viewer's pleasure frequently lies in the filmmaker's style of filming and attention to detail. As Colin Young has noted (1975: 74), in this form of documentary 'the details of our films must be a substitute for dramatic tension, and the film's authenticity must be a substitute for artificial excitement'. The delineation of character may also play a part, as it does in novels. E. M. Forster, deploring the excessive focus on story-lines in novels, wrote: 'We can [now] turn to a more interesting topic: the actors. We need not ask what happened next, but to whom did it happen; the novelist will be appealing to our intelligence and imagination, not merely to our curiosity' (1954: 43). 'The more we look at the story', he observes, 'the more we disentangle it from the finer growth it supports, the less shall we find to admire' (Forster, 1954: 26).

In a film, the quality of seeing could be said to be equivalent to the quality of writing in prose fiction. In some documentaries the filmmaker's distinctive way of viewing the world comes to approximate the first-person voices we are familiar with in novels, from that of the author in Thackeray to the voice of a character in Melville, Conrad or Nabokov. Even more concretely than in fiction films, the documentary lends itself to filmmaking in the first person. In films such as Ross McElwee's *Bright Leaves* (2003) and Jonathan Caouette's *Tarnation* (2003), filmmakers address the viewer directly, either on or off the screen. These films echo the confiding voice and uncertainty of many autobiographical essays, traceable back to Montaigne's *Essais* of the sixteenth century and developed further, as Michael Renov notes (2004: 70), in the writings of Nietzsche, Adorno and Barthes. In them, the filmmaker's self and the objects of the filmmaker's camera are mutually constitutive – or, as Montaigne puts it, 'he who touches the one, touches the other' (see Renov, 2004: 105).

In some films the voice is meditative, in others ironic and self-reflexive. It may sometimes adopt the impersonal tone of a commentator on world affairs, but in most cases the focus is on something closer to home, often involving a personal relationship with a parent, friend, spouse or lover. As in the autobiographical essay, the world is reported through a subjective response that disavows both the positivism of journalism and the truth claims of informational films. Indeed, this is often further undercut by adopting a persona of uncertainty or inadequacy, as in Michael Moore's and Nick Broomfield's films. In this respect it resembles its literary forebears, for as Renov notes: 'The essayistic bears with it a logic that questions the verities of rhetorical composition and of system, indeed, of mastery itself; the status of the subject as transcendental or originary is likewise challenged' (Renov, 2004: 106).

Good documentary filmmakers, like good novelists, combine their gifts of expression with an acknowledgement of the openness of the world, a world that cannot be fully explained by any film. Nor do they believe that the world will explain itself by virtue of being filmed. Dai Vaughan has written of an ideal but unattainable cinema 'composed of uncomposed elements' that would 'attain to a narrative significance whilst remaining random; a coherence proposed without artifice'. For Vaughan, certain fiction films, such as Olmi's *The Tree of Wooden Clogs* (1978), approach this ideal, but the films that have come closest have been documentaries, seen in their unfinished state. 'Not the rushes, yet not the fine cuts [...] but the films as they stood when their narrative structures had just begun to emerge with the patient chipping away of the surrounding substance, yet were still perceptibly of its density and of its mass' (Vaughan, 1999: 114).

Since the 1960s there has been a renewal of the sensibility that inspired the earliest filmmakers, tempered now with greater awareness of the film-maker's inevitable presence in the work. In an essay entitled 'Let There Be Lumière', Vaughan writes of one of the early Lumière films[13] that it reminds us of a moment 'when cinema seemed free, not only of its proper connotations, but of the threat of its absorption into meanings beyond it' (Vaughan, 1999:8). At the end of *Musical Elaborations*, Edward Said writes of a kind of music bearing a similar promise, a music 'whose pleasures and discoveries are premised upon letting go, upon not asserting a central authorising identity, upon enlarging the community of hearers and players beyond the time taken, beyond the extremely concentrated duration provided by the performance occasion' (Said, 1991: 105). So, too, might we regain a more searching, exploratory documentary cinema, beyond the packaged and prefabricated performances now so familiar to us.

Notes

1 John Dewey, in *Art as Experience* (1934), made a similar argument about the separation of art from experience, and how artworks have become isolated from everyday life as museum objects.

2 See Bertrand Tavernier's commentary on the Lumière films as recorded in *The Lumière Brothers' First Films* (1996).

3 This according to his wife, Frances Flaherty (see Christopher, 2005: 322).

4 In 1914 Edward S. Curtis had released a film entitled *In the Land of the Head-Hunters*, a love story set in a Kwakiutl community in British Columbia, but it relied much more on the enactment of a script than *Nanook*. An interesting predecessor to *Nanook* is *The Romance of the Far Fur Country* (1920), filmed in the Canadian Arctic in 1919 for the Hudson's Bay Company. Although essentially a chronicle of the filming expedition, it includes scenes of an Inuit man, Inqmilayuk, describing his early life, as well as an illustrative narrative sequence of Inqmilayuk's romance with a woman named Innotseak (see the *BBC News Magazine* of 21 January 2012). Another early effort was *The Transformed Isle* of 1917, filmed in the Solomon Islands, which contained narrative sequences of local warfare and 'blackbirding'.

5 The subtitle of *Nanook of the North* was *A Story of Life and Love in the Actual Arctic*.

6 This is based on Cooper's introduction to the film at the Colloquium on Ethnographic Film held at the University of California at Los Angeles in April 1968 (four decades after the making of the film).

7 Rouch's innovative ideas and practice are explored in depth in Paul Henley's magisterial study, *The Adventure of the Real* (2009).

8 There have been a few exceptions to this general trend, however – films that have adopted some of the techniques of *The Thin Blue Line* and used them intelligently. Quite a number, like Morris's film, explore the uncertainties of unresolved murder cases. They include: *Marilyn: The Ultimate Investigation into a Suspicious Death* (1999), *Mississippi Cold Case* (2007), *Interview with a Murderer* (2016) and *Natasha and the Wolf* (1995).

9 In *The First Interview* (2011), Dennis Tupicoff has created a mock filmed interview with the French scientist Michel Eugène Chevreul that actually occurred in 1886, before cinema was invented. It is based on contemporary photographs and a verbatim transcription of the interview conducted by the famous photographer Nadar. Here, Tupicoff gives us a sense of the latent potential of cinema, struggling to be born.

10 Historical re-enactments in documentaries are notorious – usually poorly reconstructed, unconvincingly acted and awkwardly filmed. For exceptions, see Peter Watkins's *Culloden* (1964) and Dennis Tupicoff's *The First Interview* (2011).

11 For example, the television programme *The Making of David Attenborough's Conquest of the Skies* (2015). Recent BBC natural history documentaries narrated by Attenborough have included an epilogue illustrating the programme's production.

12 In *Campaign Manager* (1964), a film by Richard Leacock and Noel E. Parmentel about Barry Goldwater's run for the American presidency, a group of political organisers meet over lunch and become grid-locked passing plates of steaks around the table. In *The Duchess and the Detectives* (1982), the detectives mistakenly assume that two named dogs are human members of the household. Humour in documentaries is often mixed with more serious scenes, and this is surely in keeping with the ebb and flow of emotions in daily life. At one point in *Etre et avoir* (2002) we see a boy losing a comic battle with a photocopying machine, and at another we see a boy close to tears as he describes his father's operation for cancer. Humour in documentary may be more problematic ethically than it is in fiction if it appears to be at the expense of living people. A film that succeeds in being both humorous and humane is Lasse Naukkarinen's *House of Full Service* (1994), about a small roadside bar that gradually grows to take over all the business activities of the community, including burying its dead.

13 *Barque sortant du port* (1895).

Bibliography

Astruc, Alexandre. 1948. Du stylo à la caméra et de la caméra au stylo. *L'Écran francaise*, 30 March.

Barthes, Roland. 1977. *Image–Music–Text*. Stephen Heath, trans. Glasgow: Fontana/ Collins.

Bateson, Gregory and Margaret Mead. 1942. *Balinese Character: A Photographic Analysis*. New York: New York Academy of Sciences.

— and —. 1977. Margaret Mead and Gregory Bateson on the Use of the Camera in Anthropology. *Studies in the Anthropology of Visual Communication* 4(2): 78–80.

Baumgarten, Alexander Gottlieb. 2013. *Metaphysics: A Critical Translation with Kant's Elucidations, Selected Notes, and Related Materials*. Courtney D. Fugate and John Hymers, eds and trans. London: Bloomsbury.

Bazin, André. 1967. *What Is Cinema? Vol. 1*. Hugh Gray, ed. and trans. Berkeley, CA: University of California Press.

Berenson, Bernard. 1896. *The Florentine Painters of the Renaissance*. New York: G. D. Putnam's Sons.

Berlin, Brent and Paul Kay. 1969. *Basic Colour Terms*. Berkeley, CA: University of California Press. Reprinted 1991, with an updated bibliography by Luisa Maffi.

Bond, Ruskin. 1988. The Photograph. In *Night Train to Deoli*. New Delhi: Penguin Books (India), 21–3.

Bowden, Edward M. and Mark Jung-Beeman. 2003. Aha! Insight Experience Correlates with Solution Activation in the Right Hemisphere. *Psychonomic Bulletin and Review* 10(3): 730–7.

Bryson, Norman. 1983. *Vision and Painting: The Logic of the Gaze*. London: Macmillan.

Chion, Michel. 1994. *Audio-Vision: Sound on Screen*. Claudia Gorbman, trans. New York: Columbia University Press.

Chopra, Pushpindar Singh (ed). 1996. *The Doon School Sixty Years On*. Dehra Dun: Doon School Old Boys Society.

Christopher, Robert J. 2005. *Robert and Frances Flaherty: A Documentary Life, 1883–1922*. Montreal: McGill-Queen's University Press.

de Heusch, Luc. 1962. *Cinéma et sciences sociales: panorama du film ethnographique et sociologique*, Rapports et documents de sciences socials 16. Paris: UNESCO.

Deleuze, Gilles and Félix Guattari. 1987. *A Thousand Plateaus*. London: Continuum.

Dewey, John. 1934. *Art as Experience*. New York: Putnam.

Eisenstein, Sergei. 1957. Methods of Montage. In *Film Form*. New York: Meridian Books, 72–83.

Evans-Pritchard, E. E. 1937. *Witchcraft, Oracles, and Magic among the Azande*. Oxford: Clarendon Press.

Flaherty, Robert. 1950. Robert Flaherty Talking. In *The Cinema 1950*. Roger Manvell, ed. Harmondsworth: Pelican Books, 11–29.

Forster, E. M. 1954. *Aspects of the Novel*. New York: Harcourt, Brace and Company.

Frémaux, Thierry (ed.). 1996. *The Lumière Brothers' First Films* (video-recording). Commentary by Bertrand Tavernier. Musical accompaniment by Stuart Oderman. Lyon: Institut Lumière/Association Frères Lumière.

Gage, John. 1999. *Colour and Meaning: Art, Science and Symbolism*. London: Thames and Hudson.

Gibson, E. J. and R. D. Walk. 1960. Visual Cliff. *Scientific American* 202(4): 67–71.

Godard, Jean-Luc. 1972. *Godard on Godard*. Tom Milne and Jean Narboni, eds. New York: Viking Press.

Goldberg, Vicki (ed.). 1981. *Photography in Print: Writings from 1816 to the Present*. New York: Touchstone/Simon and Schuster.

Goody, Jack. 2002. The Anthropology of the Senses and Sensations. *La Ricerca Folklorica*, No. 45, *Antropologia delle sensazioni*, April: 17–28.

Grierson, John. 1938. The Course of Realism. In *Footnotes to the Film*, Charles Davy, ed. London: Lovat Dickson, 137–61.

Grimshaw, Anna. 2001. *The Ethnographer's Eye: Ways of Seeing in Anthropology*. Cambridge: Cambridge University Press.

Grimshaw, Anna and Amanda Ravetz. 2009. *Observational Cinema*. Bloomington, IN: Indiana University Press.

Gross, Larry, John Stuart Katz and Jay Ruby (eds). 1988. *Image Ethics*. New York: Oxford University Press.

Hardy, Forsyth. 1946. *Grierson on Documentary*. London: Collins.

Henley, Paul. 2009. *The Adventure of the Real: Jean Rouch and the Craft of Ethnographic Film*. Chicago, IL: University of Chicago Press.

James, William. 1890. The Stream of Thought. In *The Principles of Psychology, Vol. 1*. New York: Holt. Reprinted in *The Writings of William James*. John J. McDermott, ed. Chicago, IL: University of Chicago Press, 1977.

Jeanne, René. 1965. *Cinéma 1900*. Paris: Flammarion.

Kounios, John, Jessica I. Fleck, *et al.* 2008. The Origins of Insight in Resting-State Brain Activity. *Neuropsychologia* 46(1): 281–91.

Leacock, Richard. 1975. Ethnographic Observation and the Super-8 Millimeter Camera. In *Principles of Visual Anthropology*. Paul Hockings, ed. The Hague: Mouton, 147–9.

—. 1997. A Search for the Feeling of Being There. 20 May. At http://www.afana.org/leacockessays.htm.

Levin, G. Roy. 1971. *Documentary Explorations: 15 Interviews with Film-makers*. Garden City, NY: Doubleday and Company.

Lovell, Alan and Jim Hillier. 1972. *Studies in Documentary*. New York: Viking Press.

MacDougall, David. 1975. Beyond Observational Cinema. In *Principles of Visual Anthropology*. Paul Hockings, ed. The Hague: Mouton, 109–24.

—. 1992. When Less Is Less. *Film Quarterly* 46(2): 36–45.

—. 1998. *Transcultural Cinema*. Princeton, NJ: Princeton University Press.

—. 2006. *The Corporeal Image: Film, Ethnography, and the Senses*. Princeton, NJ: Princeton University Press.

Malinowski, Bronislaw. 1935. *Coral Gardens and Their Magic. Volume II: The Language of Magic and Gardening*. London: George Allen and Unwin.

Marcus, George. 1990. The Modernist Sensibility in Recent Ethnographic Writing and the Cinematic Metaphor of Montage. *Society for Visual Anthropology Review* 6(1): 2–12.

Marshall, John. 1993. Filming and Learning. In *The Cinema of John Marshall*, Jay Ruby, ed. Chur: Harwood Academic Publishers.

Mead, Margaret. 1975. Visual Anthropology in a Discipline of Words. In *Principles of Visual Anthropology*. Paul Hockings, ed. The Hague: Mouton, 3–10.

Moore, Alexander. 1988. The Limits of Imagist Documentary. *Society for Visual Anthropology Newsletter* 4(2): 1–3.

Morin, Edgar. 1962. Preface. In *The Cinema and Social Science: A Survey of Ethnographic and Sociological Films*. Reports and Papers in the Social Sciences 16. Luc de Heusch, ed. Paris: UNESCO, 3–5.

—. 2005 [1956]. *The Cinema, or The Imaginary Man*. Lorraine Mortimer, trans. Minneapolis, MN: University of Minnesota Press.

Nichols, Bill. 1981. *Ideology and the Image*. Bloomington, IN: Indiana University Press.

—. 1991. *Representing Reality*. Bloomington, IN: Indiana University Press.

—. 2001. *Introduction to Documentary*. Bloomington, IN: Indiana University Press.

Oudart, Jean-Pierre. 1969. La Suture. *Cahiers du Cinéma* 211 (April): 36–9; 212 (May): 50–6.

Parry, Jonathan. 1988. Comment on Robert Gardner's 'Forest of Bliss'. *Society for Visual Anthropology Newsletter* 4(2): 4–7.

Perez, Gilberto. 1998. *The Material Ghost: Films and Their Medium*. Baltimore, MD: Johns Hopkins University Press.

Piault, Marc Henri. 2000. *Anthropologie et cinéma*. Paris: Éditions Nathan/HER.

Ramachandran, V. S. 2010. *The Tell-Tale Brain: A Neuroscientist's Quest for What Makes Us Human*. Noida: Random House India.

Renov, Michael. 2004. *The Subject of Documentary*. Minneapolis, MN: University of Minnesota Press.

Rizzolatti, G. and M. F. Destro. 2008. Mirror Neurons. *Scholarpedia* 3(1): 2055.

Roth, Philip. 2017. *Why Write? Collected Nonfiction 1960–2013*. New York: Library of America.

Rouch, Jean. 2003. *Ciné-Ethnography*. Steven Feld, ed. and trans. Minneapolis, MN: University of Minnesota Press.

Ruby, Jay. 1989. The Emperor and His Clothes: A Comment. *Society for Visual Anthropology Newsletter* 5(1): 9–11.

Russell, Bertrand. 1912. *The Problems of Philosophy*. London: Oxford University Press.

Ryle, Gilbert. 1949. *The Concept of Mind*. Chicago, IL: University of Chicago Press.

Sadoul, Georges. 1962. *Histoire du cinéma*. Paris: Flammarion.

Said, Edward W. 1991. *Musical Elaborations*. New York: Columbia University Press.

Sherrington, C. S. 1906. *The Integrative Action of the Nervous System*. New Haven, CT: Yale University Press.

Smith, Adam. 1969 [1790]. *The Theory of Moral Sentiments*. New Rochelle, NY: Arlington House.

Spiegel, Pauline. 1984. The Case of the Well-Mannered Guest. *The Independent: Film and Video Monthly*, April, 15–17.

Srivastava, Sanjay. 1998. *Constructing Post-Colonial India: National Character and the Doon School*. London: Routledge.

Strecker, Ivo. 1979. *The Hamar of Southern Ethiopia. Volume III: Conversations in Dambaiti*. Hohenschäftlarn: Klaus Renner Verlag.

—. 1982. The Short Take. *RAIN (Royal Anthropological Institute Newsletter)* 50: 10–12.

—. 2003. Co-Presence in Ethnographic Film. Unpublished manuscript.

Sussex, Elizabeth. 1975. *The Rise and Fall of the British Documentary*. Berkeley, CA: University of California Press.

Symons, A. J. A. 1934. *The Quest for Corvo: An Experiment in Biography*. London: Cassell.

Turner, Terence. 1995. Social Body and Embodied Subject: Bodiliness, Sociality, and Subjectivity Among the Kayapo. *Cultural Anthropology* 10(2): 143–70.

Vaughan, Dai. 1999. *For Documentary: Twelve Essays*. Berkeley, CA: University of California Press.

—. 2005. The Doon School Project. *Visual Anthropology* 18: 457–64.

von Hildebrand, Adolf. 1907. *The Problem of Form in Painting and Sculpture* (3rd edition). New York: G. E. Stechert and Co.

Young, Colin. 1975. Observational Cinema. In *Principles of Visual Anthropology*. Paul Hockings, ed. The Hague: Mouton, 65–80.

—. 1982. MacDougall Conversations. *RAIN (Royal Anthropological Institute Newsletter)* 50: 5–8.

—. 1986. A Provocation. *CILECT Review* 2(1): 115–18.

Filmography

Titles are listed alphabetically in the form by which they are generally best known in English-speaking countries, with the original title or translation in brackets.

51 Birch Street. 2005. Doug Block. Copacetic Pictures/HBO-Cinemax Documentary/ZDF Enterprises. USA/Germany. 90 mins.

The 400 Blows [*Les Quatre cents coups*]. 1959. François Truffaut. Films du Carrosse/SEDIF. France. 94 mins.

1900 [*Novecento*]. 1976. Bernardo Bertolucci. Produzioni Europee Associate/Les Productions Artistes Associés/Artemis Film. Italy. 317 mins.

The Act of Seeing with one's own eyes. 1971. Stan Brakhage. USA. 32 mins.

The Age of Reason. 2004. David MacDougall. Fieldwork Films/Centre for Cross-Cultural Research, Australian National University. Australia. 87 mins.

Air Post. 1934. Geoffrey Clark. GPO Film Unit. UK. 12 mins.

All the King's Men. 1949. Robert Rossen. Columbia Pictures. USA. 110 mins.

An American Family series. 1973. Craig Gilbert. WNET New York/PBS. USA. 12 episodes of 60 mins.

And Then There Were None. 1945. René Clair. Popular Pictures, Inc. USA. 97 mins.

À propos de Nice. 1930. Jean Vigo. Pathé-Natan. France. 29 mins.

L'Arrivée d'un train en gare de La Ciotat. 1896. Louis Lumière. Société Lumière. France. 50 seconds.

The Ascent of Man series. 1973. Various directors. BBC/Time-Life Television. UK. 13 episodes of 50 mins.

Ascent to the Sky [*La Montée au ciel*]. 2009. Stéphane Breton. Les Films d'Ici/Arte. France. 52 mins.

Au hasard Balthazar. 1966. Robert Bresson. Argos Films/Parc Films/Athos Films/Svensk Filmindustri/Svenska Filminstitutet. France/Sweden. 95 mins.

L'Avventura. 1960. Michelangelo Antonioni. Cino Del Duca/Produzioni Cinematografiche Europee/Société Cinématographique Lyre. Italy/France. 145 mins.

Awareness. 2010. David MacDougall and Judith MacDougall. Fieldwork Films/Rishi Valley Education Centre/Research School of Humanities and the Arts, Australian National University. Australia/India. 67 mins.

Barque sortant du port. 1895. Louis Lumière. Société Lumière. France. 50 seconds.

Bataille d'enfants à coup d'oreillers. 1897. Alexandre Promio. Société Lumière. France. 50 seconds.

Bataille sur le grand fleuve. 1952. Jean Rouch. CNRS. France. 33 mins.

Battleship Potemkin [Броненосец «Потёмкин»] [*Bronenosets Patyomkin*]. 1925. Sergei Eisenstein. Mosfilm. USSR. 72 mins.

Behind the Great Wall [*La muraglia cinese*]. 1958. Carlo Lizzani. Astra Cinematografica. Italy. 120 mins.

Berlin: The Symphony of a Great City [*Berlin: Die Sinfonie der Großstadt*]. 1927. Walter Ruttmann. Deutsche Vereins–Film. Germany. 65 mins.

Bicycle Thieves [*Ladri di biciclette*]. 1948. Vittorio De Sica. Produzioni De Sica. Italy. 89 mins.

Big Brother series. 2000–. Various directors. CBS Television. USA. Multiple 30-min episodes.

The Birds. 1963. Alfred Hitchcock. Alfred J. Hitchcock Productions. USA. 119 mins.

The Blue Angel [Der Blaue Engel]. 1930. Josef von Sternberg. UFA. Germany. 98 mins.

The Blue Lamp. 1950. Basil Dearden. Ealing Studios. UK. 84 mins.

Bright Leaves. 2003. Ross McElwee. Channel 4 Television/Homemade Movies/WGBH Boston. UK/USA. 107 mins.

Bwana Devil. 1952. Arch Oboler. Gulu Productions. USA. 79 mins.

Campaign Manager. 1964. Richard Leacock and Noel E. Parmentel. Leacock-Pennebaker Inc. USA. 26 mins.

Catfish. 2010. Henry Joost and Ariel Schulman. Supermarché/Hit The Ground Running Films. USA. 87 mins.

Celso and Cora. 1983. Gary Kildea. Independently produced. Australia. 109 mins.

The Chair. 1963. Robert Drew. Drew Associates/Time-Life Broadcast. USA. 59 mins.

Chang: A Drama of the Wilderness. 1927. Merian C. Cooper and Ernest B. Schoedsack. Paramount. USA. 90 mins.

Chronique d'un été [Chronicle of a Summer]. 1961. Jean Rouch and Edgar Morin. Argos Films. France. 90 mins.

Citizen Kane. 1941. Orson Welles. RKO Radio Pictures/Mercury Productions. USA. 119 mins.

The City. 1939. Ralph Steiner and Willard Van Dyke. American Documentary Films, Inc. USA. 43 mins.

Civilisation: A Personal View by Kenneth Clark series. 1969. Michael Gill, Peter Montagnon and Ann Turner. BBC Television. UK. 14 episodes of 50 mins.

Coal Face. 1935. Alberto Cavalcanti. GPO Film Unit. UK. 12 mins.

The Coming of the Dial. 1933. Stuart Legg. GPO Film Unit. UK. 14 mins.

Crisis: Behind a Presidential Commitment. 1963. Robert Drew. ABC News/Drew Associates. USA. 52 mins.

Crumb. 1994. Terry Zwigoff. Superior Pictures. USA. 119 mins.

Culloden. 1964. Peter Watkins. BBC Television. UK. 69 mins.

Day after Day [Jour après jour]. 1962. Clément Perron. National Film Board of Canada. Canada. 28 mins.

The Day after Trinity. 1981. Jon H. Else. KETH Television. USA. 89 mins.

Demolition [Chaiqian]. 2008. J. P. Sniadecki. Film Study Center, Harvard University. USA. 62 mins.

Il Deserto Rosso [Red Desert]. 1964. Michelangelo Antonioni. Duemila/Francoriz. Italy. 117 mins.

Dial M for Murder. 1954. Alfred Hitchcock. Warner Bros. USA. 104 mins.

Diaries: 1971–1976. 1982. Ed Pincus. Independently produced. USA. 200 mins.

Diya. 2001. Judith MacDougall. Centre for Cross-Cultural Research/Australian National University/Fieldwork Films. Australia. 55 mins.

Don't Look Back. 1967. D. A. Pennebaker. Leacock-Pennebaker Inc. USA. 96 mins.

Doon School Chronicles. 2000. David MacDougall. Fieldwork Films/Centre for Cross-Cultural Research, Australian National University. Australia. 108 mins.

Dream of a Rarebit Fiend. 1906. Edwin S. Porter. Edison Manufacturing Co. USA. 9 mins.

Drifters. 1929. John Grierson. Empire Marketing Board/New Era Films. UK. 49 mins.

The Duchess and the Detectives. Episode of *Police* series. 1982. Charles Stewart. BBC Bristol. UK. 45 mins.

L'Eclisse [Eclipse]. 1962. Michelangelo Antonioni. Cineriz/Interopa Film/Paris Film. Italy. 126 mins.

Elephant Boy. 1937. Robert Flaherty and Zoltan Korda. London Film Productions. UK. 80 mins.

Empire of the Sun. 1987. Steven Spielberg. Warner Brothers. USA. 146 mins.

Enfants annamites ramassant des sapèques devant la Pagode des Dames. c. 1899. Gabriel Veyre. Société Lumière. France. 1 min.

Enfants jouant aux billes. 1896. Director unknown. Société Lumière. France. 47 seconds.

Entre les murs [*The Class*]. 2008. Laurent Cantet. Haut et Court/France 2 Cinéma. France. 128 mins.

Equator series. 2006–7. Sophie Todd, Warren Kemp and Steven Grandison. BBC Television. UK. 3 episodes of 59 mins.

Essene. 1972. Frederick Wiseman. Zipporah Films. USA. 86 mins.

Etre et avoir [*To Be and to Have*]. 2002. Nicolas Philibert. Canal+/Centre National de Documentation Pédagogique/Gimages 4/Les Films d'Ici/Maïa Films/Arte France Cinéma. France. 102 mins.

The Eye above the Well [*Het oog bovan de put*]. 1988. Johan van der Keuken. Fonds voor de Nederlandse Film/Interkerkelijke Omroep Nederland (IKON)/Westdeutscher Rundfunk (WDR). Netherlands. 94 mins.

La Fantôme de la liberté [*The Phantom of Liberty*]. 1974. Luis Buñuel. Greenwich Film Productions. France. 104 mins.

Farrebique. 1946. Georges Rouquier. Les Films Etienne Lallier/Écran Français. France. 90 mins.

The Father of the Goats [*Der Herr der Ziegen*]. 1984. Ivo Strecker. Institut für den Wissenschaftlichen Film. Germany. 44 mins.

Fires Were Started. 1943. Humphrey Jennings. Crown Film Unit. UK. 63 mins.

The First Interview. 2011. Dennis Tupicoff. Australian Broadcasting Corporation/Jungle Pictures. Australia. 27 mins.

The Fog of War: Eleven Lessons from the Life of Robert S. McNamara. 2003. Errol Morris. Sony Pictures Classics/RadicalMedia/SenArt Films. USA. 107 mins.

Forbidden Games [*Jeux interdits*]. 1952. René Clément. Silver Films. France. 102 mins.

Forest of Bliss. 1985. Robert Gardner. Film Study Center, Harvard University. USA. 90 mins.

Freddie Flintoff Versus the World series. 2011. Various directors. ITV4. UK. 8 episodes of 60 mins.

Freeze – Die – Come to Life [*Замри, умри, воскресни*] [*Zamri, umri, voskresni!*]. 1989. Vitali Kanevsky. Lenfilm Studio/SPiEF/Studio Troitskij Most. USSR. 105 mins.

The Galloping Major. 1951. Henry Cornelius. British Lion Film Corporation/Riverside Studios Ltd/Romulus Films. UK. 80 mins.

Gandhi's Children. 2008. David MacDougall. Fieldwork Films/Centre for Cross-Cultural Research, Australian National University. Australia. 180 mins.

Garlic Is as Good as Ten Mothers. 1980. Les Blank. Flower Films. USA. 51 mins.

Gates of Heaven. 1978. Errol Morris. Gates of Heaven. USA. 85 mins.

The General Line [*Generalnaya liniya*] [re-titled *Old and New*, or *Staroye i novoye*]. 1929. Sergei Eisenstein and Grigori Aleksandrov. Sovkino. USSR. 121 mins.

Germany, Year Zero [*Germania, Anno Zero*]. 1947. Roberto Rossellini. Tevere/Sadfilm. Italy. 78 mins.

The Gleaners and I [*Les Glaneurs et la glaneuse*]. 2000. Agnès Varda. Ciné Tamaris. France. 88 mins.

Grass: A Nation's Battle for Life. 1925. Merian C. Cooper and Ernest B. Schoedsack. Famous Players-Lasky Corporation/Paramount Pictures. USA. 71 mins.

Great Indian Railway Journeys series. 2018. Cassie Farrell and Ben Rowland. BBC Television. UK. 4 episodes of 60 mins.

Great Railway Journeys of the World series. 1980. Various directors. BBC Television. UK. 8 episodes of 60 mins.

The Great Train Robbery. 1903. Edwin S. Porter. Edison Manufacturing Company. USA. 12 mins.

Il Grido. 1957. Michelangelo Antonioni. SpA Cinematografica/Robert Alexander Productions. Italy/USA. 116 mins.

A Happy Mother's Day. 1963. Richard Leacock and Joyce Chopra. Leacock-Pennebaker Inc. USA. 26 mins.

High School. 1969. Frederick Wiseman. Osti Productions. USA. 75 mins.

Hospital. 1970. Frederick Wiseman. Osti Films. USA. 84 mins.

House of Full Service. 1994. Lasse Naukkarinen. Ilokuva, Naukkarinen & Co. Finland. 53 mins.

Housing Problems. 1935. Arthur Elton and Edgar Anstey. British Commercial Gas Association. UK. 15 mins.

Imaginero – The Image Man. 1970. Jorge Prelorán. Tucuman National University/ Film Study Center, Harvard University. Argentina/USA. 52 mins.

Interview with a Murderer. 2016. David Howard. ITN Productions/Monster Films. UK. 79 mins.

In the Dark [*V temnote*]. 2004. Sergei Dvortsevoy. Making Movies Oy/Kaarle Aho. Finland. 41 mins.

In the Land of the Deaf [*Le Pays des sourds*]. 1992. Nicolas Philibert. Les Films d'Ici/La Sept/Centre Européen Cinématographique Rhone Alpes. France. 99 mins.

In the Land of the Head-Hunters. 1914. Edward S. Curtis. Seattle Film Co. USA. 65 mins.

In the Year of the Pig. 1968. Emile de Antonio. Emile de Antonio Productions/Turin Film Productions. USA. 104 mins.

The Iron Ministry. 2014. J. P. Sniadecki. Cinder Films. USA. 82 mins.

I Shot My Love. 2009. Tomer Heymann. Heymann Brothers Films/Lichtblick Film/ Westdeutscher Rundfunk (WDR)/Arte. Israel. 56 mins.

Ivan's Childhood [*Ива́ново де́тство*] [*Ivanovo Detstvo*]. 1962. Andrei Tarkovsky. Mosfilm. USSR. 97 mins.

I Was Born, But… [*Otona no miru ehon – Umarete wa mita keredo*]. 1932. Yasujiro Ozu. Shôchiku Eiga. Japan. 100 mins.

Jaguar. 1967. Jean Rouch. Les Films de la Pléiade. France. 110 mins.

Joe Leahy's Neighbours. 1988. Bob Connolly and Robin Anderson. Arundel Productions. Australia. 90 mins.

John Atkins Saves Up. 1934. Arthur Elton. GPO Film Unit. UK. 18 mins.

Le Joli Mai. 1963. Chris Marker and Pierre Lhomme. Sofracima. France. 165 mins.

Juvenile Court. 1973. Frederick Wiseman. Zipporah Films. USA. 144 mins.

Karam in Jaipur. 2001. David MacDougall. Fieldwork Films/Centre for Cross-Cultural Research, Australian National University. Australia. 56 mins.

The Kid. 1921. Charles Chaplin. First National. USA. 68 mins.

The King's Stamp. 1935. William Coldstream. GPO Film Unit. UK. 20 mins.

Kino-Nedelya [*Кино-Неделя*] [*Cinema Week*]. 1918–19. Dziga Vertov, Elizaveta Svilova, Mikhail Kaufman and others. USSR. 43 newsreels of varying lengths.

Kino-Pravda [*Кино-Правда*] [*Cine-Truth*]. 1922–5. Dziga Vertov, Elizaveta Svilova, Mikhail Kaufman and others. USSR. 23 newsreels of varying lengths.

KJ: Music and Life [*Yinyue rensheng*]. 2008. Cheung King-wai. CNEX/Hong Kong. China. 93 mins.

Land Without Bread [*Las Hurdes*]. 1933. Luis Buñuel. Ramón Acin. Spain. 30 mins.

Laveuses sur la rivière. 1897. Director unknown. Société Lumière. France. 55 seconds.

The Leader, His Driver and the Driver's Wife. 1991. Nick Broomfield. Lafayette Films. UK. 85 mins.

The Leap across the Cattle. [*Der Sprung über die Rinder*]. 1979. Ivo Strecker. Institut für den Wissenschaftlichen Film. Germany. 45 mins.

Letter from Siberia [*Lettre de Sibérie*]. 1958. Chris Marker. Argos Films/Procinex. France. 62 mins.

Let There Be Light. 1946. John Huston. US Army Pictorial Services. USA. 58 mins.

Leviathan. 2012. Lucien Castaing-Taylor and Veréna Paravel. Arrète Ton Cinéma/Harvard Sensory Ethnography Lab. USA. 87 mins.

The Lives of Others [*Das Leben der Anderen*]. 2006. Florian Henckel von Donnersmarck. Wiedemann and Berg Filmproduktion/Bayerischer Rundfunk/Arte/Creado Film. Germany. 137 mins.

The Locket. 1946. John Brahm. RCA Radio Pictures. USA. 85 mins.

Lonely Boy. 1963. Wolf Koenig and Roman Kroitor. National Film Board of Canada. Canada. 27 mins.

Long Way Down series. 2007. David Alexanian and Russ Malkin. Big Earth/Elixir Films. UK. 10 episodes of 44 mins.

Long Way Round series. 2004. David Alexanian and Russ Malkin. Elixir Rilms/Image Wizard Television. UK. 7 episodes of 42 mins.

Lost, Lost, Lost. 1976. Jonas Mekas. Independently produced. USA. 178 mins.

Louisiana Story. 1948. Robert J. Flaherty. Robert Flaherty Productions Inc. USA. 77 mins.

The Lumière Brothers' First Films. 1996. Thierry Frémaux and Bertrand Tavernier. Association Frères Lumière/Institut Lumière. France. 61 mins.

The Making of David Attenborough's Conquest of the Skies. 2015. Edward McGown. Colossus Productions. UK. 50 mins.

The Maltese Falcon. 1941. John Huston. Warner Bros. USA. 100 mins.

A Man Escaped [Un Condamné à mort s'est échappé]. 1956. Robert Bresson. Gaumont/ Nouvelles Éditions de Films. France. 101 mins.

Man of Aran. 1934. Robert J. Flaherty. Gaumont-British Picture Corporation. UK. 77 mins.

Man vs. Wild series. 2006–11. Various directors. Diverse Productions. UK. 79 episodes of 43–58 mins.

Man with a Movie Camera [Человек с кино-аппаратом] [Chelovek s kino-apparatom]. 1929. Dziga Vertov. VUFKU. USSR. 68 mins.

The March of Time series. 1935–51. Various directors. Time Inc. USA. c. 209 episodes of 20–30 mins.

Marilyn: The Ultimate Investigation into a Suspicious Death. 1999. Jean Durieux and Fabienne Verger. Sunset Presse. France. 51 mins.

Marjoe. 1972. Sarah Kernochan and Howard Smith. Cinema X/Mauser Productions. USA. 88 mins.

A Matter of Life and Death. 1946. Michael Powell and Emeric Pressburger. Universal-International. USA. 104 mins.

La Mémoire dure. 2000. Rossella Ragazzi. Independently produced. France. 80 mins.

The Mike Wallace Interview series. 1957–8. Various directors. Newsmakers Productions/ American Broadcasting Corporation. USA. 71 episodes of 30 mins.

Mississippi Cold Case. 2007. David Ridgen. Canadian Broadcasting Corporation. Canada. 45 mins.

Moana: A Romance of the Golden Age. 1926. Robert J. Flaherty. Paramount Pictures. USA. 64 mins.

Moi, un noir. 1958. Jean Rouch. Les Films de la Pléiade. France. 70 mins.

Momma Don't Allow. 1956. Karel Reisz and Tony Richardson. British Film Institute. UK. 22 mins.

A Month in the Life of Ephtim D. 1999. Asen Balikci and Antoni Dontchev. Production company not identified. Bulgaria. 56 mins.

The Most Dangerous Man in America. 2009. Judith Ehrlich and Rick Goldsmith. Kovno Communications. USA. 92 mins.

Murmur of the Heart [Le Souffle au coeur]. 1971. Louis Malle. Nouvelles Éditions de Films (NEF)/Marianne Productions/Vides Cinematografica/Franz Seitz Filmproduktion. France. 118 mins.

My Father's Glory [La Gloire de mon père]. 1990. Yves Robert. Gaumont/Les Productions de la Guéville/TF1 Films Production. France. 105 mins.

Naim and Jabar. 1974. David Hancock and Herb Di Gioia. American Universities Field Staff. USA. 50 mins.

Nanook of the North. A Story of Life and Love in the Actual Arctic. 1922. Robert J. Flaherty. Revillon Frères. USA. 70 mins.

Natasha and the Wolf. 1995. Olga Budashevska and Kevin Sim. Yorkshire Tyne Tees Television/Corporation for Public Broadcasting/WGBH 'Frontline' series. UK/ USA. 90 mins.

The New Boys. 2003. David MacDougall. Fieldwork Films/Centre for Cross-Cultural Research, Australian National University. Australia. 100 mins.

Night and Fog [*Nuit et brouillard*]. 1956. Alain Resnais. Argos Films. France. 32 mins.

Night Mail. 1936. Harry Watt and Basil Wright. GPO Film Unit. UK. 25 mins.

No Country for Old Men. 2007. Ethan Coen and Joel Coen. Paramount Vantage/Miramax Films/Scott Rudin Productions/Mike Zoss Productions. USA. 122 mins.

North Sea. 1938. Harry Watt. GPO Film Unit. UK. 24 mins.

Nosferatu [*Nosferatu, eine Symphonie des Grauens*]. 1922. F. W. Murnau. Jofa-Atelier Berlin-Johannisthal/Prana-Film. Germany. 94 mins.

La Notte. 1961. Michelangelo Antonioni. Nepi Film/Sofitedip/Silver Films. Italy. 122 mins.

The Nuer. 1971. Hilary Harris and George Breidenbach. Film Study Center, Harvard University. USA. 73 mins.

Los Olvidados. 1950. Luis Buñuel. Ultramar Films. Mexico. 80 mins.

On the Waterfront. 1954. Elia Kazan. Columbia Pictures. USA. 108 mins.

Panorama du Grand Canal vu d'un bateau. 1896. Alexandre Promio. Lumière Brothers. France. 40 seconds.

Passing Fancy [*Dekigokoro*]. 1933. Yasujiro Ozu. Shikoku Kinema. Japan. 101 mins.

The Passion of Joan of Arc. 1928. Carl Dreyer. Société Générale des Films. France. 114 mins.

Peeping Tom. 1960. Michael Powell. Anglo-Amalgamated. UK. 101 mins.

People's Park. 2012. Libbie D. Cohn and J. P. Sniadecki. Harvard Sensory Ethnography Lab. USA. 78 mins.

Pett and Pott. 1934. Alberto Cavalcanti. GPO Film Unit. UK. 31 mins.

Photographic Memory. 2011. Ross McElwee. St Quay Films/French Connection Films/Arte. France. USA/France. 87 mins.

The Plow That Broke the Plains. 1936. Pare Lorentz. US Resettlement Administration. USA. 25 mins.

Point of Order! 1964. Emile de Antonio. Point Films. USA. 97 mins.

Pole to Pole series. 1992. Roger Mills and Clem Vallance. BBC Television/Passepartout Productions/Prominent Television. UK. 8 episodes of 50 mins.

Polyester. 1981. John Waters. New Line Cinema. USA. 86 mins.

Porte de France. 1896–7. Alexandre Promio. Lumière Brothers. France. 40 seconds.

Portrait of Jason. 1967. Shirley Clarke. Shirley Clarke Productions/Graeme Ferguson Productions. USA. 105 mins.

Primary. 1960. Robert Drew. Drew Associates/Time Inc. USA. 60 mins.

Project 20 series. 1954–70. Various directors. NBC Television. USA. 34 episodes of 60 mins.

La Pyramide humaine. 1961. Jean Rouch. Les Films de la Pléiade. France. 90 mins.

Le Quattro Volte. 2010. Michelangelo Frammartino. Invisibile Film/Ventura Film/Vivo Film/Essential Filmroduktion. Italy/Germany/Switzerland. 88 mins.

Rear Window. 1954. Alfred Hitchcock. Patron Inc. USA. 112 mins.

Le Règne du jour. 1967. Pierre Perrault. Office National du Film du Canada. Canada. 118 mins.

Rien que les heures. 1926. Alberto Cavalcanti. Neo Films. France. 47 mins.

The River. 1938. Pare Lorentz. US Farm Security Administration. USA. 31 mins.

The Romance of the Far Fur Country. 1920. Harold M. Wyckoff. Hudson's Bay Company. UK. c. 120 mins.

Russia with Simon Reeve series. 2017. Freddie Martin, Eric McFarland and Chris Mitchell. BBC Television. UK. 3 episodes of 60 mins.

Salesman. 1969. Albert Maysles, David Maysles and Charlotte Zwerin. Maysles Films. USA. 85 mins.

Scent of Mystery. 1960. Jack Cardiff. Michael Todd Company. USA. 125 mins.

SchoolScapes. 2007. David MacDougall. Fieldwork Films/Centre for Cross-Cultural Research, Australian National University. Australia. 77 mins.

See It Now series. 1951–8. Don Hewitt and other directors. CBS Television. USA. 188 episodes of 30–48 mins.

The Selling of the Pentagon. 1971. Peter Davis. CBS Television. USA. 60 mins.

Seven Up! 1964. Paul Almond. Episode of *World in Action* series. Granada Television. UK. Originally broadcast at 45 mins, later reduced to 30 mins.

Shipyard. 1935. Paul Rotha. Gaumont-British Instructional. UK. 24 mins.

Shoah. 1985. Claude Lanzmann. BBC Television/Historia/Les Films Aleph. France/ UK. 566 mins.

Shoeshine [*Sciusciá*]. 1946. Vittorio De Sica. Alfa/ENIC. Italy. 93 mins.

Some Alien Creatures. 2005. David MacDougall. Fieldwork Films/Rishi Valley Education Centre/Centre for Cross-Cultural Research, Australian National University. Australia. 74 mins.

Songhua. 2007. J. P. Sniadecki. Sensory Ethnography Lab, Harvard University. USA. 28 mins.

The Song of Ceylon. 1934. Basil Wright. Ceylon Tea Propaganda Board/GPO Film Unit. UK. 40 mins.

The Spirit of the Beehive [*El espíritu de la colmena*]. 1973. Victor Erice. Elías Querejeta Producciones Cinematográficas S.L./Jacel Desposito. Spain. 97 mins.

Spy Kids 4: All the Time in the World in 4D. 2011. Robert Rodriguez. Dimension Films/ Troublemaker Studios/Mulberry Square Productions. USA. 89 mins.

The Staircase [*Soupçons*] series. 2004. Jean-Xavier de Lestrade. Maha Productions. France. 8 episodes of 47 mins.

Strangers on a Train. 1951. Alfred Hitchcock. Warner Brothers. USA. 101 mins.

Sulfur [*Soufre*]. 2005. Florian Geyer. Arte. France. 52 mins.

The Suri. 2005. James Smith. Episode 2 of *Tribe* series. BBC Television. UK. 60 mins.

Survivor series. 1997–. Various directors. Survivor Productions/Castaway Television/Mark Burnett Productions. USA. Over 525 episodes of 43 mins.

Sweetgrass. 2009. Ilisa Barbash and Lucien Castaing-Taylor. Harvard Sensory Ethnography Lab. USA. 102 mins.

Tarnation. 2003. Jonathan Caouette. Production company not identified. USA. 88 mins.

Tempus de Baristas [*Time of the Barmen*]. 1993. David MacDougall. Fieldwork Films/ BBC Television/Istituto Superiore Etnografico della Sardegna. Australia/UK/Italy. 100 mins.

La Terra Trema: episodio del mare. 1948. Luchino Visconti. Universalia Film. Italy. 160 mins.

The Thin Blue Line. 1988. Errol Morris. Third Floor Productions/Channel 4 Television/ American Playhouse. USA. 101 mins.

The Things I Cannot Change. 1967. Tanya Ballentyne. National Film Board of Canada. Canada. 55 mins.

The Third Violin. 2010. Björn Reinhardt. Maramurese Filmarchive. Romania. 90 mins.

Thursday's Children. 1954. Lindsay Anderson and Guy Brenton. World Wide Pictures/ Morse Films. UK. 21 mins.

Titicut Follies. 1967. Frederick Wiseman. Bridgewater Film Co. USA. 84 mins.

To Live with Herds. 1972. David MacDougall. University of California at Los Angeles. USA. 70 mins.

Toni. 1935. Jean Renoir. Les Films Marcel Pagnol. France. 71 mins.

The Transformed Isle. 1917. R. C. Nicholson. Methodist Missionary Society of Australasia. Australia. 49 mins.

The Tree of Wooden Clogs [*L'albero degli zoccoli*]. 1978. Ermanno Olmi. RAI Radiotelevisione Italiana/Italnoleggio Cinematografico. Italy. 186 mins.

Tribe series. 2005–7. Various directors. BBC Television. UK. 15 episodes of 60 mins.

Tropic of Cancer series. 2010–11. Dominic Ozanne and others. BBC Television. UK. 6 episodes of 59 mins.

Turkana Conversations trilogy. David MacDougall and Judith MacDougall. 1977–81. Fieldwork Films. USA/Australia: *The Wedding Camels.* 1977. 108 mins. *Lorang's Way.* 1979. 70 mins. *A Wife among Wives.* 1981. 75 mins.

The Twisted Cross. 1956. Episode of *Project 20* series. Donald B. Hyatt. NBC Television. USA. 53 mins.

Umberto D. 1952. Vittorio De Sica. Rizzoli Film/Produzione Films Vittorio De Sica/ Amato Film. Italy. 89 mins.

Unknown White Male. 2005. Rupert Murray. Court TV/FilmFour/Spectre Films. USA/ UK. 88 mins.

Vermont People series. David Hancock and Herb Di Gioia. University of California at Los Angeles/ Vermont Center for Cultural Studies. USA: *Duwayne Masure.* 1971. 40 mins. *Chester Grimes.* 1972. 50 mins. *Peter Murray.* 1975. 50 mins. *Peter and Jane Flint.* 1975. 120 mins.

Vernon, Florida. 1981. Errol Morris. Errol Morris Films/WNET Channel 13 New York/ ZDF Television. USA/West Germany. 55 mins.

Victory at Sea series. 1952–3. M. Clay Adams. NBC Television/US Navy. USA. 26 episodes of 30 mins.

La Vie est immense et pleine de dangers [*Life Is Boundless and Full of Dangers*]. 1995. Denis Gheerbrant. Les Films d'Ici/La Sept/Arte, l'INA. France. 80 mins.

Viridiana. 1961. Luis Buñuel. Unión Industrial Cinematográfica (UNINCI)/Gustavo Alatriste/Films 59. Spain/Mexico. 90 mins.

Vivre sa vie [*My Life to Live*]. 1962. Jean-Luc Godard. Les Films de la Pléiade/Pathé Consortium Cinéma. France. 85 mins.

Le Voyage dans la lune [*A Trip to the Moon*]. 1902. Georges Méliès. Star-Film. France. 14 mins.

We Are the Lambeth Boys. 1959. Karel Reisz. Graphic Films. UK. 53 mins.

Weather Forecast. 1934. Evelyn Spice. GPO Film Unit. UK. 18 mins.

Weekend. 1967. Jean-Luc Godard. Comacico/Les Films Copernic/Lira Films/Cinecidi. France/Italy. 105 mins.

West of the Tracks [*Tie Xi Qu*]. 2003. Wang Bing. Wang Bing Film Workshop/Hubert Bals Fund. China/Netherlands. Three parts: *Rust.* 240 mins. *Remnants.* 176 mins. and *Rails.* 135 mins. 551 mins total.

White Paper series. 1960–89. NBC Televison. USA. 34 episodes of 60 mins.

Why We Fight. 1942–5. Frank Capra. US War Department. USA. 7 films of 41–76 mins.

A Wife among Wives. 1981. David MacDougall and Judith MacDougall. Fieldwork Films. Australia. 75 mins.

The Wind Will Carry Us. 1999. Abbas Kiarostami. MK2 Productions. Iran/France. 118 mins.

With Babies and Banners: Story of the Women's Emergency Brigade. 1979. Lorraine Gray. Women's Labor History Film Project. USA. 45 mins.

With Morning Hearts. 2001. David MacDougall. Fieldwork Films/Centre for Cross-Cultural Research, Australian National University. Australia. 110 mins.

The Yellow Bank. 2010. J. P. Sniadecki. Film Study Center, Harvard University. USA. 27 mins.

You Bet Your Life series. 1950–61. Robert Dwan and Bernie Smith. FilmCraft Productions/ NBC Television. USA. 203 episodes of 30 mins.

Zerda's Children. 1978. Jorge Prelorán. Ethnographic Film Program, University of California at Los Angeles. USA. 52 mins.

Zero for Conduct [*Zéro de Conduite*]. 1933. Jean Vigo. Argui Films. France. 44 mins.

Index

Note: Page references in *italic* refer to illustrations.